LIBERATION
ETHICS

Barbara Rau

Union Seminary, b. Sept 1995

LIBERATION ETHICS

Sources,
Models,
and
Norms

Thomas L. Schubeck, S.J.

Fortress Press
Minneapolis

LIBERATION ETHICS
Sources, Models, and Norms

Scripture quotations unless otherwise noted are from the Revised Standard Version of the Bible, copyright © 1946, 1952, and 1971 by the Division of Christian Education of the National Council of Churches. Used with permission.

Cover design and interior art: McCormick Creative
Cover art: One of the world's most beautiful birds, the endangered quetzal of Guatemala flourishes in the wilderness but dies in captivity. According to Mayan legend, the quetzal lost its voice when the Spaniards arrived. For the indigenous peoples of the region it remains a powerful symbol of hope, mirroring their own ongoing struggle for life and liberation.

Library of Congress Cataloging-in-Publication Data

Schubeck, Thomas L. 1936-
    Liberation ethics : sources, models, and norms / Thomas L. Schubeck.
      p.   cm.
    Includes bibliographical references and index.
    ISBN 0-8006-2755-5 (alk. paper) :
    1. Liberation theology.   2. Christian ethics—Catholic authors.
I. Title.
BT83.57.S367   1993
230'.046—dc20   CIP
                                                         93-15946

The paper used in this publication meets the minimum requirements of American National Standard for Information Sciences—Permanence of Paper for Printed Library Materials, ANSI Z329.48-1984. ∞™

Manufactured in the U.S.A.   AF 1-2755

97   96   95   94   93   1   2   3   4   5   6   7   8   9   10

To Ignacio Ellacuría, Amando López Quintana,
Juan Ramón Moreno Pardo, Ignacio Martín Baró,
Joaquín López y López, Segundo Montes Mozo,
Celina Maricet Ramos, and Elba Julia Ramos.

✠

San Salvador

November 16, 1989

Contents

Part Three
Models of Ethics

Part Four
Norms

Acknowledgments

Many institutions, colleagues, and friends have assisted me in beginning, continuing, and finally finishing this book. The project never would have been launched without grants from both the Association of Theological Schools and the Jesuit School of Theology at Berkeley. These generous gifts allowed me to begin my library research as a visiting fellow at the Woodstock Theological Center in Washington, D.C., and to travel to nine Latin American countries in order to interview theologians, bishops, social scientists, and organizers of neighborhoods and church base communities. Howard Gray, then provincial superior of the Detroit Province of the Society of Jesus, provided additional financial support that made it possible to continue my research and writing at Woodstock Center for another year. John Carroll University granted financial aid for graduate assistants who did the exacting work of checking endnotes, proofreading, and indexing.

A delightful aspect of the research was meeting professional and congenial librarians, who continually uncovered valuable materials that I had overlooked or that had just been published. I am grateful to Eugene Rooney of the Woodstock Theological Center Library, Georgette Magassy Dorn at the Library of Congress, and Ruth Reider, Marcella Milota, and Rose Bell of Grasselli Library of John Carroll University.

Woodstock Center was an ideal place to write not only because of the uninterrupted solitude and splendid library facilities, but especially because of the lively conversation, breadth of interest, and commitment to social justice expressed by the Woodstock fellows. I received invaluable assistance from these colleagues who clarified my thinking and steered me away from unforseen pitfalls in our bimonthly "brown-bag" seminars: Dean Brackley, James Connor, Leon Hooper, John Langan, and Thomas Reese. I would also like to acknowledge the generous and expert help of other scholars who read specific chapters with a critical eye and offered many helpful suggestions: Michael Buckley, John Donahue, Verghese Chirayath, John Haughey, David Hollenbach, Leon Hooper, Philip Land, Donna Markham, Arthur McGovern, Dennis McNamara, Lucien Richard, and Edward Vacek. I am especially indebted to Lisa Cahill and Arthur McGovern for their careful reading of the entire manuscript.

I would also like to express appreciation to my colleagues in the Department of Religious Studies at John Carroll University who read a section of the book and made incisive comments at a department colloquium: Paul Lauritzen, Joseph Kelly, Arthur Lelyveld, David Mason, and Joan Nuth. I thank David Bell, William Bichl, Ann Klonowski, and David Staples for their careful proofreading of the text and Rita Moore for her assistance in making stylistic changes.

The inspiration for *Liberation Ethics* arose from the commitment of men and women in Latin America who have dedicated their lives to the liberation of the poor and oppressed. Limited space does not permit my mentioning all those courageous and caring persons I met in Lima, Santiago, Buenos Aires, Montevideo, São Paulo, Rio de Janeiro, Managua, and San Salvador. I wish to thank the following theologians for taking the time to be interviewed and for the rich contributions they made to my study: Ricardo Antoncich, Marcello Azevedo, María Clara Bingemer, Clodovis Boff, Teresa Calvacanti, Ignacio Ellacuría, Gustavo Gutiérrez, Bernardino Leers, J. B. Libanio, Carlos Mesters, Tony Mifsud, José Míguez Bonino, Francisco Moreno, Antonio Moser, Jorge Pixley, Juan Carlos Scannone, Juan Luis Segundo, Jon Sobrino, Ana María Tepedino, and Enrique Vaz.

I received fresh perspectives and insights from conversations with many social scientists, pastors, and grass-roots leaders, including Frank Chamberlain, Fernando D'Avila, Fernando Cardenal, Matt Garr, Javier Iguiñez, Francisco Ivern, Nancy Mangaviera, Peter Marchetti, Jill Marshall, Joseph Mulligan, Juan Hernández Pico, Haroldo Rahm, and Vicente Santuc.

Research and writing frequently demand more time than the author initially anticipates. The entire process of travel, interviews, and writing met with unforeseen obstacles, delays, and illness that gave me a taste of what Latin Americans encounter daily. I would like to extend my deep appreciation to that special group of friends who by their constant encouragement and creative suggestions helped me to surmount those obstacles and to bring the book to its completion: Michael Buckley, Arthur McGovern, and Donna Markham. Finally, I am grateful to Fortress editor Michael West for his patience and encouragement as he waited for the first draft to arrive on his desk.

Introduction

As the country priest made the rounds in his parish, he peered at the miserable little houses crowded together under a bleak November sky in a poor French village. A thought struck him as he trod along the muddy road under a steady drizzle: "My parish is bored stiff." Like dust, the boredom is sifted fine. Slowly, almost imperceptibly, it coats the faces, hands, and lungs of the villagers. The priest wondered whether human beings have ever before experienced this contagion of boredom where people languish in apathy and loneliness. The disease has also infected the priest, who anguishes over his own incapacity to act. Later that night he recorded in his diary: "My parish, yes, but what could I do?"[1]

In France in the 1930s, boredom gripped the people. For centuries in Latin America, fatalism and political despair imprisoned its inhabitants. Boredom would almost be a luxury for these downtrodden. Fatalism oppressed both young and old, men and women, Afro-Americans and Amerindians. These indigenous and black Latin Americans, unlike the French villagers, inherited from their enslaved and colonized ancestors an alien religion and political-economic conditions that continue to prey upon them. The patterns of exploitation from the early sixteenth century to the present have engraved on the people a servile consciousness paralyzing body and soul. The marks are visible: backs bent in defeat, eyes lowered before the landlord's gaze, and speech hesitant and muffled.

Nonetheless, the people demonstrate resiliency and courage. Many today survive by selling pottery, beads, or blankets on the village streets.[2] Women wash clothes in the river. Teenage girls work as domestics in the homes of the affluent. Farm workers labor long hours planting, watering, and harvesting crops on vast wealthy estates for 60 cents a day. Children shine shoes or beg

1. Georges Bernanos, *The Diary of a Country Priest* (Garden City, N.Y.: Image Books, 1954), 1–2.
2. United Nations Children's Fund, *The State of the World's Children 1989* (Oxford: Oxford University Press, 1989), 94–95. Many of these poor do not survive. In Peru in 1987, 89 infants (under 1 year) died for every 10,000 live births, and 126 children (under 5 years) died for every 10,000 live births. In the United States in the same year, infant mortality and under-five mortality rates were 13 and 10 per 10,000 live births, approximately one-tenth of Peru's rate.

for money on the streets of Rio or Lima. Others compete side by side with vultures for food at the city dump. Stone-faced like the vultures, adults and children watch with these harbingers of death as bulldozers push mounds of rancid, dripping garbage in the city dump. Then they wade into it, knee deep, clawing for recyclable tin cans or vegetables for soup.[3] Thus, they suffer miserable days that extend into years and years that become a lifetime. Enduring such indignities without protest recalls the apt perception of Shakespeare's Duchess of Gloucester: "Call it not patience, Gaunt, it is despair."[4]

There are diaries other than this from Georges Bernanos—diaries that come out of the soil and struggle of Latin America. Three diaries—those of a Brazilian bishop, a Peruvian novelist, and a Salvadoran writer—chronicle the cancerous fatalism that arises from an oppressive existence.

Diaries

The country bishop, Dom Helder Câmara, scans his parish in Recife in northeastern Brazil. His parish consists of a vast countryside divided into large, rich estates and poor villages. Most of his parishoners live in shantytowns. Around midnight this prophetic bishop opens his diary to reflect on the day spent visiting his people. He recalls a chat with one peasant, who in many respects typifies his parishioners.

"His name," says Dom Helder, "is Severino of the Northeast, son of Severino, grandson of Severino." Like his ancestors, Severino does not live; he vegetates. He passes his days not like a shady tree, its roots filled with the sap of life, but like the cactus that survives in arid soil. So far this unemployed farm worker has not rebelled. Raised by illiterate parents and instructed in the faith by the priest in the dusty chapel, Severino learned from them to suffer patiently. Thus, he imitates the Son of God, who saved him by yielding his life to unjust persecutors. Severino's belief supported his resignation to a world in which things could not be otherwise. "Some are born rich and others poor," he says. "Such is the will of God."[5] This conviction stifles any thoughts of fighting back. Daily he paces the muddy streets of his *favela*, humbled by unemployment while his family goes hungry. For Severino, hope of a better life lies on the other side of the great divide. Until then, Jesus counsels patience and offers strength to endure.

    3. *National Geographic*, "Brazil: Moments of Promise and Pain" (March 1987): 358–60.
    4. William Shakespeare, *Richard II*, act I, scene 2, line 29.
    5. Helder Câmara, *Revolution Through Peace* (New York: Harper & Row, 1971), 22.

Diary from Lahuaymarca

On the eve of the fiesta, writes novelist José María Arguedas, a priest from a neighboring town entreats an old mestizo to assist him with the fiesta mass. The mestizo wants to defer in favor of the Indian sacristan. But the priest rejects his suggestion, not wanting to deal with the Indians, neither the male sacristan nor the female singer:

> "That Indian doesn't know anything," the priest told him the night before the fiesta. "He repeats the words like a parrot, and he's almost not a Christian. You're a mestizo and the organist, and you can answer in Latin. The mass will be a bigger affair with you."[6]
>
> "I'm suffering, Father," the mestizo sacristan answered. "The church inside my breast is burning. How am I going to be able to sing? This Gertrudis sings like an angel."
>
> "This Gertrudis doesn't think about God; she's too melancholy when she sings, yeah, because she's deformed."
>
> "Look, Father, you don't understand the soul of the Indians. Gertrudis, even though she doesn't know God, belongs to God. If not, then who gave her that voice that can even wipe away sin? She consoles the sad people and makes the happy person think; she can remove the filth from any blood."
>
> "Okay, you obstinate old fool. I can't make you. That old hunchback has something, something strange, it hurts."
>
> "It's God, Father. She's suffered among the masters. The God of the masters has no equal. He makes people suffer without letting up. . . . She's arrived all jaundiced, broken, without even her cap. She's come back with those same old clothes, but in her eye, there's God."
>
> "What God? How do you know?"
>
> "God is hope. God is happiness. God is life. When he came he was sickly, weak, and beaten down. He left firm and strong, like an eagle. He was a true man. God is here now in Lahuaymarca. He's left the town of San Pedro, I imagine forever."
>
> "Why you're not even a real Christian, my child![7] And you've been a sacristan all these years! You think like one of the witch doctors.[8] God is everywhere! Everywhere!"

6. Excerpt from José María Arguedas, *Todas las Sangres*, reprinted in Spanish in Gustavo Gutiérrez, *A Theology of Liberation: History, Politics, and Salvation*, rev. ed., trans. and ed. Caridad Inda and John Eagleson (Maryknoll, N.Y.: Orbis Books, 1988). Excerpt translated by T. Matt Garr.

7. Translator Matt Garr points out that *hijo* means "son" but in this context carries a negative, paternalistic meaning. Hence, it is better translated "my child." The next four notes (8–11) are comments of the translator.

8. *Brujo* literally means "witch." There is a hierarchy of various religious practitioners among the Indians, but for the upper-class priest, they are all just witch doctors.

The old sacristan from San Pedro shook his head to say no. "Was God in the hearts of those who broke the body of our innocent school-teacher, Bellido? Is God in the body of the engineers who are killing our Emerald Mountain?[9] Is God with our politicians[10] who took away the corn from the rightful owners where the Virgin used to play with her Son during every harvest?[11] Don't make me cry, Father! I'm walking around like a dead man too. God's with Don Demetio, and he's with that hunchback when she sings; God fights with the devil in Don Bruno; but for me there's no comfort, not from nobody!"

Like Severino, the old sacristan walks in darkness. He experiences religious and political oppression at the hands of the wealthy entrepreneurs who destroyed the sanctuary of Esmeralda, took away the farmers' cornfields, and killed a schoolteacher who dared to protest. Most painful for the old man is God's absence. Yet he believes in the incomprehensible mystery that God makes even good people, like Gertrudis, suffer interminably. True enough, God is hope and life. But no one in Lahuaymarca thinks of God as liberator. Neither the old mestizo nor the people cry to God to free them from misery or to crush the exploiters of their mountain and land. The old sacristan and the Lahuaymarcan peasants perceive their future as depending on the decisions of powerful agents: the politician, the entrepreneur, even God.

Fatalistic though he be, the old sacristan manifests better biblical insight into God's presence than does the priest, who repeats an abstract theological thesis about God's omnipresence—"God is everywhere." The wise, though uneducated, mestizo knows better. God does not participate in the evil machinations of the entrepreneurs. Their unjust deeds—snuffing out the life of Bellido and desecrating the Emerald Mountain—spell a type of atheism. God must be present, however, in good people, like Gertrudis, for she consoles the desolate and challenges the contented. She may not know God; yet God lives in her heart and speaks through her gifts.

For all his keen theological insight and compassionate understanding, the sacristan lives in torment. Nothing can soothe his burning breast. The old man walks about aimlessly without hope of release from captivity.

9. *La Esmeralda* refers to a mountain. The mountains for the Indians are where the local deities (the *Apukuna* or Lords) live. Hence in destroying the mountain, the engineers are not only ruining its natural beauty, but are destroying the habitat of their gods.

10. *Señor autoridad*—literally, "sir authority"—refers to low-level politicians. Its formalization here conveys the notion that the lower class are forced to be respectful of higher authority.

11. This illustrates Indian syncretism, in which the Christian Indians meld together their Christian and popular religious beliefs. Here the mestizo is referring to the Virgin Mary and the child Jesus, but he also alludes to the real goddess of the harvest, Mother Earth or *Pachamama*.

Diary from San Salvador

Writer Manlio Argueta invites a Salvadoran campesina from San Miguel to speak. "My alias is Beatriz. Ticha is my nickname. I am twenty-four and come from a peasant background. Currently living in San Miguel, though I travel frequently to San Salvador."[12]

How does Ticha survive? "We peasants grind corn using the strength of our arms. Using a pestle, we mash corn that has been cooked in water and ashes. The ashes help to soften it." After pounding the corn into a spongy white dough, she kneads the dough and shapes it into a tortilla. She then bakes it on a clay griddle. "The tortilla is our bread. It is life."

Ticha knows the fatalism of Severino and the sacristan. Her survival depends on warding off diseases and staying clear of governmental forces. Over half the small children in a family die from rickets, diarrhea, and starvation. "Maybe that's why we always want big families. It's a kind of defense to keep the race alive. Besides, the more hands a family has, the better its chances to earn its daily bread."[13]

Turning her attention to governmental authorities, she speaks solemnly: "They're after us. They murder us." She and her neighbors share grisly episodes about unannounced midnight visits by the national guard dressed in mufti, who kidnap then murder their father or brother. Stories abound about mysterious disappearances, the torture of the innocent, the arrest of peasants on trumped-up charges. Her friends have felt the policeman's club and the interrogator's electric cattle prod. Repressive measures have taught Ticha and her friends street smarts and political savvy.

Years ago, she accepted without question the opprobrium heaped upon her by the authorities. They must be right; therefore, she had to be wrong. Now she recognizes the deceit in their voices. Their lies justify a corrupt power structure consisting of an oligarchy of landowners, the army, and political officials. Governmental and military officers blame the social ills of El Salvador on the peasants. "You're the plague, you poor people are a curse from God. You've been multiplying like the fish and loaves. It's time to wipe out poverty."[14] Wiping out poverty, in their minds, means killing the peasants, both vagrants and those who would join land and labor organizations. The military criticizes the peasants for making the rich unhappy and so hunts them down, just as

12. Manlio Argueta, *Cuzcatlán*, trans. Clark Hansen (New York: Vintage Books, 1987), 3.
13. Ibid., 4.
14. Ibid., 5.

the conquistadors did over five hundred years ago. In the past decade, decapitation, dismemberment, and disappearance have ended the lives of tens of thousands.

The widow Ticha explains why her neighbors were slain. At first, the police incarcerated them for refusing to work for the landowner. Police charged them with vagrancy and making trouble. But in recent years, the peasants were murdered for refusing to work. "Our history is sad and boring. Maybe the authorities are not interested in hearing about it." Yet beneath her sadness and fatalism lies a spark of hope. "We are interested in our history because it gives us strength and teaches us how to survive. We've learned to survive. That's why I use an alias."

The fatalism of Severino, the old mestizo, and Ticha comes from many causes: from living in wretched social and economic circumstances, from accepting their lot as powerless before the landowners and government forces, from internalizing "the man's" racist views and policies, from superstitious religious beliefs, and from the conviction that God wills their suffering. Paulo Freire thinks the key to their fatalism stems from domination. An oppressed consciousness, he observed, lacks the capacity to distance itself from reality and thus be critical of the social system. Poor peasants in Brazil could not objectify facts and problematic situations in their everyday life. Therefore, they would attribute certain phenomena to a superreality or to something deficient within themselves. Explanations for problems lay in a superior power or in a person's natural incapacity. They resorted to magic. "Before harvest time or sowing, Latin American peasants perform magical rites, often of a syncretistic religious nature."[15] In the presence of the landowner, the poor majorities in Latin America remained silent. They moved about in a culture of silence.

The Rise of Liberation Theology

In its twenty-five years of existence, liberation theology has exercised an enormous influence over the conscience of the world. Born in Latin America in the early 1960s as a grass-roots church movement, this theology engaged in its reflections the people's life of faith within the struggles of oppressive living conditions.[16]

15. Paulo Freire, *Cultural Action for Freedom*, Monograph Series, (Cambridge: *Harvard Educational Review*, 1970), 36.

16. Enrique Dussel, "Sobre la Historia de la Teología en América Latina," in *Liberación y Cautiverio*, (Mexico City: Organizing Committee, 1975), 19–68. Dussel divides the history of liberation theology into three periods, the first of which he calls the preparatory period (1962–68); the second, the formulation of the theology of liberation (1968–72); and, the third, the captivity period (from 1972 to the present).

Liberation movements and popular organizations had already sprung up everywhere in Latin America, engendering the hope that the whole continent might be liberated. In Cuba in 1959, Fidel Castro and Che Guevara overthrew the dictator Fulgencio Batista. Their revolution inspired other widespread movements from the short-lived socialist revolution in Chile (1970–73) to the socialist revolution in Nicaragua (1979). In rural Brazil, a mass-based education program developed by Paulo Freire in the late 1950s taught illiterate adults to read and so assume active control over their lives. In the cities of Brazil and Peru, Catholic university students organized themselves. Leaders from among these youth groups participated in popular education for adults, the development of a critical consciousness among urban workers, and the organization of workers' unions.[17] Priests who ministered directly to the poor took prophetic stands against social injustices.[18]

The basic ecclesial community (BEC) began in Brazil in the mid-1960s and then mushroomed throughout Latin America. BECs grew out of the efforts of clergy and religious, who helped the people relate their faith to concrete needs.[19] Each community, consisting of fifteen to twenty families, gathered once or twice a week to hear the word of God, to share their common problems, and to work in solidarity toward a solution.[20]

The ecclesial, political, and educational movements served as the milieu in which liberation theologians reflected and wrote. From these situations emerged a new way of doing theology: reflecting on Christian faith from the perspective of the poor and the oppressed.

International Influence

The influence of Latin American theology quickly spread to other continents, creating dialogue among theologians, church workers, political activists, educators, and students in North America, Africa, and Asia.[21] In the United

17. Scott Mainwaring, *The Catholic Church and Politics in Brazil, 1916–1985* (Stanford: Stanford University Press, 1986), 64–66.
18. Peruvian Bishops' Commission for Social Action, *Between Honesty and Hope*, trans. John Drury (Maryknoll, N.Y.: Maryknoll Publications, 1970).
19. Marcello deC. Azevedo, *Basic Ecclesial Communities in Brazil*, trans. John Drury (Washington, D.C.: Georgetown University Press, 1987), 35.
20. Leonardo Boff, *Church: Charism and Power*, trans. John W. Diercksmeier (New York: Crossroad, 1985), 125–26.
21. For the impact that Latin American liberation theology has had on other Third World countries, see Deane William Ferme, *Third World Theologies: An Introductory Survey* (Maryknoll, N.Y.: Orbis Books, 1986); Marc H. Ellis and Otto Maduro, *The Future of Liberation Theology* (Maryknoll, N.Y.: Orbis Books, 1989).

States, this radical theology has had a major impact on the development of many theology projects: Asian, black, Hispanic, indigenous people's, and women's. These groups were brought together through the efforts of an exiled Chilean priest, Sergio Torres, who encouraged people living in North America to develop a liberation theology rooted in their own experience.[22] They shared with Latin American theology certain methodological perspectives: the goal of liberating human beings from oppressive structures, the process of reflecting on lived experience as upon a primary source for doing theology, and the use of social analysis for transforming social structures.[23]

Liberation theology has had greater impact on North American grassroots organizations and pastoral centers than on North American scholarly writings and church documents, though some important theological and church writings have come under its influence.[24] On the pastoral-practical level, this theology has given impetus to the U.S. sanctuary movement that sheltered, supported, and defended Central American refugees.[25] Under its influence, the Mexican-American Cultural Center (MACC) in San Antonio has educated many church leaders in Hispanic ministry since its beginning in 1972.[26]

Some important theologians and philosophers in the United States and Canada have integrated liberation theology into their own theological method and have developed it further within a North American context. These authors include Gregory Baum, Robert McAfee Brown, Lee Cormie, Allan Deck, Virgil Elizondo, Roger Haight, Alfred Hennelly, Arthur McGovern, Rosemary Radford Ruether, and Elisabeth Schüssler Fiorenza.[27]

22. John and Sheila Collins, "Theology in the Americas Holds First Inter-Ethnic/Indigenous Dialogue," *TIA Newsletter* 6, no. 3 (August 1981): 3. The authors give the origins of the network called "Theology in the Americas": "At first composed largely of white, male academics and professional church workers, the network has grown to encompass organizers, workers, students, educators, and political activists from the diversity of ethnic, cultural and national backgrounds which make up the Americas."

23. For some of the early history of these theological projects, see "Theology in the Americas," *The Response of First World Churches*, June 17–19, 1978. For a summary of the recent history, see Rosemary R. Ruether et al., "Liberation Theology Here and Now," *Christianity and Crisis* (June 12, 1989).

24. I am grateful to Lee Cormie for this insight. Professor Cormie, a theologian from St. Michael's College, Toronto, made important contributions on the theoretical and organizational levels toward the creation of "Theology in the Americas."

25. Ignatius Bau, *This Ground Is Holy* (New York: Paulist Press, 1985), 176–82.

26. The Mexican-American Cultural Center has invited liberation theologians to its summer-school programs, including Gustavo Gutiérrez, Paulo Freire, Enrique Dussel, Jon Sobrino, and Leonardo Boff.

27. Other theologians or philosophers who have made important contributions

Reasons for Its Appeal

Within the Roman Catholic Church, liberation theology has influenced, though in a qualified sense, the U.S. bishops' pastoral letter on the economy, *Economic Justice for All*, and another document, *The National Pastoral Plan for Hispanic Ministry*, which arose from the reflections of leaders within the Hispanic movement in the United States. In *Economic Justice* the bishops adopted, in a modified form, liberation theology's principle of preferential option for the poor as a criterion for evaluating national economic policies.[28] The Hispanic movement directed by the Catholic church leaders engaged in reflection-action encounters (*encuentros*) that manifest traits of liberation theology's methodology. Allan Deck has pointed out that Hispanic Catholic communities in the United States "have singled out the BEC as an especially effective instrument of evangelization."[29]

Liberation theology has exerted a significant influence on two diverse kinds of publications: the *Monthly Review Press* and *Sojourners*. The *Monthly Review Press*, which represents the secular left, has made important efforts in its publications to understand liberation theology as a genuinely transformative theology that calls upon people to work for a just society.[30] *Sojourners*, an independent Christian journal, has for many years reported and analyzed the struggles of the poor and oppressed in Latin America from a liberationist perspective.[31]

---

in further developing and applying liberation theology within the North American context include Dean Brackley, Orlando Espín, Roberto Goizueta, Christine Gudorf, Beverly Harrison, and Richard Shaull.

28. National Conference of Catholic Bishops, *Economic Justice for All* (Washington, D.C.: United States Catholic Conference, 1986), par. 319. For further discussion on how the preferential option for the poor has influenced churches outside Latin America, see Azevedo, *Basic Ecclesial Communities in Brazil*, 51–52 n. 37.

29. Allan Deck, *The Second Wave* (New York: Paulist Press, 1989), 71. Deck identifies three waves in the Hispanic movement that held three *encuentros* or national conferences (1972, 1977, and 1985).

30. William K. Tabb, "Introduction: Transformative Theologies and the Commandment to Do Justice," *Churches in Struggle: Liberation Theologies and Social Change in North America*, ed. William K. Tabb (New York: Monthly Review Press, 1986), xvi–xvii.

31. For examples of this journal's analysis of political events in Latin American countries, see the following articles in *Sojourners*: Brian Jaudon, "A Land of Danger and Hope" [El Salvador] (November 1988): 22–26; Jo-Marie Burt, "Convulsion in the Andes" [Peru] (February 1989): 8–10; Penny Lernoux, "The Struggle for Nicaragua's Soul" (May 1989): 14–23.

In addition to its commitment to the poor, liberation theology has exerted international influence for another reason—namely, its methodology. It distinguishes its approach from pre-Vatican II Roman Catholic theology, which separated theory from practice. Following an Aristotelian scholastic tradition, seminarians first learned theory—dogma and natural law principles—and then applied it to hypothetical situations, or cases. The case method served to test the students' grasp of theory, but it never allowed the pastoral practice to challenge or modify the theory. Moral theory was based on a fixed view of human nature and natural law principles understood as codified law. It used Scripture as a static system of laws that served as proof texts for the principles.[32] The strength of this moral system was its coherence within a natural law framework. However, this ethics prevented a critical and prophetic spirit from flourishing. It even allowed some Spanish philosophers to justify the conquest and enslavement of the Amerindians on the basis of natural law principles.[33] Moreover, the oppressive treatment of women by church members in Latin America and elsewhere would go unchallenged for many centuries. Indeed, some moral manuals rationalized racial and sexual domination.[34] Imbued with this kind of dogma and moral theology, with its disjunction between theory and praxis, the Latin American church allied itself with the oppressor class.

The new theology coming out of Latin America in the 1960s has rejected the manual-based framework upon which the static view of human nature and natural law was in large part based. For liberation theology, praxis is not just one of three categories of knowledge, as it is for Aristotle. Praxis extends into all areas of knowledge, including *theoria* and *poesis*. Theory, whether dogmatic or ethical, is fashioned by praxis from within the very context where theological and social problems arise. Urgent questions and new ideas emerge, generated by crises and created by the collective wisdom of communities. Liberation theology's original contribution, then, involves an insistent integration of theology and lived faith, of contemplation and action, and of ethical theory and prophetic praxis.

32. Bernhard Häring, *Free and Faithful in Christ*, vol. 2: *General Moral Theology* (New York: Seabury Press, 1978), 47.

33. Lewis Hanke, *The Spanish Struggle for Justice in the Conquest of America* (Boston: Little, Brown, and Company, 1965), 11–132. Hanke presents the debate between Bartolomé de Las Casas and Juan Gínes de Sepúlveda. The latter based his justification of the conquest and subjugation of the Amerindians on the basis of a Gospel passage according to Luke (14:23), Aristotle's justification of slavery, and Thomas Aquinas's principles of a just war.

34. Regarding the justification of slavery, see Häring, *Free and Faithful in Christ*, 47. On sexist attitudes and the denial of rights to women, see Margaret Farley, "New Patterns of Relationship: Beginnings of a Moral Revolution," *Theological Studies* 36, no. 4 (December 1975): 629.

Critics of Liberation Theology

Liberation theology possesses great appeal because of its solidarity with the poor, the personal commitment of its theologians, and its integrative method. But it also has its critics. Strong voices accuse it of being Marxist, fostering violence, and being methodologically weak. The critics include bishops and theologians as diverse as Cardinal Joseph Ratzinger and James Gustafson, Peter Berger and Elisabeth Schüssler Fiorenza, Cardinal Alfonso López-Trujillo and Marciano Vidal. Whatever their profound differences, all these critics have raised questions about a single issue: the ethical foundations of liberation theology.

Cardinal Ratzinger, writing as prefect of the Congregation for the Doctrine of the Faith, charged that certain liberation theologies adopted the praxis of class struggle as ethically normative. Presented as an objective and necessary law, this praxis calls into question the very nature of ethics.[35] Sociologist Peter Berger objected to the way in which liberation theologians use social analysis, arguing that the theologians' insistence on commitment prior to and during scientific investigation skews the investigation.[36] Biblical scholar Elisabeth Schüssler Fiorenza criticized liberation theologian Juan Luis Segundo's use of Scripture as a source. Segundo does not evaluate critically the biblical texts, thus failing to distinguish liberative from oppressive interpretations. Finally, Spanish moral theologian Marciano Vidal faults liberation theologians for not developing autonomous moral reasoning distinct from theological reasoning. The absence of the former results in reducing faith to its ethical demand.[37]

The problem, as critics view this influential theology, lies in the way its theologians use the sources and the way they establish moral criteria from the sources. These criticisms urge a systematic investigation of the foundations of the ethics in liberation theology.

As an initial response, liberation theologians maintain that Christian ethics should first concern itself with the ethos and power structures of society that shape moral norms and ethical reasoning. Doing ethics principally requires analyzing and then assessing the values, ideologies, and structures within society. Moral judgments depend upon a vision of the good and just society

35. Sacred Congregation for the Doctrine of the Faith (CDF), *Instruction on Certain Aspects of the "Theology of Liberation"* (Vatican City: Vatican Polyglot Press, 1984), pt. VIII, nos. 7, 9.

36. Peter Berger, "Different Gospels," *This World* 17 (Spring 1987): 11.

37. Marciano Vidal, "Is Morality Based on Autonomy Compatible with the Ethics of Liberation?" *The Ethics of Liberation—The Liberation of Ethics,* ed. Dietmar Mieth and Jacques Pohier, *Concilium* 172 (Edinburgh: T & T Clark, 1984), 80–86.

within which decisions based on justice are to be made. Setting forth such a vision calls for a coherent presentation of perspectives, evidence, and values based on the primary sources of truth: revelation, scientific investigation, and everyday experience or praxis. Liberation theologians call these sources "mediations," because they interconnect God's word and political reality. Clodovis Boff identified three mediations, which liberation theologians generally acknowledge to be the foundational sources for doing theology and ethics: praxis, social analysis, and Sacred Scripture.

The Ethics of Liberation

The present book pursues an important question raised by the critics: How coherent in its methodology and how comprehensive in its use of sources is the ethics of liberation theology? This question emerges from a consideration of the history of liberation theology in chapter 1. A balanced history must show both how liberation ethics arose and how its critics have been roused to counter it. The first section examines the foundational sources of liberation ethics. Chapters 2 and 3 address praxis as a source of ethics. Chapter 2 treats the long history of "praxis" and its many shades of meaning from Aristotle to the liberation theologians. Gustavo Gutiérrez's work provides an example of appropriation and expansion of the Hegelian-Marxian notion of praxis by the liberation theologians. Chapter 3 examines how praxis conditions the method and the moral content.

Although praxis itself involves reflection, liberation theologians call for a deeper, scientifically rigorous type of analysis to explain the intricate working of institutions and systems. Chapter 4 examines three analyses of key institutions in liberation theology. The first analysis, done jointly by Clodovis and Leonardo Boff, evaluates the pastoral letter of U.S. Catholic bishops on the American economy. The second analysis, done by José Comblin, studies the doctrine of national security in relation to the church. The third analysis, done by Ignacio Ellacuría, investigates a conflict involving the redistribution of farmland in El Salvador. Chapter 5 presents a variety of ways in which two theologians, Gustavo Gutiérrez and Jorge Pixley, use Scripture in ethics. These initial chapters, then, discuss what each of these three sources—praxis, social analysis, and Scripture—contribute to the ethics of liberation.

Part Three (chapters 6 and 7) investigates different approaches to ethics in liberation theology. It studies the implied models in the writings of Jon Sobrino and José Míguez Bonino. The ethics of Sobrino employs a method of moral discernment undertaken by the followers of Christ. The ethics of Míguez Bonino deals with the ethics of political power and revolutionary change.

The book concludes with an evaluation of the ethics of liberation theology, focusing especially on the role of moral norms. In the course of evaluating the normative dimension of liberation ethics, I suggest what needs to be done to strengthen liberation ethics. Both the appraisals and the recommendations are offered in the spirit of profound respect for the theologians who collectively have made a monumental contribution to broadening the horizon of Christian social ethics. My critiques are made in the spirit of constructive criticism. I have drawn my material chiefly from the theologians' writings and from personal interviews with many of the theologians treated in this book.

Personal Reflection

Whatever the criticisms I will offer, this theology has deeply influenced me. Liberation theology's emphasis on the creative imagination as an indispensable resource for liberation first drew my attention in 1972.[38] Brazilian theologian Rubem Alves called for a new theological language created by the imagination that would identify freedoms now absent in order to break the spell of oppressive forces all too present.[39] In a similar vein, Peruvian theologian Gustavo Gutiérrez wrote about the necessity of the creative imagination for creating a new kind of person living in a qualitatively different kind of society.[40] These and other theologians have helped me to see that a lively moral imagination must be the handmaiden of analysis in ethics.

Second, liberation theologians have encouraged me to reflect on theological and moral issues from within the social context. Their insistence that social location conditions theological and ethical perspectives led to my working in a prison before writing about prisoner rehabilitation. My experience in prison ministry confirmed what these theologians maintain: I think and write differently about rehabilitation of prisoners because of my personal experiences inside the walls of San Quentin.[41]

Third, the consistent affirmation that policies, structures, and social change must be evaluated by means of their impact on the lives of the poor has subtly changed my own way of examining issues. I read U.S. governmental

38. Thomas L. Schubeck, "Liberation and Imagination: A New Theological Language in Response to the Marxist Critique of Religion" (diss., Ann Arbor, Mich.: Ann Arbor Microfilms, 1975).

39. Rubem A. Alves, *A Theology of Human Hope* (Cleveland: Corpus Books, 1969), 166.

40. Gutiérrez, *Theology of Liberation,* 136–38.

41. Thomas L. Schubeck, "Reconciliatory Response to Crime," in *Who Is the Prisoner?* ed. George Anderson et al. (New Orleans: Institute of Human Relations, 1985), 63–69.

policy in terms of its influence upon vulnerable groups within American society and upon less-developed nations. Visiting various countries in Latin America has afforded me a glimpse of how peoples of Central and South America view the United States. In their eyes, the United States is not God's chosen people called to lead the poorer nations to development. These viewpoints, some of which will be presented in this book, have collectively encouraged me to examine with suspicion whether stated governmental policies in fact contribute to the development of our southern neighbors.

Ideological suspicion, however, as Segundo and his colleagues insist, is only the beginning. Intuition must be challenged by hard evidence and rigorous reasoning. Before turning to the evidence and to the reasoning, we must look briefly at how this theology began. It arises from simple stories of the poor whose misery and faith draw them from a state of apathy to an awareness of a more humane way of living. Chapter 1 tells this amazing tale.

Part
One

ORIGINS
of Liberation Theology

1

Emergence of Liberation Theology

Cracks began to break open the silent world of the impoverished peasants in the twentieth century. Major crises shook the world like earthquakes: two world wars, the 1929 depression, the Cuban revolution, and violent military coups in many countries of Latin America. These political and economic upheavals loosened the tongues of the oppressed. Some even dared to protest, though not in any effective, enduring manner that led to social change. Effective, concerted action for justice and freedom would first require an interior transformation and social organization.

Story about Liberation

Leonardo Boff tells a new kind of story in which a people broke the spell of its fatalism and assumed responsibility for shaping its life. A country pastor, Father Carlos Alberto, gathered his people in a rural parish of Brazil. These men and women were impoverished "nonpersons"—regarded as chattel by the wealthy. Their religious beliefs and level of self-awareness matched those of Severino, the old mestizo, and Ticha. Sitting in the simple church, a small group of them listened meditatively to a gospel passage read by one of them.[1] At the conclusion, Father Carlos asked them what this passage meant. His question was met by silence. One person finally broke the silence. Then another spoke, followed by a third. Each one described how he or she saw the gospel addressing concrete problems in their lives: getting enough food, finding work, caring for their sick children. As they reflected on these issues, they gradually became aware that they were persons, not things or animals. These weekly sharing sessions engendered self-confidence and bonds of trust within the

1. Leonardo Boff, *Passion of Christ, Passion of the World*, trans. Robert R. Barr (Maryknoll, N.Y.: Orbis Books, 1987), 118–20.

group. Individuals acquired a critical awareness about the causes of their plight, aided by the Bible's liberating message.

Reflecting on the gospel as a community, the people came to understand the kingdom of God as a life of love, justice, and hope. They saw that the kingdom was already present among them. This realization encouraged them to stand up for themselves and to unite with their neighbors suffering from hunger, diseases, and affronts to their dignity. They organized themselves to address these issues, insisting on their human rights: the right to health services, schools, housing, and water. In short, they believed that living the kingdom demanded that they as a community participate in remolding their village. Such activity was not only human activity; it was God's work.

Father Carlos had cautioned them that their efforts to live the gospel in this fashion would generate conflict, just as Jesus' ministry had done. Just as the preaching and actions of Jesus encountered resistance, even violent opposition, from religious and political authorities, so might the people's commitment elicit hostile reaction. Such meditations on the mission of Jesus reshaped the people's thinking on the meaning of the cross. Previously they had understood that Jesus died because of blind fate or because of eternal, divine decrees. Now they understood that Jesus was crucified because his preaching and deeds exposed the sinful and unjust actions of the powerful authorities.

Turning to the squalid conditions in which they lived, this newly awakened people now began to see that God did not create this misery. Human hands constructed it. Wealthy owners in Brazil supported by foreign investors set up structures that took over their land and minerals. Thereupon these peasants dared to question why vast landholdings came into the hands of a select few. "If God has given the earth to everyone, then why do just a few persons possess nearly all of it? Why do we plant and reap, and then the landowner gets practically the whole thing?"[2]

Group reflection on the gospel gradually drew the people out of apathy and fatalistic thinking. They rejected their former belief that God foreordained that some persons be rich and others poor. Despondency gave way to a critical awareness and to hope. They joined farm-workers' unions, created food programs for children, and demanded running water for their pueblo.

As predicted, the people's new attitude and bold action enkindled white-hot anger in the landowners. They threatened the farm workers for attending the priest's school, for joining the unions, and for turning "communist." When the peasants persisted in their actions, the owners drove the organized workers

2. Ibid., 118.

off the land and burned the crops on their plots. They waged war on the chief instigator of all this subversion, Father Carlos.

The landowners and their sympathizers stopped coming to his church. After slandering the priest throughout the area, they made accusations to the bishop, charging the priest with involvement in politics and with fomenting revolutionary activities. The people stood firmly behind Father Carlos. Tensions mounted. Leaders of the Bible-reflection group were arrested, many incarcerated, and some tortured. Families were given death threats. Finally, Father Carlos was arrested, interrogated, and tortured for many days. Upon his release, he was assigned to another parish, where he began all over again to form another reflection group.

Although the display of violence and hatred frightened the peasants, they demonstrated remarkable courage and solidarity. Face to face with the power structure, the people learned firsthand how it operated. They saw collaboration among the landowners, politicians, and the national guard aimed at grinding down the opposition. Landowners tried to force their will on the people, the priest, and the bishop. Yet the experience gave the people a sense of their own collective power and instilled in them a vigorous determination to fight for justice. Fatalism gave way to hope. The peasants grew in their belief that Jesus accompanied them in their struggle for liberation. A major breakthrough was achieved.

There is another scene besides the stories recounted in such diaries. It is the scene photographed and reported by the press: six priests and two co-workers lying lifeless on the lawn outside their home, brutally murdered during the early hours of the morning on November 16, 1989.[3] These Jesuits were assassinated because they, like Father Carlos, supported the cause of the disenfranchised and addressed El Salvador's social, political, and economic problems, including land reform.[4] They also insisted on a political settlement between the guerrilla and government forces in a ten-year-old war. One of the assassinated was Father Ignacio Ellacuría, whose analysis of land distribution in El Salvador we shall investigate in chapter 4. Ellacuría and his companions gave witness to gospel values that constitute the bedrock of a liberation ethics: solidarity with the poor, equality for all, and basic human rights for the oppressed. These men spoke truthfully, debated issues openly and reasonably. For this, these Jesuits from the Central American University

3. Lindsey Gruson, "Six Priests Killed in a Campus Raid in San Salvador," *New York Times*, November 17, 1989, 1.

4. Phillip Berryman, "What Was Jesuits' Crime?" *Cleveland Plain Dealer*, November 20, 1989, sec. B.

had their brains blown out by assassins' bullets. Thus, hostile agents chose to mock the use of reason that sought solutions by negotiation.

Framework of a New Ethics

Such events gave birth to the theology of liberation and its ethics. The stories stir today's Latin American theologians the way biblical parables roused the first disciples of Jesus. The parables of Jesus, spoken in homespun, familiar language, serve as carriers of the Spirit. They place in sharp relief evil and good deeds, presenting what biblical scholar John Donahue calls "a vision of reality which becomes a presupposition to ethics."[5] Similarly, today's stories, contemporary parables, describe the topography of injustice in Latin America. They also provide the elements for sketching a vision of a new social order. Created from lived experience, parables of the people serve as the point of departure for the ethics of liberation.

The contemporary parables unveil an absurd situation. Starving, diarrhetic children dressed in rags rummage through garbage cans and city dumps. Landless farmers pick cotton or coffee beans under a blistering sun for a pittance of what they deserve. Women missioners are raped, then murdered, for building self-help communities among the indigent. Giant foreign corporations exploit through their mining operations the precious resources of many nations. Wealthy and powerful oligarchies monopolize farmland for export crops in El Salvador and repress with violent measures all popular organizations that protest their actions.[6] In Brazil, students are tortured on the "parrot's perch" for organizing urban workers.[7] In Argentina and El Salvador, thousands of its citizens "are disappeared."[8] The theologians themselves, like Father Ellacuría and his companions, are brutalized and murdered for speaking on behalf of the oppressed. One ghastly tale follows another.

5. John R. Donahue, *The Gospel in Parable* (Philadelphia: Fortress Press, 1988), 17.

6. Raymond Bonner, "The Failure of Land Reform," in *El Salvador: Central America in the New Cold War*, ed. Marvin E. Gettleman et al., rev. (New York: Grove Press, 1986), 289–300.

7. Joan Dassin, ed., *Torture in Brazil*, introd. Joan Dassin, trans. Jaime Wright (New York: Vintage Books, 1986): "The parrot's perch consists of an iron bar wedged behind the victim's knees and to which his wrists are tied; the bar is then placed between two tables, causing the victim's body to hang some 20 to 30 centimeters from the ground. This method is hardly ever used by itself: its normal 'complements' are electric shocks, the *palmatoria* [a length of thick rubber attached to a wooden paddle], and drowning" (16).

8. John Simpson and Jana Bennett, *The Disappeared and the Mothers of the Plaza* (New York: St. Martin's Press, 1985).

Return to First Principles

These long-standing violations of human dignity and basic human rights led theologians and pastoral agents to project new theologies and modes of evangelization radically different from traditional ones. As Aristotle said in his discussion of the dialectic, if a conclusion is absurd, something must be wrong with its first principles.[9] In a similar vein, theologians reasoned, if severe oppression and poverty characterize so much of Latin American life, something must be awry with the infrastructure, and with the theology and morality that fail to challenge it. Severino's understanding of the cross, the old mestizo's view of hope, and Ticha's notion of providence reflect a type of theology that fosters passive resignation. Hopelessness etched on their faces raised questions for the theologians about the church's traditional theology.

As for the infrastructure, low growth rates and an increasing national debt in Argentina, Brazil, Peru, and Mexico led certain Latin American social scientists to criticize the political-economic theory called development that had forecast steady economic growth for Third World countries. Contrary to the predictions of the developmentalists, today's data reveal little growth in Latin America. The statistics indicate a widening gap in gross national product between developed and so-called developing countries. Social scientists in Latin America have argued that the economic relationship between the developed and Latin American nations is one of dependency and not of development. André Gunder Frank explained this dependency as a structural underdevelopment resulting from imperialist expansionism by dominant foreign nations.[10] Fernando Henrique Cardoso and Enzo Faletto presented a more sophisticated analysis of dependency. The structural links between rich and poor, they showed, are not based on mere external structures of exploitation and dominance between developed and underdeveloped nations, but between international centers of power and local dominant classes who are challenged by the local dominated classes and groups.[11]

Theologians considered these analyses of dependency in recasting the foundations of theology and ethics. They rejected the commonly accepted

9. Aristotle, "Topics," in *The Works of Aristotle*, ed. W. D. Ross, trans. W. A. Pickard-Cambridge (London: Oxford University Press, 1928), vol. 1, pt. VIII, sec. 11.

10. André Gunder Frank, *Capitalism and Underdevelopment in Latin America*, rev. (New York: Monthly Review Press, 1969), xxi.

11. Fernando Henrique Cardoso, *Dependency and Development in Latin America*, trans. Marjory Mattingly Urquidi (Berkeley: University of California Press, 1979), xvi.

explanation that Latin American countries were moving along a path of economic development following the pattern of developed nations. In considering the analyses of the infrastructure and the policies of foreign conglomerates, theologians adopted social analysis as a source that traditional theologies and ethics had for the most part neglected. This new emphasis contributed significantly to the distinctive method of liberation theology.

For these new theologians, reshaping theology and ethics included (1) selecting the foundational sources that serve as evidence for theological and moral truth; (2) constructing a new perspective for interpreting the sources; and (3) reinterpreting a fundamental theological metaphor that gives liberation ethics its distinctive Christian character: the kingdom of God. These three components formed the principal agenda of the ethics of liberation theology.

Distinctive Sources

From its birth, liberation theology emphasized methodology, which meant selecting foundational sources or fonts of knowledge and developing a way of correlating these sources. In the past, Catholic and Protestant traditions have created theology and ethics from four sources: Scripture, tradition, philosophical reasoning, and experience.[12] While attending to all these fonts, certain traditions have given greater authority to one or two of them. The Lutheran tradition emphasized Sacred Scripture; the Roman Catholic tradition operated from within a natural law philosophical framework. Liberation theology, Protestant as well as Roman Catholic, stressed praxis and reason based on social analysis.

Theological ethicist Lisa Cahill refers to the four sources as "complementary reference points for Christian ethics" that reciprocally correct and enrich each other. Liberation theologians would concur with Cahill that these primary sources both complement and challenge one another, though the liberation theologians begin with praxis and insist that praxis inform all theory, whether it be Scripture, tradition, philosophy. Thus reflective action serves as the test of theoretical claims and explanations. Juan Luis Segundo has developed a hermeneutical method that scrutinizes theory, testing whether political doctrine, theology, or moral principles are grounded in reality. Chapter 3 will examine his hermeneutics, especially as he uses it in ethics.

12. Lisa Cahill, *Between the Sexes* (Philadelphia: Fortress Press, 1985), 5; David Hollenbach, "Fundamental Theology and the Christian Moral Life," in *Faithful Witness*, ed. Leo J. O'Donovan and T. Howland Sanks (New York: Crossroad, 1989), 173.

Liberation theology correlates its primary sources in a distinctive manner. It differs from pre-Vatican II Catholic theology and morality, which first constructed theological theses and moral principles according to a hierarchical sequence of steps. Traditional or neo-scholastic theology began its investigation of a question by examining its biblical basis. It then considered the teaching of the church fathers and dogma. Aided by natural law reasoning, theologians formulated theological truths and moral norms for guiding and regulating Christian life and worship.[13] Thus dogma, moral principles, and canon law developed from the primary sources (revelation and philosophy) served as guides to good pastoral practice. Pastoral practice served as a secondary source in Catholic theology and ethics. Popes, bishops, and theologians did not call upon the practice of faith, as liberation theology does, either to inform dogma or moral teaching, to gain a new perspective, or to corroborate its theory or to challenge it.[14]

Liberation theology reversed the starting point of classical theology by beginning with the people's praxis.[15] Historical praxis must be interpreted through social analysis and then scrutinized in light of revelation. Praxis, as seen in Father Carlos's basic community, reveals a people's unique problems, values, and aspirations. Their reflective activity raised questions for them, such as the meaning of the kingdom of God.

The ethics of liberation, like its theology, begins with praxis. This starting point accounts for the fact that differences of social status and self-understanding create diversity in moral practices, which in turn conditions ethical theory.[16] Many liberation theologians maintain that their own direct communication with the people and involvement in their struggle affords a perception of the Christian message that eludes other approaches.

13. Cahill, *Between the Sexes*, 5, 12 n. 7. Cahill shows that historically Christian theology has relied on four primary sources or fonts: Scripture, church tradition, philosophy, and empirical science. In her examination of moral teaching on sexuality, Catholic theologians (e.g., Thomas Aquinas) have emphasized church tradition and philosophy, whereas Protestant theologians (e.g., Martin Luther) have stressed Scripture and science.

14. Arthurus Vermeersch, *Theologiae Moralis*, vol. 1: *Theologia Fundamentalis*, 3d ed. (Rome: Pontifical Gregorian University, 1933), 13–14. Vermeersch lists the following as primary sources for moral theology: Scripture, tradition, church magisterial teaching (ecumenical councils, papal encyclicals), and human authorities (papal letters, works of certain theologians such as Thomas Aquinas and Alphonsus Liguori). Experience is not mentioned as a source.

15. Gutiérrez, *Theology of Liberation*, 5.

16. Clodovis Boff, "The Social Teaching of the Church and the Theology of Liberation," in *Christian Ethics: Uniformity, Universality, Pluralism*, ed. Jacques Pohier and Dietmar Mieth (Edinburgh: T & T Clark, 1981), 17.

Perspective of the Poor

Liberation theologians try to interpret reality through the eyes of the poor, and to work actively toward the liberation of the oppressed. The choice to assume this stance, called "preferential option for the poor," emerged as the new principle and foundation of liberation theology. The option functions as a hermeneutical tool for interpreting reality and theological sources. Theologians such as Clodovis Boff and José Míguez Bonino claim that this commitment gives them a vantage point for reading the Bible and church teaching, for selecting a particular mode of social analysis, and for interpreting the everyday experiences of the poor.

The option for the poor also serves as the principle and foundation for the ethics in liberation theology, and does so in a number of ways. It functions as the fundamental choice that undergirds all other moral decisions. Like the theological concept called "fundamental option," developed by Karl Rahner and other contemporary theologians, the preferential option becomes the basic moral decision that gives meaning and direction to more specific, concrete choices. The latter choices, such as the decision to defend human rights, make concrete and deepen the fundamental commitment to the poor.

Making this commitment involves a conversion, which changes the perspective and motive of theologians. In the language of Thomas Aquinas, liberation theologians maintain that until a person has an ordered appetite, he or she will make decisions swayed by narrow self-interest. Hence, commitment to the poor serves as the cornerstone of liberation ethics because it transforms the moral decision maker's horizon and sense of purpose. This option becomes the moral choice prior to and determinative of specific object choices.

Certain observers have raised the question whether an ethics built on a preferential option for the poor can remain impartial in evaluating alternatives for moral choice involving the poor. Whether preferential option for the poor can serve as the core element in a universal standard of justice is an important question and one that will be discussed later. Liberation theologians, and indeed many biblical exegetes, locate the basis of this option in God's gratuitous love expressed for the poor throughout the Bible.[17] God's free self-commmunication creates the "graced" human being who is then given the motivation and the capacity to love others freely as he or she has been loved. So gifted, persons are moved to commit themselves without desire for compensation or feeling of ethical superiority to indigent and exploited persons.[18] The experience of

17. God's preferential option may be seen in such passages as Deut. 6:20-25; Zeph. 3:12-13; Isa. 42:3-4, 6; Matt. 5:3-12; 25:31-46; and Luke 6:20-23; 7:22-23.

18. Jon Sobrino, *Spirituality of Liberation*, trans. Robert R. Barr (Maryknoll, N.Y.: Orbis Books, 1988), 38.

gratuitous love, Sobrino says, serves as a reminder that those transformed by God's love are the forgiven ones. Hence they must wage revolution as a people forgiven.[19] Sobrino speaks of this gift of love as holiness that guides a person's political-ethical choices. Like Sobrino, Gustavo Gutiérrez and Segundo Galilea have developed spiritualities based on this fundamental commitment to the poor.[20] Gutiérrez views spirituality as the heart of ethics. The poor, says Chilean theologian Galilea, are the "preferential sacrament" of Christian hope, because they who lack human hope receive the gospel of hope and happiness.[21]

Option for the poor gives a prophetic quality to liberation ethics. In the spirit of the biblical prophets, liberation theologians analyze, then judge certain social structures and policies in terms of how they assist or exploit the poor. The ultimate standard on which they base these judgments is the reign of God, which by proclaiming God's covenant of love and justice serves as the standard of human behavior. Liberation theologians Ignacio Ellacuría, Leonardo Boff, and others specify the general values of the kingdom in terms of the common good and human rights. The common good, Ellacuría says, is "a process which must extend to the liberation of oppressed people and classes."[22] A true common good must be equitably shared by all those who make up the human community. International trade that boosts the economy of developed nations at the expense of less developed nations violates the common good. Both poor and rich nations must prosper.

Liberation theology focuses on universally held values found in other ethical systems, such as the dignity of the human person, freedom, and human rights. Yet the option for the poor gives an emphasis and priority to these values different from the other systems.[23] Liberation theologians approach human rights on a hierarchically arranged set of priorities that begins with the right to life, which is the most basic right of all. The poor, whose lives are threatened by hunger, disease, and repression, constitute the majority in Latin America. The second right and corresponding duty calls for restitution for injuries inflicted and for goods unjustly taken. Third, the violation of individual

19. Ibid., 38. Sobrino borrowed this expression from José Ignacio González Faus.

20. Gustavo Gutiérrez, *We Drink from Our Own Wells*, trans. Matthew J. O'Connell, (Maryknoll, N.Y.: Orbis Books, 1984), 95–106; Sobrino, *Spirituality of Liberation*, 84–86; Segundo Galilea, *Spirituality of Hope* (Maryknoll, N.Y.: Orbis Books, 1988), 36–39.

21. Galilea, *Spirituality of Hope*, 36–37.

22. Ignacio Ellacuría, "Human Rights in a Divided Society," in *Human Rights in the Americas: The Struggle for Consensus*, ed. Alfred Hennelly and John Langan (Washington, D.C.: Georgetown University Press, 1982), 63.

23. Bernardo Cuesta, "Nuevo enfoque de la moral: la perspectiva de la teología moral latinoamericana," *Ciencia Tomista* 114, no. 374 (September–December 1987): 18.

rights—the right to speak, to organize, and even to protest against unjust treatment—occurs more often in the Third World than anywhere else. Boff holds that these rights limit the right to private property. Property may not be obtained or possessed through the exploitation of the weak and powerless.[24]

Ultimate Standard

Liberation theology presents us with an ethics in which eschatology plays a central role. Entrance into the kingdom is the saving or liberating event. But liberation theology sees the saving event occurring not simply at the end time (final judgment) but in the everyday events of history. In emphasizing liberation throughout history, it presents a shift away from traditional eschatologies in Latin America, which interpreted the kingdom as a future reality realized only in the next world. The peasants, like Severino, viewed it as a future reward for patiently suffering the misery of life on earth. Accepting their lot as God's will, they came to terms with their poverty. Such an interpretation creates a dualism by overemphasizing the future reality as contrasted with the present and by underemphasizing human participation in response to God's action.[25]

Liberation theology tries to correct this dualism by showing that the kingdom of God is more actively present in the midst of the people. The perspective of the peasants in Father Carlos's community embodies this shift in eschatology. The peasants view liberating events within their present existence as indications that "the kingdom of heaven is at hand." The nearness of the kingdom invites the people to participate fully in the work of the kingdom. The old mestizo from Lahuaymarca seems to recognize God's active presence in the healing work of a woman named Gertrudis. Yet he does not believe that he himself might also be God's agent called to proclaim the kingdom. The people in the community of Father Carlos begin to understand this vocation. They become aware that their graced efforts participate in God's saving activity.

Liberation theology builds on the eschatology of the Second Vatican Council, which taught that "earthly progress can contribute to the better ordering of human society." To the extent that progress does provide a better order, the council says, it is of vital concern to the kingdom of God.[26] The phrase "is of vital concern to the kingdom" is ambiguous. The council says

24. Leonardo Boff, *When Theology Listens to the Poor*, trans. Robert R. Barr (San Francisco: Harper & Row, 1988), 55.

25. Gerhard Lohfink, "The Exegetical Predicament Concerning Jesus' Kingdom of God Proclamation," *Theology Digest* 36, no. 2 (Summer 1989): 104–5.

26. *Gaudium et Spes*, par. 39.

that human transformative activity relates to the kingdom. It leaves unresolved whether human transformative action actually contributes to the coming of the kingdom of God or is a sign of its presence.

Liberation theologians advance the position that human beings do contribute to the work of the kingdom as they participate in planning for and constructing a new, free, and just society.[27] Gutiérrez says that the growth of the kingdom occurs historically in liberation, understood as greater human fulfillment rooted in God's love.[28] Acts of human love operate like Christ's sacraments. God loves efficaciously through deeds of love and justice. As a pure gift of God, the kingdom is totally and completely God's work. Insofar as God chooses to work through human agents, the kingdom is totally and completely human work.[29] How will the kingdom of God come about? Not by magic, says Leonardo Boff; "it will come as a result of the human effort that helps gestate the definitive future."[30] Does such emphasis on action arrogate to human agents salvific work that is exclusively God's? No, the work carried out by followers of Christ receives its power from God. The divine empowerment is received in contemplation. As Gutiérrez states it: "God is contemplated and practiced." A people's union with God in prayer and worship enables it to view the world with God's eyes. This same people "practices" God by living out God's word.

Liberation theology also emphasizes that the kingdom is a social as well as a personal reality. God invites each person to enter the kingdom. This experience of God's gratuitous love, communicated through personal invitation, moves the person to assist others. One neighbor joins another in a common pursuit to make their lives more humane, dignified, and meaningful. Thus, individuals graced by the experience of love in turn become transformed into grace for others.[31] Disenfranchised and isolated individuals form a community that prays and reflects together and engages in concerted action, as Father Carlos's basic ecclesial community did. In this community, people experienced an abiding peace despite the fact that they daily encountered conflict with landowners.

Voices of the Critics

Observers from the United States, Europe, and from within Latin America itself have voiced criticism of this theology's ethical dimension. This last

27. Boff, *Passion of Christ*, 118.
28. Gutiérrez, *Theology of Liberation*, 104.
29. Lohfink, "The Exegetical Predicament," 105.
30. Boff, *Passion of Christ*, 125.
31. Sobrino, *Spirituality of Liberation*, 69.

section highlights certain critiques of the way liberation theology uses its theological and nontheological sources to make moral judgments. The first set of critiques faults liberation theology for its lack of moral norms; the other critiques focus on liberation theology's use of praxis, analysis, and Scripture to illuminate ethical issues.

Is Its Ethics Situationist?

The first group of critics asks whether liberation theology has developed concrete moral norms for evaluating institutions and human behavior. As mentioned in the previous section, liberation theologians appeal to values that revelation associates with the kingdom of God: freedom, love, justice, and solidarity with the poor. Critics press the question whether these general values are given any moral content so as to help the process of moral discernment.

Brian Hebblethwaite wrote that the ethics of liberation theology, which operates on the basic principle of love as justice, runs the risk of being manipulated and controlled by circumstances. Is it a situational ethics? He fears that Marxism may exert undue influence over this theology, bringing it to support violent revolution and guerrilla warfare. Hebblethwaite thinks that liberation theology must develop sound theological judgment that remains "faithful to basic Christian doctrine and to the ideal of justice." It must also strive for a practical wisdom that both correctly reads the situation and proposes realistic measures for liberating the poor.[32]

Spanish theologian Marciano Vidal criticized liberation theology for its lack of appropriate distance between ethics and its theological foundation. He contends that liberation theology has failed to distinguish between two distinct, though inseparable, aspects of theological ethics: first, independent moral reasoning, which forms the hermeneutical channel for the establishment of ethical standards; and, second, specifically theological reasoning, which establishes Christian concepts and their axiological application. In blurring the distinction between theological and moral reasoning, liberation theology does not sufficiently respect the different, though related, functions of faith and morality. It tends to reduce faith to its ethical demand, thereby diminishing faith's character as offer and celebration; it risks giving religious sanction to political decisions.[33] Vidal appears to be saying that the absence of philosophical reasoning in liberation theology needs to be addressed.

32. Brian Hebblethwaite, *Christian Ethics in the Modern Age* (Philadelphia: Westminster Press, 1982), 94–96.
33. Vidal, "Is Morality Based on Autonomy Compatible with the Ethics of Liberation?" in *The Ethics of Liberation—The Liberation of Ethics*, 83–84. Vidal writes

James Gustafson, a Christian ethicist who appreciates liberation theology's theocentric perspective of "God acting in history," has raised a question about its political-ethical component. "There is a strong tendency in this movement," Gustafson says, "to eschew the precision of political ethical concepts." The theologians do this by moving from a theological interpretation of events to showing the consequences this interpretation has for human action. Moral discernment is bypassed.[34] Gustafson thinks that theologians should employ precise formal principles in order to develop stronger arguments about the existing social situation in Latin America.

Dennis McCann and Charles Strain follow on the heels of Gustafson's critique that liberation theology does not engage in "ethics in a more limited sense"; that is, it lacks precise normative principles. They apply this criticism to the ethics of three liberation theologians: Enrique Dussel, Juan Luis Segundo, and José Míguez Bonino.[35] These critics find Dussel's ethics deficient because it fails to support its moral judgments about institutions (e.g., transnational corporations) on the basis of ethical principles.[36] Dussel's system, they say, lacks a disinterested perspective of alternative modes of action needed to balance the author's passionate moral involvement. His ethics consists of a basic political option that both criticizes the ethos of the status quo and then calls for the ethos of a liberated society. Moral theology is dismissed as an application of dogma to praxis, which only serves to distort what is being evaluated.

Turning to Segundo's *Liberation of Theology*, McCann and Strain see a small advance over Dussel's ethics. Segundo constructed a framework based on faith and ideology that potentially would allow for ethical reflection. He defines faith as an unconditional commitment to ultimate meaning and value, and ideology is a relative system of values. The absolute value of faith adopts certain ideologies as normative for criticizing other ideologies suspected of being distortions of reality. After criticizing an ideology that is distorting, Segundo constructs a new ideology thought to be more representative of the situation.

---

that "the particular role of theological ethics has been usurped by liberation theology as a whole. On the one hand this has resulted in excessive confusion between ethics and theology, and on the other it has hindered the diversification of theological/moral knowledge within the general framework of theology."

34. James M. Gustafson, *Ethics from a Theocentric Perspective*, vol. 1: *Theology and Ethics* (Chicago: University of Chicago Press, 1981), 72–73.

35. Dennis P. McCann and Charles R. Strain, *Polity and Praxis* (Minneapolis: Winston Press, 1985), 42–43, 145–52.

36. Ibid., 148.

McCann and Strain show the weakness of Segundo's method in the latter's treatment of violence. Segundo's Christian morality finds inadequate the pacifist ideology that links love with nonviolence and egoism with violence. An adequate ideology, he says, recognizes the presence of violence as one of the necessary consequences of love. Choosing to help one group, for example, necessarily means denying help to another group in need. This putting another at arm's length is an act of violence, says Segundo, because the other is treated as a thing. Segundo justifies violence on the basis of a principle of proportionality. It states, "use the least amount of violence compatible with truly effective love."

McCann and Strain note two problems with this principle. First, no exegetical warrants are given to support it; second, adequate ideologies grounded in and expressive of faith function as a hermeneutic that clear up distortions in theology but do not serve to identify moral principles. The latter are necessary for working out the ethical ambiguities in specific situations, such as those that revolutionary violence presents. Consequently, Segundo does not, in the final analysis, engage in ethical reflection on the normative level. His ethics consists of a kind of metaethics, which McCann and Strain call "ideological discourse."

These critics appraise more positively Míguez Bonino's work, *Toward a Christian Political Ethics*. Unlike Dussel, Míguez Bonino sees the importance of ethical reflection as a resource for social transformation of society. His method differs from Segundo's in appealing to ethical guidelines for engaging in a dialectic with praxis. McCann and Strain identify approvingly two of his general moral norms: first, a principle of social justice that protects the rights of the poor; second, a utilitarian standard that evaluates social activity on the basis of its maximizing universal human possibilities and minimizing human costs.[37] These principles relate dialectically with praxis.

McCann and Strain evaluate Míguez Bonino's social ethics as "promising," because of his efforts to show how and why practical theology, conceived as critical reflection on religious praxis, requires distinctive norms for social action. At the same time, the role of ethics remains ambivalent. The critics want Míguez Bonino to clarify the relationship between "ethics in a more limited sense and critical reflection on religious practice."

In summary, all these critics focus on the normative dimension, demanding of liberation theology that it establish concrete moral norms and that it develop moral reasoning to support its judgments.

37. Ibid., 150–51.

Is Praxis an Absolute?

Other critics focus upon liberation theology's use of praxis as a source, criticizing it because of the close association with the Marxist understanding of praxis. Two critics in particular deserve attention: the Congregation for the Doctrine of the Faith (CDF) and theologian Dennis McCann.

The congregation criticized certain theologies of liberation for defining the norm of charity according to a political criterion that is rooted in the class struggle. "As a result," the congregation said, "participation in the class struggle is presented as a requirement of charity itself."[38] Associating the Christian virtue of charity with the praxis of class struggle, as the CDF sees it, causes conceptual strain and practical difficulties, if not an irreconcilable opposition.

Dennis McCann cites the liberation theologians' use of the dialectical method as the origin of a fundamental contradiction, or incoherence, within their theology. He argues that the liberation theologians have adopted Paulo Freire's dialectical method, which, he contends, is fundamentally Marxist. Freire's pedagogy of conscientization and dialectical vision threatens to eliminate theology altogether. In this pedagogy, illiterate and oppressed adults are encouraged to identify with, and then to struggle against, limit-situations by means of praxis. The praxis entails a reflection-action struggle of the oppressed against the oppressor. The dialectical vision underlying the praxis is problematic, writes McCann, because it views history "as a struggle for freedom without defining the content of that freedom, save as overcoming all possible limit-situations."[39] Praxis, in other words, operates as an absolute principle that bulldozes its way through all limit-situations, including Christian dogma and moral principles.

Consequently, the dialectical-oriented theologians (Gutiérrez, Segundo, Sobrino), should they follow the Freirean method rigorously, would "conscienticize" any obstacle hindering a people's full liberation, including both theology and theological ethics. McCann asks whether a conscienticizing evangelization can be formulated in a coherent theological doctrine. He frames his question of coherence in a dilemma in which he thinks liberation theologians are caught. They must choose between a radical method and Christian content. If liberation theologians opt for the Freirean method developed by Gutiérrez, then liberation theology would grow increasingly apart from its mainstream Christian sources. If they choose the content, the theology would be much the same as the progressive theology of Vatican II. Choosing the method,

38. CDF, *Instruction*, pt. IX, nos. 4–7.
39. Dennis P. McCann, *Christian Realism and Liberation Theology* (Maryknoll, N.Y.: Orbis Books, 1981), 170.

McCann suggests, would lead liberation theologians along the path that the Young Hegelian philosophers pursued in eliminating theology in the mid-nineteenth century.[40] I shall return to this dilemma in chapter 3.

Is Analysis Objective?

Another group of critics has attacked liberation theology for its lack of objective social-scientific analysis. Lying at the heart of this criticism are two major questions: first, whether a theology can employ a Marxist social analysis without at the same time accepting Marxism's anti-Christian elements; second, whether a theologian's preferential option for the poor interferes with a detached, objective scientific analysis.

Like the Congregation for the Doctrine of the Faith, Colombian bishop López-Trujillo objects to the use of Marxist analysis. Liberation theology's approach, he says, involves analyzing a society according to dominance-dependence polarities. It assumes that liberation is equivalent to revolution.[41]

The CDF carried López-Trujillo's criticism further in its 1984 "instruction" on liberation theology. It criticized certain liberation theologies for questioning the very nature of ethics by subordinating the theological criteria for truth to a political criterion. The congregation asserted that these theologies of liberation (unnamed, but clearly of Latin America) have adopted the Marxist model of scientific analysis without first examining the relationship of the analysis to its materialist and atheistic value system. The congregation insisted that any theology that borrows an analytical method from another discipline must first do a critical study of its philosophical presuppositions. Failure to do so results in accepting the values and presuppositions of that analytical tool. This document thinks it impossible to separate the worldview of Marxism (which is judged incompatible with Christian faith) from its analysis.[42] Therefore, theologians should not use Marxist analysis. Chapter 4, which treats liberation theology's use of social analysis, will examine whether and to what extent liberation theologians do employ a Marxist analysis. Chapter 8 examines whether it can be used without accepting Marxist values.

U.S. sociologist Peter Berger attacks liberation theology on a number of fronts, including its use of Marxist analysis. In addition to this critique, Berger also faults liberation theology for its lack of impartial and objective analysis. Berger contends that liberation theology's emphasis on a preferential

40. Ibid., 165–75.

41. Bishop Alfonso López-Trujillo, *Liberation or Revolution?* (Huntington, Ind.: Our Sunday Visitor, 1977), 39.

42. CDF, *Instruction*, pt. VII, nos. 9–10.

option for the poor renders a value-neutral analysis difficult, if not impossible. The scientific observer should be detached from his or her own values for the sake of understanding the reality.[43] Chapters 3 and 4 will address Berger's criticism.

Is Scripture Used Adequately?

Biblical exegetes raise various issues about liberation theology's use of Scripture as a source. They raise hermeneutical questions about how the liberation theologians use the Bible to interpret how God lives and acts in the world. Furthermore, they criticize the theologians' exegesis of specific passages used to support their theological and ethical claims.

Vincent MacNamara questions the way liberation theologians apply the Bible to contemporary moral situations. He thinks that the theologians' attempts to find moral standards in the Bible for settling specific contemporary issues are unwarranted. He says that "Ellacuría seems to claim biblical warrant for revolutionary violence." Then Segundo and other liberation theologians argue that the Bible supports the choice of socialism over capitalism. MacNamara casts doubt on making such specific biblical claims.[44]

Liberation theologians like Gutiérrez, José Severino Croatto, and Jorge Pixley use the exodus to illuminate how God today leads the poor and oppressed Latin Americans out of a kind of bondage toward freedom. The exodus also serves as biblical evidence for showing God's preferential option for the poor. Critics respond in various ways.

Roman Catholic exegete Norbert Lohfink, who takes a generally favorable attitude toward liberation theologians' use of Exodus, faults them for interpreting Exodus as a message of political liberation and not as the creation of a people of God. What God specifically creates, says Lohfink, is the "contrast society of the people of God."[45]

Jewish exegete Jon Levinson takes a more critical stance than Lohfink on liberation theology's use of the exodus.[46] He berates liberation theologian Jorge

43. Peter L. Berger. "The False Consciousness of 'Consciousness Raising,' " *Worldview* (January 1975): 37–38. See also Berger's article "Different Gospels: The Social Sources of Apostasy," *This World* (vol. 17: Spring 1987): 11.

44. Vincent MacNamara, *Faith and Ethics* (Washington, D.C.: Georgetown University Press, 1985), 139.

45. Norbert F. Lohfink, *Option for the Poor: The Basic Principle of Liberation Theology in the Light of the Bible*, ed. Duane L. Christensen, trans. Linda M. Maloney (Berkeley: BIBAL Press, 1987), 51.

46. Jon D. Levinson, "Liberation Theology and the Exodus," *Midstream* 35, no. 7 (October 1989): 30–36.

Pixley for his construction of a historical scenario in which the liberated people are viewed not as the Jewish people established in the land of Israel (Levinson's view), but as any group of political victims who have found new freedom from oppression (allegedly Pixley's view).

The basic problem is Pixley's "selective attention" to Exodus which sees only part of the picture. Reading the book as a revolutionary class struggle leading to an egalitarian society prevents Pixley from seeing a number of important realities contained therein. Besides overlooking the presence of slavery and male dominance, Pixley fails to understand that the liberated are an ethnic group freed from oppression and led to a land promised them by God. Exodus means more than an emancipation from slavery; it fundamentally involves a surrender, a kind of slavery, in which the chosen people hand themselves over to God.

Levinson notes other flaws in Pixley's interpretation of Exodus: a contradiction in his hermeneutical principles, a failure to apply the hermeneutics of suspicion to the socialist tradition, and an inaccurate reading of certain passages of Exodus. Chapter 5 will examine how well Pixley uses the book of Exodus.

These critiques taken as a whole point to four major concerns in the ethics of liberation theology. The first involves a question of objectivity in the ethics of liberation theology, given its use of praxis as commitment and a Marxist social analysis as sources for doing ethics. The second concern asks about the coherence and compatibility between a Marxist dialectical approach and Christian doctrine. The third concern questions the criteria for interpreting Scripture, especially as a source for interpreting complex social structures today. The fourth inquires whether concrete norms play any role in moral reasoning. The four concerns, in effect, probe liberation theology's use of sources to do ethics: "How solidly grounded in its critical use of sources and how coherent in its methodology is the ethics of liberation theology?" The present book pursues this fundamental question of using sources adequately. The next chapter examines how its theologians understand the term "praxis." Chapter 3 shows how they employ praxis as a source to do ethics.

Part
Two

SOURCES
of Ethics

2

Meaning of Praxis

Certain liberation theologians identify their theology as a Christian political ethics.[1] They call their ethics "Christian" because it analyzes and evaluates human decisions on the basis of Christian revelation, and "political" because it treats social action of agents seeking to shape the polis.[2] This broad sense of political differs from its more common notions, such as an orientation to power and as partisan activity of political parties.[3]

Thus, liberation theology and ethics include as their material object a wide range of social activity aimed at challenging existing structures and constructing a new societal order. This theology considers, for example, resistance and guerrilla movements, protests against government oppression, denunciation of institutional policies by bishops, organizing people in church base

1. Clodovis Boff, *Theology and Praxis: Epistemological Foundations*, trans. Robert R. Barr (Maryknoll, N.Y.: Orbis Books, 1987), xxv. José Míguez Bonino, *Toward a Christian Political Ethics* (Philadelphia: Fortress Press, 1983), chap. 1. Enrique Dussel, *Ethics and Community*, trans. Robert R. Barr (Maryknoll, N.Y.: Orbis Books, 1988), chap. 1. Clodovis Boff refers to liberation theology as a "theology *of* the political" rather than a "political theology." The proposition "of" keeps what it unites at an appropriate distance—that is, it more clearly than the adjectival form (*political* theology) respects the relative autonomy of theology and politics. Míguez Bonino sometimes uses the same expression as Boff, though generally he describes his theology as "Christian political ethics." Dussel prefers the term "ethics of community" or "communitarian ethics" to stress that ethical discourse and corresponding political action should occur within a Christian community of faith, or *koinonia*.

2. Gustavo Gutiérrez, *The Truth Shall Make You Free: Confrontations*, trans. Matthew J. O'Connell (Maryknoll, N.Y.: Orbis Books, 1990), 129–30, 191 n. 101.

3. José Comblin, *The Church and the National Security State* (Maryknoll, N.Y.: Orbis Books, 1979), 39–40; Míguez Bonino, *Toward a Christian Political Ethics*, 17–21. Both theologians distinguish between politics in the wide sense as referring to public or social life generally, and politics in the strict sense that pertains to the possession and exercise of power by groups, such as private corporations and the state.

communities and neighborhood associations, and planning for social change. Such political activities comprise what liberation theologians generally call "praxis." They regard praxis as a "mediation," or foundational source, which serves as a font for theological and ethical questions about a Christian people's understanding of faith, church, sacraments, and social justice. Accordingly, the theologians define their theological project as a critical reflection on praxis in light of the word of God.[4]

Problem of Ambiguity

Yet theologians describe praxis in varied ways, referring to it as "historical," "liberating," "orthopraxis," and "heteropraxis."[5] In addition, certain theologians seem to use it interchangeably with "experience" and "practice."[6] A principal type of praxis negates the negative, instanced in bishops and priests denouncing monopolization of land or violation of human rights. A second principal type expresses a positive type of action, such as the nonpoor committing themselves to the poor.

Moreover, praxis as a source appears to be a font of moral values and norms when theologians employ the term "orthopraxis." Spanish theologian Marciano Vidal has pointed out the obscurity of this term in the writings of liberation theologians, who speak of orthopraxis as follows: (1) "the absolute criterion for ethics is 'liberate the poor and the oppressed' " (Enrique Dussel); (2) "the basic criterion for ethical judgment is the human life of the real, concrete man" (Pablo Richard); (3) "knowing God means practising justice, and finding concrete expression in the praxis of love for the 'other,' for the 'nonperson,' for the 'stranger' " (Gustavo Gutiérrez). Each of these expressions, Vidal suggests, conveys something different about the normative quality of praxis.[7]

Although Vidal does not try to interpret the meaning of orthopraxis from the context of each theologian's writing, he does alert us to the conceptual ambiguity in each use of the term praxis. Pablo Richard includes all concrete

4. C. Boff, *Theology and Praxis*, xxi. Gustavo Gutiérrez, *The Power of the Poor in History: Selected Writings*, trans. Robert R. Barr (Maryknoll, N.Y.: Orbis Books, 1983), 200–201.

5. Gutiérrez, *Theology of Liberation*, 5–12.

6. Liberation theologians in the mid-1980s began using the term "practice" in place of "praxis." This shift in terminology may be largely due to criticism by the CDF over liberation theology's use of praxis because of its Marxist overtones. Other theologians continue to use the term.

7. Vidal, "Is Morality Based on Autonomy Compatible with the Ethics of Liberation?" in *The Ethics of Liberation—The Liberation of Ethics*, 84.

human activity under praxis, thereby making the term as extensive as "experience," or what sociologist Alfred Schutz calls the world of "everyday life." Schutz's notion encompasses the practical day-to-day coping of a people guided by the maxims of a common wisdom.[8] Like Schutz, Richard sees maxims arising from everyday life, but refers to them as basic imperatives or fundamental human rights to employment, food, shelter, and education. Yet explicit ethical content is absent from his definition.[9] What Richard is asserting when he identifies "the human life of the concrete man" as the criterion for moral judgment is not a moral norm but a foundational source from which norms are derived. In other words, praxis is a source for imperatives just as everyday life is a source for maxims in the sociology of Schutz.

In contrast to Richard, both Enrique Dussel and Gustavo Gutiérrez include ethical concepts in their definition of orthopraxis. However, Dussel and Gutiérrez are talking about orthopraxis on different levels of ethical discourse. Dussel is enunciating an ethical imperative expressed as an absolute: "liberate the poor and oppressed"; whereas Gutiérrez is stating that the ground of this same imperative is faith in God. Knowing or believing in God means doing justice.

Not all praxis, liberation theologians point out, is morally right or just. Certain types of change can be misguided and even oppressive. Therefore, one must distinguish humanizing praxis from dehumanizing action.[10] Juan Luis Segundo and José Míguez Bonino employ the terms "orthopraxis" and "heteropraxis" in order to distinguish a just or liberating praxis from that which exploits persons and groups.[11] Because of its moral ambiguity, they develop a theology that analyzes and evaluates praxis.

Further ambiguity lies in the various descriptions ascribed to praxis. In his early writings, Gutiérrez used the term in a variety of ways, calling praxis "pastoral activity," "political practice," "historical" and "liberating." Historical praxis must be viewed critically, he says, implying that not all of it is of the Spirit. Yet in calling other activity "liberating," he implies that it is morally

8. Alfred Schutz, *Collected Papers*, vol. 1: *The Problem of Social Reality*, ed. and introd. Maurice Natanson, preface by H. L. Van Breda (The Hague: Martinus Nijhoff, 1962), 208–29; John A. Coleman, "A Response to Ellen Leonard: 'Experience as a Source for Theology,' " *Catholic Theological Society of America Proceedings* 43 (1989): 63.

9. Pablo Richard, "La ética como espiritualidad liberadora en la realidad eclesial de América Latina," *Moralia* 4 (1982): 109.

10. Matthew Lamb, "Orthopraxis and Theological Method: Lonergan," *Catholic Theological Society of America Proceedings* 35 (1980): 79.

11. Juan Luis Segundo, "The Shift within Latin American Theology," lecture presented at Regis College, Toronto (March 22, 1983), 5–7. See also Alfred T. Hennelly, *Theologies in Conflict* (Maryknoll, N.Y.: Orbis Books, 1979), 87–96.

good. In his later writings, he defines praxis as "a transformative activity that is influenced and illumined by Christian love."[12] Similarly, Leonardo and Clodovis Boff speak of praxis as a positive and righteous act: "action always driven and guided by faith and by the Gospel present in the life of the people."[13]

The writings of other liberation theologians reveal additional connotations. Women liberation theologians, including Yvone Gebara of Brazil, Nelly Ritchie of Argentina, and Elsa Tamez of Costa Rica, prefer the term "experience" over "praxis," though they use the terms interchangeably.[14] Tamez says that women theologians address concrete experience by "dealing with things of daily significance, and that means also dealing with the relationships between men and women."[15] These relationships embody both oppressive and liberating elements. So she emphasizes in her writings praxis as direct, or face-to-face experience, that must be transformed.

This chapter aims to clarify the meanings of praxis within Western thought and how liberation theology developed and expanded these meanings. After tracing roots of praxis, I shall show the principal ways praxis is understood by liberation theology. Finally, I shall indicate how these different usages of praxis are used in the ethics of liberation theology.

Historical Development from Aristotle to Vatican II

In the history of Western thought, all praxis, whether Aristotelian, Hegelian, Marxian, or Christian, consists of knowledge and action. Yet these traditions have given various meanings to knowledge and action, and have established their reciprocal relationship within praxis in different ways. This section will review the meanings that Aristotle, Hegel, Marx, Freire, and contemporary Catholic social teaching have given to praxis.

12. Gutiérrez, *Truth Shall Make You Free*, 99.

13. Leonardo Boff and Clodovis Boff, *Liberation Theology: From Confrontation to Dialogue*, trans. Robert R. Barr (San Francisco: Harper & Row, 1986), 62.

14. Ana María Tepedino, "Feminist Theology Marked by 'Practice of Tenderness,' " *Latinamerica Press*, October 13, 1988: 3; Rosanna Panizo, "Women's Theology Is Search for Consensus in Community: Interview with Argentine theologian Nelly Ritchie," *Latinamerica Press*, January 5, 1989: 5.

15. Elsa Tamez, *Through Her Eyes: Women's Theology from Latin America*, (Maryknoll, N.Y.: Orbis Books, 1989), 4.

Aristotle and Praxis

The taproot of praxis grows out of ancient Greek soil.[16] Pythagoras described the philosopher's contemplation of the divine and eternal as *theoria*. One who lived the "theoretical" life was closest to the gods and so the happiest.[17] Aristotle adopted Pythagoras's interpretation of *theoria* as knowledge or contemplation. *Theoria*, or theory, designates those disciplines, such as metaphysics and mathematics, concerned with knowing for their own sake. Aristotle's understanding of theory differs from today's general use of the term, understood as abstract ideas or mere thinking. For Aristotle theory meant contemplating the universal and the timeless; a divine activity attainable by certain humans, the philosophers.

Aristotle related theory to two other kinds of activity: *praxis*, or the activity of "doing," such as moral conduct and politics; and *poesis*, or "making," such as building a house or sculpting a statue. Praxis had its own end—namely, good action; while the end of *poesis* was something other than itself, such as the making of a ship.[18] Thus, the philosopher distinguished three kinds of science—*theoria, praxis,* and *poesis*—on the basis of their respective objectives of knowing, doing, and making.[19] They correspond to three kinds of life: the life of contemplation, the political life, and the life of enjoyment.[20] While praxis had action rather than knowing as its end, it nevertheless required knowledge for doing something well. This knowledge that guided ethico-political activity, Aristotle said, was of a practical, not of a theoretical nature.[21] Hence, a practical knowledge, not *theoria*, guided praxis.

The tension between theory and practice was not, as Marx would maintain against Hegel, between reason and its thought-objects abstracted from actual life and social institutions. It was an opposition between the divine and the strictly human in persons. Theory and practice were two dimensions of human life that came together in the philosopher, who, as a human being, had to live in the polis while striving as a philosopher to transcend the political and human dimension of existence. Although both dimensions were embodied in one person, they stood in opposition to each other. The contemplative life

16. Gutiérrez, *Truth Shall Make You Free*, 91–93.

17. Nikolaus Lobkowicz, *Theory and Practice: History of a Concept from Aristotle to Marx* (Notre Dame: University of Notre Dame Press, 1967), 7.

18. Richard McKeon, ed., *Nicomachean Ethics* in *The Basic Works of Aristotle* (New York: Random House, 1941), 1026–27.

19. Richard McKeon, *Introduction to Aristotle* (Chicago: University of Chicago Press, 1973), xviii, 348–50.

20. McKeon, *Nichomachean Ethics*, 937–38.

21. Ibid., 952–53.

did not build upon and complete the ethico-political life. Indeed, the incompleteness of the contemplative was rooted in the human.[22]

Plotinus restricted *theoria* to contemplation, or the intuitive union with the absolutely transcendent God. The speculative element, or scientific knowledge (*logos*) became conceptual thought that was discursive and predicative. Knowledge could never measure up to theory with its richness and immediacy of lived, intellectual experience.[23] With Plotinus and his followers, praxis was regarded as less perfect existence than the life of contemplation.

Hegel and Praxis

Georg Wilhelm Friedrich Hegel maintained that nothing lies beyond the reach of human thought, in opposition to Immanuel Kant, who held that only the appearances of things (phenomena) and not things in themselves (noumena) can be known. Consequently, Hegel interpreted the Kantian gulf between the phenomena and the noumena not as unbridgeable, but as an opposition between what already is known and what still is waiting to be known.[24] Spirit (*Geist*) as reason pervades the universe, seeking to contemplate even things previously believed to lie beyond the realm of human experience.

Reason contemplates the motion of concepts or things, a composite movement consisting of a double negation that proceeds dialectically through various stages or forms of self-differentiation.[25] Hegel uses the image of the phoenix to convey the unending struggle of spirit with itself, a struggle that undergoes negations and death, and then arises from its ashes into a life transfigured. "The Spirit, devouring its worldly envelope, not only passes into another envelope, not only arises rejuvenated from the ashes to its embodiment, but it emerges from them exalted, transfigured, a purer Spirit."[26] As the Spirit devours its own existence, it makes known a deeper meaning of existence, the embodiment of which is a new reality. In this dialectic, the subject matter develops from an undifferentiated simplicity into a second form that negates the first while preserving its truth. The alienation between the two forms is negated in a second movement, but the mediate form is preserved, and transcended in a way that it contributes to the creation of a new embodiment. In

22. Lobkowicz, *Theory and Praxis*, 26–27, 32.

23. Ibid., 53.

24. Ibid., 145.

25. Michael J. Buckley, *Motion and Motion's God* (Princeton: Princeton University Press, 1971), 215–16.

26. G. W. F. Hegel, *Reason in History*, trans. with introduction by Robert S. Hartman (Indianapolis: Bobbs-Merrill, 1953), 89.

similar dialectical process, the self-differentiation and self-realization of all concepts, persons, and institutions occur by means of perpetual struggle and self-destruction.[27]

Reason grasps the dialectical movements that give rise to new self-determinations of the subject matter. It apprehends the intelligibility inherent in the dialectical struggle. Thus, history unfolds as a totality of thought, not in a general and abstract way, but concretely and in great detail. The totality reveals a narrative that tells how freedom and self-determination develop from an abstract or indeterminate form to a concrete reality in persons and in institutions through a struggle with limitations that must be overcome.[28]

A vignette in Hegel's monumental work *The Phenomenology of Mind* describes the dialectical development of self-consciousness and freedom. Two actors struggle to establish their own self-certainty by means of receiving recognition from the other. The conflict begins with a life-and-death struggle that is resolved at one stage by one becoming master and the other his slave. In the second stage both master and slave realize neither is truly free. The master by enslaving the other is himself enslaved because the very recognition he sought from the other is not a fully conscious and free one. Because the bondsman works for the lord out of great fear of his absolute power, he has no awareness of himself as a self-existent being.

In the course of laboring for the master, the bondsman's own consciousness awakens. His labor fashions objects, instilling something of himself in them. His consciousness expresses itself in the products he brings forth. This externalization of his self-existence makes him aware of his alienated situation. It further awakens him to the fact that he has a mind of his own. He recognizes that he himself exists in his own right.[29] Paradoxically, the beginning of the slave's liberation grows out of a contradiction: freedom arises out of the situation of slavery.

By means of this dialectical process, Hegel interprets the totality of history. The Spirit produces, objectifies, and thereby alienates itself. It then overcomes the forms of alienation by integrating the contradiction into a larger

27. Richard J. Bernstein, *Praxis and Action: Contemporary Philosophies of Human Activity* (Philadelphia: University of Pennsylvania Press, 1971), 21.

28. Ibid., 30.

29. G. W. F. Hegel, *The Phenomenology of Mind*, trans. J. B. Baillie (New York: Harper Colophon Books, 1967), 238–40. Hegel summarizes the three moments of the dialectical process: "In the master, the bondsman feels self-existence to be something external, an objective fact (*an sich*); in fear self-existence is present within himself (*für sich*); in fashioning the thing, self-existence comes to be felt explicitly as his own proper being, and he attains the consciousness that he himself exists in his own right and on his own account (*an und für sich*)."

whole. For Hegel, praxis consists of this self-activity of Spirit realizing itself in history.[30] Hegelian praxis transforms material and social realities by imposing upon them the mark of rationality.[31] In this sense, praxis is for the sake of theory. Theory does not guide praxis, but simply comprehends the actual.

Marx and Praxis

Marx accepted Hegel's dialectical method, but rejected the interpretation that Spirit alienated itself and subsequently overcame the alienation. This interpretation, Marx maintained, concealed the true source of the alienation as well as the subject who transformed it. The source of alienation lies in the historical, sociopolitical, and economic structures. The transforming subject is the human being, not Spirit.[32]

Marx disagreed with Hegel on the meaning of alienation. For Hegel objectification meant alienation. In its various stages of development, Spirit divided itself and then overcame its division in the dialectic. All forms of objectification had to be negated and transcended. Marx distinguished between objectification and alienation. Objectification referred to the overcoming of limits found in the condition of human existence; alienation was a specific kind of historical objectification occurring in capitalist society.[33]

Marx agreed with Hegel that human beings were shaped by what they did. Just as Hegel maintained that the bondsman was and was not his product, so Marx held that alienated workers in one sense were and in another sense were not the expression of their products. Although the commodities manufactured by workers represented the distinctive attribute of laboring activity, the commodities assumed an alien, hostile dimension in capitalist society that dehumanized laborers. Marx maintained against Hegel that the cause of the alienation lay in political structures that had to be changed radically before the contradiction could be overcome.

Marx characterized alienation as an abstraction, meaning that one part or member became isolated from the whole so that the estranged part assumed an independent existence. An alienated worker became cut off from the product, his or her activity, and fellow workers. For Marx, the three relations of person to product, person to labor, and person to other workers defined what it meant to be human or dehumanized.[34] As regards the product, Marx said

30. Ibid., 34.
31. Lobkowicz, *Theory and Practice*, 153.
32. Bernstein, *Praxis and Action*, 40.
33. Ibid., 45.
34. Bertell Ollman, *Alienation: Marx's Conception of Man in a Capitalistic Society* (Cambridge, England: Cambridge University Press, 1971), 134.

that the worker puts his or her life into the product. In capitalist society, however, the life invested no longer belonged to the worker but to the product. It failed to express the worker's true potentialities. The relation was severed. Consequently, the product assumed an independent existence and controlled the worker by making him or her adjust to the product.[35]

Workers can also become alienated from their productive activity, or labor. Marx defines work as human beings acting on nature, incorporating nature into themselves. For Marx, work is praxis: sensuous human activity directed toward a goal. Praxis constitutes the most basic and distinctive quality of human beings. In a more specific sense, praxis involves the production of things to satisfy basic needs, such as food, housing, or medical care. Nonalienated praxis expresses the combined operation of human powers, affords the opportunity of developing these powers, and establishes new possibilities for fulfillment by transforming nature. What people produce by acting on nature represents and forms their humanity.[36]

In capitalist political economy, the operation of human powers becomes narrowed and its potential for development blocked because of the specialization of tasks and the repetitive nature of the work. Capitalist labor consumes the powers of the workers without replenishing them. Moreover, it exhausts nature by producing slums, a polluted environment, and dirty factories.[37]

Emancipation from this situation lies in changing the political-economic conditions causing the alienation. This is possible because alienation, for Marx, is brought about by a set of political and economic institutions and practices, and is not due to sinful human tendencies or to psychological causes.[38] The term "revolutionary praxis" connotes activity aimed at radically changing society. It involves understanding the profound political-economic causes of the alienation by means of criticism and removing existing conditions responsible for the alienation.[39]

In summary, Marx speaks of two types of praxis: a nonalienated type of work that affords persons the opportunity to express and develop their human powers as they satisfy their basic needs; and a revolutionary type that seeks to uproot the political-economic conditions that impede human growth. Both types of praxis consist of action guided by a goal.

35. Karl Marx, *Capital*, in *The Marx-Engels Reader*, ed. Robert C. Tucker (New York: Norton, 1978), 407–15.
36. Bernstein, *Praxis and Action*, 42.
37. Ollman, *Alienation*, 136–40.
38. Bernstein, *Praxis and Action*, 48.
39. Marx, "Theses on Feuerbach," in *Marx-Engels Reader*, 144.

Freire and Praxis

Paulo Freire incorporated into his own concept of praxis Hegel's transformation of consciousness and Marx's transformation of nature. Following Hegel, Freire developed the notion of conscientization wherein persons grow in self-awareness and self-determination. Following Marx, Freire insisted that new awareness must go hand in hand with the transformation of social structures. The Hegelian-Marxian influences are evident in his three steps of educating the poor and oppressed people of Latin America: first, an empirical investigation of the stages of consciousness of the illiterate adults; second, a self-awakening and critical process that helps learners to grow in awareness of themselves as subjects of their lives while learning to read; third, a dialogical method of discovering contradictions in their own situation, posing them as problems and then trying to change their reality.[40]

One may think of the entire process of conscientization as Freire's distinctive type of praxis. Conscientization involves a concurrent growth in self-awareness and critical awareness of the social reality. As the participants share their views about problems they perceive in their world, they grow in personal self-awareness of their capacity to act as agents in changing history.[41] The process is gradual. The poor of Latin America have over many years interiorized the cultural values and thinking patterns of the dominators. If the oppressed are to develop, they must struggle to free themselves from a dominated consciousness. They achieve heightened awareness by objectifying their familiar, but not yet thematized, world. This can be done only within a supportive environment called a "cultural circle." Here the illiterate peasant gradually develops into a knowing subject who makes observations, asks questions, and carries on dialogue with other learners. As the peasants grow in trust of one another, they grow increasingly more confident of their ability to analyze their own situations.

This development entails their becoming aware of contradictions in their daily lives. They recognize the contradiction in the paternalistic and overbearing way a landowner speaks to the workers while the workers react passively in silence. The owner's demeaning remarks grate against their new self-esteem as free, creative agents, and not as chattel. Their newly awakened consciousness

40. Denis Collins, *Paulo Freire* (Mahwah, N.J.: Paulist Press, 1977), 83.
41. Paulo Freire, *Cultural Action for Freedom*, Monograph Series (Cambridge: *Harvard Educational Review*, 1970), 27. Freire defines conscientization as "the process in which men, not as recipients, but as knowing subjects, achieve a deepening awareness both of the socio-cultural reality which shapes their lives and of their capacity to transform that reality."

calls the peasants to transform the oppressive master-slave relationship of the latifundium.[42]

As the peasants critically analyze their situation, they may arrive at solutions for transforming these structures, but the solutions may be in conflict with each other. Some may desire higher wages; others, more radical change of working conditions. In dialogue the solution emerges as a dialectical synthesis of the two positions, so that the demand for higher wages can be sought as an initial step within a more long-range, pervasive radical strategy.

Freire, like Marx, defines praxis as critical reflection and action. Action flows out of insight and back into insight. If structural change is absent, criticism becomes empty chatter; if reflective criticism is lacking, activism results. Freire differs from Marx regarding the relation of the transformation of consciousness to political-economic change. For Marx, consciousness begins to form in the political struggle for change, but takes on a new form of freedom only after alienating structures have been transformed. For Freire, conscientization begins even prior to political praxis, in the literacy program when the oppressed first objectify and analyze their own situations.

Thus, Freire expands and humanizes praxis by showing the integral relationship between personal growth in self-awareness, and freedom and commitment to political change. Awareness of oneself as creative subject is born when illiterate peasants learn the power of the word. They begin by mastering the building blocks of words. Then they learn how familiar words are constructed and how they can create new words. The process of learning to read and write leads to a deeper realization that the word possesses generative qualities.

Freire's use of "word" as *logos* connotes the creative capacity of the Hebrew understanding of *dabar*: it bears a message that is performative. The person as subject has the power to "name" things, meaning she or he possesses power to transform reality. Freire's expression "naming the reality" means exercising creative freedom and participating in a program for social change. The poor learn how certain political mechanisms may be exploiting them. Then they develop strategy for dealing with the exploitive practice. Finally, the oppressed and those in solidarity with them must propose an alternative. Freire calls the twin activities of denunciation and annunciation a "utopian" pedagogy because they try to imagine a new vision of the world by creatively overcoming the present.[43]

42. The term latifundium means a large privately owned landholding with primitive agriculture and labor often in a state of partial servitude.
43. Freire, *Cultural Action for Freedom*, 20.

In summary, Freire presents praxis as a process of conscientization that simultaneously attends both to growth in human subjectivity and to transformation of cultural-political-economic structures. He emphasizes personal freedom gained through dialogue and collaboration in working for social change. Freire's emphasis on the word as generative and on the word that denounces oppression and announces more humane structures evokes images of the biblical prophet. In fact, he alludes to the biblical word, though he does not incorporate the faith dimension into his notion of praxis. As we shall see later in the chapter, liberation theologians expand praxis to include faith and charity as distinctive elements of Christian praxis.

Praxis from Vatican II to Medellín

Official Catholic church documents began using the formula "scrutinizing signs of the times" to designate an approach to pastoral transformation similar to the Freirean method. The expression "signs of the times" was first used by Pope John XXIII in his Christmas message of 1961. He gave birth to an idea that the Second Vatican Council (*Gaudium et Spes*) and Pope Paul VI (*Octogesima Adveniens*) developed as a method of moral discernment.[44]

The "signs of the times," Pope John said, are "distinctive characteristics" enmeshed within events, achievements, or currents of thought. The signs include both positive and negative currents that indicate a contradiction or crisis. For example, Pope John XXIII made an observation, similar to Freire's thinking, that women and men were increasingly claiming their dignity and rights in the socioeconomic sphere (a positive indicator) in opposition to those who would treat them as irrational and unfree objects (a negative indicator).[45]

Pope Paul VI and the Second Vatican Council delineated the steps in John XXIII's signs-of-the-times approach. Reading the signs meant identifying the symptoms of a crisis, probing into the causes by means of the social sciences, and reflecting on the human values at stake illumined by the gospel. The reflective process provided guidelines for pastoral action.[46] *Gaudium et Spes*

---

44. Pope John XXIII, *Humanae Salutis, The Encyclicals and Other Messages of John XXIII*, ed. staff of *The Pope Speaks* (Washington, D.C.: The Pope Speaks Press, 1964), 387.

45. Pope John XXIII, *Pacem in Terris,* in *The Gospel of Peace and Justice: Catholic Social Teaching since Pope John*, presented by Joseph Gremillion (Maryknoll, N.Y.: Orbis Books, 1976), pars. 40–41.

46. Second Vatican Council, *Gaudium et Spes*, par. 44; Pope Paul VI, *Octogesima Adveniens*, par. 1. Both documents in *Gospel of Peace and Justice*. Both proceed in a similar manner, first by beginning with an analysis of the problem, second by interpreting human values and aspirations, third by doing a theological–ethical reflection on the problems, and finally by issuing a call to action. Liberation theology builds its own method on this framework.

(1965) identified a number of signs in the mid-1960s, such as the contradiction between great wealth, natural resources, and economic power existing alongside abject poverty, hunger, and illiteracy.[47]

Viewed theologically, the signs are pointers where human events and divine action intersect, inviting openness to the call of God. The signs bridge the divine and the human realities.[48] But because signs are subject to a variety of interpretations, Paul VI set down conditions for doing Christian discernment, such as seeking the guidance of the Holy Spirit and the counsel of other people of goodwill, including nonbelievers.

Paul VI emphasized the need for a judicious use of Sacred Scripture. By "judicious" he meant employing Scripture as a spiritual source to inspire one's mission and as a theological-ethical resource for developing a vision of justice, while avoiding prescriptive uses as though the Bible were a moral recipe book. Christian communities should be self-critical and be aware that their judgments are shaped by ideological class and cultural influences. Finally, Christian organizations have a responsibility for collective action in helping to transform society.[49] These guidelines of Paul VI influenced the methodology of the Latin American bishops and theologians in significant ways.[50]

The Latin American bishops appropriated and further developed the signs-of-the-times approach. The discernment called for seeing, judging, and acting. Seeing (ver) the signs entails recognizing them and trying to understand the causes that brought about the crisis. Judging (juzcar) involves evaluating the practices and attitudes of institutions and agents contributing to the crises. Acting (actuar) calls for drawing up criteria for responsible action.

The Latin American episcopate went beyond the Second Vatican Council by calling for a special commitment to work toward liberating the poor. They also stressed more than the council the importance of doing a social analysis in order to gain a deeper understanding of poverty and oppression. Although the Latin American bishops at Medellín never used the term praxis in their official writings, their call for transformative social action conveyed essentially the same meaning that liberation theologians gave to praxis. The bishops emphasized that working for justice and peace demanded the establishment of

47. *Gaudium et Spes*, par. 4.
48. Ricardo Antoncich, *Christians in the Face of Injustice: A Latin American Reading of Catholic Social Teaching*, trans. Matthew J. O'Connell (Maryknoll, N.Y.: Orbis Books, 1987), 64.
49. Pope Paul VI, *Octogesima Adveniens*, pars. 50–51.
50. Segundo, "The Shift within Latin American Theology," 2.

a just order brought about by the "dynamic action of awakening and orga-nization of the popular sectors."[51]

We generally think of praxis as the final stage of acting, but the entire three-step process of seeing-judging-acting may be considered a type of praxis inasmuch as it begins by examining historically the concrete reality of Latin American people in the early 1960s, and in light of this analysis directs its own theological reflection to the future praxis of the Christian people. The people's past efforts included the building of cooperatives, initiating agrarian reform programs, and encouraging literacy campaigns; the organization of college student associations; the formation of groups of priests and women religious working with the poor; the creation of lay reflection groups.

Expansion of Praxis in Liberation Theology

This historical development within Western philosophy and the social teaching of the church help us see how liberation theologians use the term "praxis." These theologians move away from the ancient Greek notion of praxis and develop a new meaning based on insights from Hegel, Marx, Freire, and contemporary Christian social thought. Under the combined influence of Aristotle and Plotinus, early Christian thought conferred a greater dignity on theory. Doctrine assumed a primacy, sometimes even an exclusiveness, over praxis in Christian life.[52] In their critique of the Greek emphasis on theory, liberation theologians have deliberately sought to develop a theology that better integrates theory and praxis, doctrine and pastoral action, contemplation and active service of others.

Liberation theologians depart from the Aristotelian meaning of praxis as solely ethico-political activity. They hold that the goal of praxis is not simply any good action in the political world, but liberative action that frees people to participate in the polis. Furthermore, praxis does not stand apart from theory as for Aristotle, but relates to it dialectically. It involves transforming awareness and reflection leading to political change.

Drawing from Hegel's notion of praxis, the liberation theologians em-phasize the growth of consciousness within a person's lifetime and throughout history. Hegel's historical development of the enslaved subject, undergoing consciousness-raising through a historical struggle with the master, resonates

51. Second General Conference of Latin American Bishops (CELAM), "Peace," in *The Church in the Present-Day Transformation of Latin America in the Light of the Council*, vol. 2: *Conclusions* (Bogotá: General Secretariat of CELAM, 1970), par. 18.
52. Gutiérrez, *Truth Shall Make You Free*, 92.

in the writings of Latin American theologians.[53] They also speak of an oppressed people's struggle against the oppressor that eventually will change the consciousness of both groups. Hegelian liberation does not go far enough. The theologians accept Marx's critique of Hegel that critical theory and action are needed to transform alienation resulting in institutional oppression. Action nurtures theory, while critical theory guides action.[54] These twin components of praxis correlate dialectically in liberation praxis. Liberation theologians also speak of two types of praxis enunciated by Marx: praxis as creative work that satisfies basic needs, and praxis as revolutionary work that changes alienating structures. The theologians recognize the importance of Freire's conscientizing praxis, which builds on Hegelian and Marxian foundation stones. Following Hegel, Freire underscores the importance of praxis that heightens awareness and changes human patterns of thinking and acting. Following Marx, he recognizes that changing institutions is a necessary ingredient of consciousness-raising and liberation. His distinguishing praxis as denunciation and annunciation will be adopted by certain liberation theologians.

Although liberation theologians have adopted this dialectical development of praxis from Hegel to Marx to Freire, they have fashioned their understanding of praxis in light of contemporary theology and church social teaching, especially that of the Second Vatican Council and of Paul VI. Accordingly, praxis in its most profound level becomes an active-reflective charity in response to God's active presence among the people, especially with the poor.

Gustavo Gutiérrez stands out among the Latin American theologians as the grand synthesizer of these philosophical and theological traditions. Since many of his Latin American colleagues acknowledge and follow his conceptual structure of the threefold liberation process, his schema shall serve as a guide.[55] Praxis finds expression in three distinct, interdependent dimensions: the level of political institutions, human freedom, and faith. Understanding this threefold meaning of praxis helps clarify how he and liberation theologians generally use praxis.

53. Gutiérrez, *Theology of Liberation*, 19.
54. Juan Luis Segundo, *Humanist Christology of Paul*, ed. and trans. John Drury (Maryknoll, N.Y.: Orbis Books, 1986), 223 n. 251.
55. Ismael García, *Justice in Latin American Theology of Liberation* (Atlanta: John Knox Press, 1987), chap. 2. The author coordinates the views of justice of Hugo Assmann, José Míguez Bonino, and José Miranda within Gutiérrez's three meaning levels of liberation (55).

Three Dimensions of Praxis

Gutiérrez maintains that a true, integral liberation is a single, historical process consisting of three interrelated and inseparable dimensions of meaning and three corresponding forms of praxis. The levels of meaning are (1) *socio-political-economic*, which expresses the aspirations of a people to break from oppressive social, political, and economic structures; (2) *historical-utopian*, which expresses the intention of people to assume responsibility for their own destiny; (3) *Christian* or *faith*, which interprets liberation as freedom from sin and communion with God and neighbor.[56]

Praxis on each of these levels relates to and enriches the others. On the first level, political praxis involves criticism and change of institutions within society. Historical praxis, which presupposes political activity, emphasizes human transformation—that is, the growth in self-awareness and in self-determination that frees people to change the course of history. The praxis of love, which expresses itself in and through the first two forms of praxis, expresses itself by word and deed in the service of God and one's neighbor.[57]

Gutiérrez refers to all three forms taken together as a liberating praxis because they move toward an integral freedom for the exploited.[58] The process includes an emancipation from alienating and unjust elements, and a movement toward the realization of personal and social goods. Focusing on the growth dimension within Gutiérrez's three meaning levels of liberation, theologian Dean Brackley observed how the process moved from the pursuit of the more visible and material needs and desires of people (e.g., food, housing, and medicine) to the less apparent and yet deeper needs and aspirations (e.g., the right to speak and to organize) to the most profound level of forgiveness and love (e.g., solidarity in community and unconditional love).[59]

Similarly, one may interpret the process of liberation as a movement from exterior freedom to interior freedom. On the political level, freedom moves from external political-economic oppression to social structures that are just; on the historical level, freedom moves from the psychological conflicts, low self-esteem, and passivity to freedom to decide, speak, and shape one's own history; on the faith level, freedom moves from egoism and selfishness to communion with God and solidarity with others. The following section

56. Gutiérrez, *Theology of Liberation*, 24–25, 135–40.
57. Ibid., 138–39.
58. Gustavo Gutiérrez and Richard Shaull, *Liberation and Change*, ed. Ronald H. Stone (Atlanta: John Knox Press, 1977), 84.
59. Dean Brackley, "Salvation and the Social Good in Maritain and Gutiérrez" (diss., University of Chicago), 160–61.

will elaborate on these levels of freedom and praxis showing at different points how other liberation theologians relate to the scheme of Gutiérrez.

Political praxis   Although liberation theologians sometimes call praxis on this level "social" or "pastoral," they most frequently call it political praxis. It expresses the desire for freedom from institutional practices that exploit human beings, whether the exploitation be sexual, racial, economic, or political. The political for Gutiérrez means all types of social activity directed toward building a new society and new patterns of relationships. It frequently calls for social scientific analysis as well as concerted action.

More concretely, political praxis in Latin America has included revolutionary change, nationalization of private industry, and building bonds of solidarity within neighborhood groups. It has been engaged in by priests, sisters, and Christian lay leaders, who have organized the poor into ecclesial base communities, introduced new educational programs, and reorganized ecclesial structures in order to minister more effectively to the poor.

Political praxis involves conflict. The church has encountered violent resistance by dominating forces both within and outside Latin America. Members of ecclesial base communities have met with military harassment, torture, and death as they pursued their right to nonexploitive labor, employment practices, fair wages, and the right to form unions. Fellow Peruvian theologian Ricardo Antoncich refers to the people's experience of and resistance to such abusive practices as "negative contrast experiences."[60] Antoncich borrows the term from Dutch theologian Edward Schillebeeckx, who used it to capture the alienating and dehumanizing experiences that stir the conscience to protest. The resistance, Schillebeeckx says, implies the presence of positive values (e.g., human beings should be respected), though these are not yet articulated.[61] This expression sheds light on Pablo Richard's notion of orthopraxis as the concrete life of human beings that reveals imperatives dealing with basic human rights.

Historical-utopian praxis   A truly liberating praxis call for more than the change of political structures. It requires personal transformation in self-awareness, a corresponding growth in freedom, and the creation of qualitatively new kinds of human relationships between men and women and between different groups of people. This level expresses the aspiration to personal

60. Antoncich, *Christians in the Face of Injustice*, 58–59.
61. Edward Schillebeeckx, *God the Future of Man*, trans. N. D. Smith (New York: Sheed and Ward, 1968), 153.

growth of persons and humane social relationships. Gutiérrez speaks of liberation as the freedom to become creators of history.[62] Freedom is self-determination achieved by struggle against oppressive forces and by assuming greater responsibility. The liberative process bears the marks of the Hegelian struggle for freedom: two hostile groups striving for mutual recognition who must overcome contradictions in dialectical stages. Gutiérrez speaks of the conquest of freedom, which suggests active, though not necessarily armed, combat. Freedom is not a once-and-for-all achievement, but a lifelong process.

Historical-utopian praxis expresses the philosophical and psychological aspects of freedom. Gutiérrez integrates both Hegel's historical development of self-consciousness achieved by persons and groups through the dialectical struggle for recognition and Freud's psychological investigation of the unconscious determinants that block a person's fulfillment. Both theorists use conflict as a germinal explanatory category and growth in awareness as a step toward greater freedom.[63] Although Gutiérrez emphasizes the psychological aspect as an important element in the liberation process, few liberation theologians have written about it. In recent years, theologians, especially women, have focused more on this interior aspect of freedom.[64]

Gutiérrez sometimes calls this dimension of liberation historical and utopian. By history he means two things. In a general sense, it refers to the concrete events and personal experiences of a people. In a more technical sense, history represents what people intentionally create, such as a new awareness embodied in alternative ways of living, bonds of solidarity, and social structures. Because of this intentionality, history is oriented more toward building the future than remembering the past. Historical praxis involves a critical analysis of the past and present for the purpose of bringing about a new society and a new consciousness at a level Latin Americans have never experienced. History is no longer simply the agent of social change; it is the object of change because human beings alter its course.[65]

The utopian element conveys the imaginative and creative dimension necessary to bring in the genuinely new: new kinds of social relations among men and women, new political economy, and new forms of worship. Utopian thinking builds on rational, scientific thinking and planning in order to construct something qualitatively different from what presently exists. The creative imagination proposes alternative ways of relating, acting, and building. An

62. Gutiérrez, *Theology of Liberation*, 24, 138.
63. Ibid., 19–20.
64. Ivone Gebara, "Women Doing Theology in Latin America," in *Through Her Eyes*, ed. Elsa Tamez, 130.
65. Gutiérrez and Shaull, *Liberation and Change*, 84.

oppressed people must learn to move beyond the mere repetition of other people's ideas, traditions, and structures, and create their own neighborhood organizations, women's groups, and religious rituals.

Historical-utopian praxis consists of transforming one's self-awareness as well as bringing about a new way of being man and woman in history.[66] It requires resistance to imitating socialist systems of other nations, macho human relationships prevalent in its own culture, and traditional catechesis that perpetuates the oppression.

Historical-utopian praxis, like Freire's conscientizing praxis, endeavors to change the human agent as the agent changes society. It includes participation in sociopolitical activity, growth in self-awareness and social awareness, and in a person's capacity to make decisions. Juan Luis Segundo uses the phrase "conscientizing praxis," which is similar to Gutiérrez's historical-utopian praxis. Conscientization for Segundo means becoming critically aware of ideologies that seek to protect the status quo, thereby protecting the interests of dominant groups.[67] One achieves greater social awareness in Segundo's theology by discovering how ideological interpretations of Christian faith mirror and therefore reinforce dominant ideologies in society.[68] This methodological search aims to free theology and ethics from its anti-Christian and oppressive elements. Even more important, this liberation of theology frees the thinking of people burdened by an ideological theological doctrine.

Praxis as charity   At the faith level, liberation means freedom from sin, communion with God, and solidarity with one's neighbors. Human beings, in their striving for self-determination and for a freedom based on solidarity with others, are handicapped by the presence of sin in their lives—that selfish and disordered tendency that Hegel, Marx, Freud, and Freire failed to take into account. Sin, because of its self-focus, ruptures a person's relationship with God and neighbor.[69] Sin lies at the base of operations of the exploitive institution, affecting its values, its treatment of people, and its policies. Liberation theologians are intent upon showing that the ethos and policies of institutions do not arise by chance, but by the personal and collective will of their owners and managers. Consequently, authentic transformation requires both personal conversion and institutional change.[70]

66. Gustavo Gutiérrez, "Faith as Freedom: Solidarity with the Alienated and Confidence in the Future," *Horizons* 2, no. 1 (Spring 1975): 37.

67. Juan Luis Segundo, *Hidden Motives of Pastoral Action* (Maryknoll, N.Y.: Orbis Books, 1978), 21.

68. Segundo, "Shift within Latin American Theology," 5.

69. Gutiérrez, *Theology of Liberation*, 24.

70. Gutiérrez and Shaull, *Liberation and Change*, 84.

Liberation theologians have emphasized the existence of social sin and social conversion. Highlighting the social aspect of sin recognizes that social sin is a reality sui generis and as such cannot be addressed as though it possessed the same dynamic as does individual behavior.[71]

Transformation of a person from a life of selfishness to a life of serving others leads a person to the deepest dimension of freedom and to the core of what Gutiérrez means by praxis. Freedom moves from emancipation from external constraints to self-determination to a relationship between two persons. Gutiérrez likes Dietrich Bonhoeffer's statement on freedom: "being free means being free for the other, because the other has bound me to him."[72] Freedom to love the other happens because the other had previously loved one unconditionally. Freedom is a gift, not a personal achievement. As a consequence, one has the capacity to go out of oneself and to love others in return.

The gratuitous quality of the experience of being loved motivates and enables a person to love gratuitously. One loves others unconditionally because one has been given God's gift. God manifests a preferential love for the poor, not because they are necessarily better than others, but simply because they are poor and living in an inhuman situation.[73]

Charity represents the heart of praxis, which Gutiérrez calls the praxis of love. It takes concrete, historical form in persons living in solidarity with dispossessed and marginal people in society. This kind of praxis constitutes justice. Injustice is a break with friendship and love; justice is solidarity built on love. Asked about his emphasis on changing the capitalist structures, Gutiérrez responded: "My question is not about capitalism. My question is about poverty of persons and cultures. This is not an ideological question." For Gutiérrez, any loving action taken on behalf of the poor and oppressed constitutes "praxis." *Word* made concrete in *gesture* constitutes the praxis of love. It shapes attitudes and is celebrated in thanksgiving.[74] Gutiérrez defines Christian praxis as "transforming activity marked and illuminated by Christian love."[75]

71. Clodovis Boff and A. Libanio Christo, "Pecado Social y Conversión Estructural," published by *Conferencia Latinoamericana de Religiosas (CLAR)*, November 1978, 23–59.

72. Gutiérrez, *Theology of Liberation*, 25. Gutiérrez quotes Dietrich Bonhoeffer, *Creation and Fall: Temptation* (New York: Macmillan, 1966), 37.

73. Gustavo Gutiérrez, *On Job: God-Talk and the Suffering of the Innocent*, trans. Matthew J. O'Connell (Maryknoll, N.Y.: Orbis Books, 1987), 94.

74. Gustavo Gutiérrez, *Power of the Poor in History*, trans. Robert R. Barr (Maryknoll, N.Y.: Orbis Books, 1983), 37.

75. Gutiérrez, *Truth Shall Make You Free*, 138.

In a similar manner, Leonardo and Clodovis Boff refer to praxis as fundamentally Christian when it is "driven and guided by faith and by the Gospel present in the life of the people."[76] Segundo uses the term "orthopraxis" to describe liberative activity that issues from faith and the spirit of the gospel. Orthopraxis is "efficacious action in accordance with the Gospel."[77] Its opposite is "heteropraxis," which yields oppressive consequences that contradict gospel teaching.[78] Heteropraxis may include superstitious religious practices or unfair international policies of foreign trade.[79] For example, the cult of suffering among some Latin Americans supports a fatalistic resignation and superstitious religious practices.[80] Suspicious-looking praxis, therefore, must be scrutinized through analysis and theological reflection.

An Integral Praxis

This chapter examined the meaning of praxis as a step toward understanding how the term functions as a source for ethics in liberation theology. Influenced by Hegelian, Marxian, and Freirean philosophies, and especially by the Second Vatican Council, liberation theologians have expanded the meaning of praxis to make more explicit its human and faith dimensions. Although this theology does not provide a single definition acceptable to all, perhaps Gutiérrez's definition of praxis as a "transforming activity marked and illuminated by Christian love" best captures its meaning. This definition implies intentionality—that is, praxis, motivated by love, works toward a goal. For liberation theology, praxis aims at the integral liberation of the poor and oppressed. Gutiérrez specifies the objectives of this general goal within the political, historical, and religious dimensions. These objectives include establishing just institutions that allow access to and equal opportunity for all people; freedom to speak and to create one's own history; and solidarity with one's neighbors rooted in a communion with God. The praxis of charity informed by faith adds a distinctive religious notion to the historical and political dimensions of praxis.

Gutiérrez's three-dimensional structure of liberation together with its corresponding levels of praxis removes much (though not all) of the ambiguity

76. Boff and Boff, *Liberation Theology*, 61–62.

77. Alfred T. Hennelly, *Theologies in Conflict*, preface by Juan Luis Segundo (Maryknoll, N.Y.: Orbis Books, 1979), 92.

78. Segundo, "Shift within Latin American Theology," 6.

79. Gustavo Gutiérrez, "The Meaning of Development," *In Search of a Theology of Development* (Geneva, Switzerland: Ecumenical Centre, 1969), 167.

80. Segundo, "Shift within Latin American Theology," 6.

in the notion of praxis. As the concrete expression of the liberation process, praxis strives toward freedom on all the basic dimensions of human existence: the political-economic, cultural, psychological, and spiritual.[81] Gutiérrez's structure provides a comprehensive and coherent explanation of praxis by showing how love can motivate persons to work toward the liberation of the needy and downtrodden on many levels of human life. He further integrates the political and religious dimension by means of the human-utopian dimension. It processes the information and inspiration it receives "from below" (political involvement) and "from above" (divine revelation) and acts in accordance with these insights. Thus, praxis on the utopian level keeps politics and faith in a healthy symbiotic relationship by communicating insights from one to the other.

Although Gutiérrez's synthesis clarifies much about praxis, two areas of ambiguity lurk in the background. The first relates to orthopraxis and the second to experience. The way liberation theologians use the term "orthopraxis" becomes confusing because it connotes both a morally right practice and a true practice (theory meshes with reality). Earlier in the chapter, we saw that Enrique Dussel stated it as a principle of orthopraxis to liberate the poor. But he also writes of "orthopraxia . . . [as] true and proper acting."[82] Orthopraxis, he says along with Gutiérrez, should verify doctrine. Orthopraxis for Dussel and Gutiérrez serves as a standard of verification of whether theological teaching is true. But what determines whether praxis is right or just? Gutiérrez responds that the ultimate criterion for judgment is based on revelation and not on praxis.[83] Liberation theologians use the term "orthopraxis" in a moral sense to describe human acts that are just and in an epistemological sense as the basis for truth and true theological teaching. All theory, to be valid, must be grounded in reality. What they assume is that distortion of the truth generally results in an exploitation of groups in society.

The second ambiguity relates to using experience interchangeably with praxis. Although liberation theologians generally use the terms "praxis" and "practice" in the sense of transformative activity undertaken for the liberation of the poor, sometimes they substitute the word "experience" for "praxis." Ricardo Antoncich speaks of negative contrast experience, and Clodovis Boff talks about a praxis consisting of the totality of everyday experiences of people within the community of faith, which can be both positive and negative. These

81. Pope Paul VI, *Evangelii Nuntiandi* (Washington, D.C.: United States Catholic Conference, 1976), par. 31.
82. Dussel, *Ethics and Community*, 225–26.
83. Gutiérrez, *Theology of Liberation*, 180 n. 34.

would include prayer, family, sexuality, politics, and history.[84] For Antoncich, negative contrast experiences imply human resistance to oppressive activity, which is the beginning of transformation. Many female liberation theologians use the term "experience" instead of "praxis" because it better expresses what people have personally lived and, therefore, have been involved in. It also conveys a relational dimension, face-to-face encounters where men and women may share their experiences or directly confront offensive behavior.[85]

Finally, one should note that liberation theologians link knowledge to the transformation of reality. If the practice has moved beyond theoretical explanation, doctrine, or law, then it may call for changing the theory. Knowing is not a purely intellectual exercise. Knowledge of God leads to a change in the way one relates to God and to the poor. Gutiérrez says, "This preaching of a God who loves all persons equally should become flesh in history. . . . God becomes truth in the heart of a society when the social classes question themselves and take the part of the poor of the grass-roots classes, of the despised races, of the marginated cultures."[86] Knowledge of the exploitive practices of certain transnational corporations should impel people to transform the institutions.

This study of the meaning of praxis suggests three ways in which liberation theologians use praxis as a source in ethics. First, praxis serves as a method of doing theology. Theological reflection begins and ends in praxis, and praxis serves to verify the validity of teaching, laws, and doctrine. Second, praxis as a process of consciousness-raising transforms the moral agent. Third, as intentional transformative activity, praxis implies values that impel one to resist certain human acts and that guide one toward constructive change. The next chapter will investigate these three uses of praxis in ethics.

---

84. Clodovis Boff, *Feet-on-the-Ground Theology: A Brazilian Journey*, trans. Phillip Berryman (Maryknoll, N.Y.: Orbis Books, 1987), xi–xvi.

85. Gebara, "Women Doing Theology in Latin America," 126–28.

86. Gutiérrez and Shaull, *Liberation and Change*, 90.

3
Praxis and Ethics

The preceding chapter identified three roles that praxis plays in liberation ethics. Praxis first shapes the method of doing theological ethics. Second, in dialogue with revelation, praxis identifies human goods (e.g., solidarity) and norms (e.g., option for the poor) for moral decision making. Finally, as a consciousness-raising process (conscientization), praxis transforms the moral agent. This chapter investigates these three roles of praxis in order to show more precisely how praxis serves as a source in ethics and to evaluate how coherently liberation theologians use praxis as a source. The first two sections examine the objective dimension of ethics, addressing method and moral norms. The first of these considers how praxis methodically fashions liberation theology's style of doing ethics. The second explores how praxis helps identify certain human goods and norms. The chapter's third section delves into the subjective dimension of ethics, consciousness-raising, that distinctive praxis peculiar to liberation theology. Inasmuch as consciousness-raising brings about a change in self-awareness, freedom, and a sense of responsibility (a transformation of the subject's moral identity), praxis indirectly influences moral decision making.

As we saw in the last chapter, the concept of praxis within liberation theology connotes many things. Its principal meaning, as liberation theologians use the term, involves a decision to transform a structure, whether that structure be an agribusiness, a traditional way of doing theology, or a people's fatalistic worldview. An impoverished people chooses to change these structures because it has experienced their oppressive consequences—exploitation, domination, misery, terror, and brutality—and because it seeks a life that is meaningful, loving, and just. Praxis therefore involves a conscious decision and implies a moral judgment about a structure that should be changed. The judgment, however, does not necessarily include a moral argument, but operates somewhat like the Hegelian negation of a negation that happens as a people becomes aware of its alienation over a period of time and concomitantly recognizes its capacity to do something about it. Propelling this praxis are deep, though often unarticulated, convictions of what it means to be human, such as the right to have a voice and to work in conditions that are fair. With this notion of praxis in mind, we examine how praxis seeks to transform theology, ethics, and the moral agent.

Praxis Conditions the Method of Ethics

The method of liberation theology for many theologians unfolds like a four-act play. In its opening act, the play poses a problem that arises from the people's or theologian's praxis. Act two then analyzes the problem, examining causes, the network of actors involved, and consequences for the poor and society in general. The third act presents a theological reflection on a specific theme or issue connected with the problem. The final act draws up a new way of understanding Christian faith, a new method for doing theology, or perhaps guidelines for a new type of praxis.[1]

Whose Praxis?

Most liberation theologians share this four-act pattern of theological and ethical reflection that begins and ends with praxis. They differ, however, over whose praxis should serve as the point of departure, whether the subject matter for reflection should be the struggle of the poor against miserable living conditions, or whether contemporary theology and ethics seem unable to abet that struggle (and even appear to obstruct it). Mainline liberation theologians take two positions on this issue. Theologians like Gustavo Gutiérrez, Clodovis Boff, and Yvone Gebara generally begin with the praxis of the poor: their life of faith and spirituality, perspectives on love and justice, and problems of nutrition, housing, and education.[2] Other theologians, like Juan Luis Segundo

---

1. Francisco Moreno Rejón, "Seeking the Kingdom and Its Justice: the Development of the Ethic of Liberation," in *The Ethics of Liberation—The Liberation of Ethics*, ed. Dietmar Mieth and Jacques Pohier, *Concilium* 172 (Edinburgh: T & T Clark, 1984), 36.

2. Ignacio Ellacuría, "La teología de la liberación frente al cambio socio-histórico de América Latina," *Revista Latinoamericana de Teología* 4, no. 12 (1987): 241–43. Gutiérrez, Boff, and Gebara attend to the struggles and faith life of the people, seeking to give voice to the poor in their theology. This demands more direct contact with the poor, either by living within their environment or by maintaining regular contact with the people. These theologians learn from the praxis of the poor, while reflecting objectively and critically on their struggle.

and José Míguez Bonino, begin with the prevailing theology and try to transform it.[3]

This section concentrates on the second position, ably represented by Juan Luis Segundo, which starts by identifying and criticizing certain theologies suspected of supporting the status quo in Latin American society. I choose Segundo's work as a model because it coherently and clearly demonstrates how praxis challenges theory at each important step in his method and how the praxis–theory dialectic evokes human goods and principles that guide moral judgments. A second reason for concentrating on Segundo's method is that even though he attends more to hermeneutics than to ethics, he uses the hermeneutic circle to transform the method of doing ethics. He sketches the outlines of a social ethic based on efficacious love to replace what he sees as a predominantly individualistic ethics rooted in an interpersonal charity. Third, his theological-hermeneutical investigation concentrates on social criticism and structural transformation, which links it with social ethics. His social critique consists of unmasking oppressive ideologies and constructing new ones aimed at bringing about a new culture in Latin American society.

Segundo's method, the "hermeneutic circle," begins with praxis and ties praxis to theory at every point in the process, making his method thoroughly praxis grounded. Like Gutiérrez, Segundo thinks of liberating praxis as a reflective, transformative action guided by faith and motivated by love.[4] Segundo, however, gives his own seal to praxis by calling it "efficacious love." Theresa Lowe Ching's excellent study of Segundo's theology demonstrates

3. Juan Luis Segundo, "Shift within Latin American Theology," lecture presented at Regis College, Toronto (March 22, 1983). Segundo explains that in the beginning of the liberation movement, his students, collaborators from within the middle class, and he set out to fight for the liberation of the poor, but changed their tack after discovering that Christian beliefs and doctrines themselves impeded the path toward liberation. Traditional church doctrine reinforced the dominating ideologies of the ruling class. Consequently, the radical theologians refocused their objective on transforming theology itself, thinking that a liberating theology could have a deep and lasting impact on certain teachings and practices of the churches. Creating a new theology, they felt, was a prerequisite for the liberation of the poor. Therefore, they committed themselves to identifying the anti-Christian elements in the church's theology and to replacing them with a new theology capable of fostering liberating pastoral activities within the church. Although Segundo does not reject the other approach, he thinks theologians tend to lose critical objectivity and creativity when they immerse themselves in the life situation of the poor.

4. The other leading liberation theologians agree with Segundo that praxis means reflective transformative action illumined by faith and motivated by love. See Gutiérrez, *Truth Shall Make You Free, 99;* Boff and Boff, *Liberation Theology, 61–62.*

that "efficacious love" best describes his praxis. She rightly argues that Segundo's concept of efficacious love organizes his theological reflection by "providing its starting point, its goal, and the criterion of its development."[5] Efficacious love is the total self-gift of God revealed in Jesus of Nazareth and is also the source of human love, which ought to move everyone to pursue the truth and guide persons in making moral choices. Segundo calls this love "efficacious" because it transforms persons and institutions using the means available in the concrete situation.

Ideologies and Their Relation to Faith

The concepts of ideology and faith are central in the hermeneutics of Segundo. He ascribes three shades of meaning to ideology. First, in its most basic and neutral sense, ideology is a means to an end—"the systematic aggregate of ideas used to attain some goal."[6] The end gives meaning and direction to the means and in this sense justifies the means. All institutions, whether the church, the state, or private corporations, employ ideologies to accomplish their ends, though not all institutions appeal to faith to guide their policies.

In its second and negative sense, ideology denotes any idea or system of thought that disguises, distorts, or even sacralizes a certain political or economic system for the sake of certain special interests.[7] Marxism and liberalism exemplify these distorted or "one-sided" ideologies because both systems lack an external or transcendent reference point necessary for self-criticism. One-sided ideologies have blind spots. For example, Marxist critics may correctly criticize capitalism for its justification of the power arrangements of the wealthy owners and for its masking structural alienation among workers. But Marxists remain blind to the distortion brought about by their own scientific interpretation of the political economy. They fail to see and acknowledge an outside reference point or ultimate value necessary to evaluate both the superstructure and the infrastructure. Segundo calls this ultimate value "faith."

Finally, Segundo uses ideology in a third and positive sense to denote a means that accurately represents the actual situation or the consensus of a majority to change its institutions according to a set of values widely shared. Unlike the negative, one-sided ideology, the positive form possesses flexibility

5. Theresa Lowe Ching, *Efficacious Love: Its Meaning and Function in the Theology of Juan Luis Segundo* (Lanham, Md.: University Press of America, 1990), 49.
6. Juan Luis Segundo, *Faith and Ideologies*, trans. John Drury (Maryknoll, N.Y.: Orbis Books, 1984), 16.
7. Ibid., 97.

to be simultaneously normative and open to self-criticism and change.[8] The major task of Segundo's hermeneutic circle involves criticizing one-sided ideologies and replacing them with more adequate ones that express the true state of affairs. For ideologies to be positive—that is, nondistortional—they must be guided by faith. Ideologies by definition are always the means, while faith is always an end. In this third and positive sense, ideology functions as the efficacious and relative means for expressing the absolute end of faith.

Segundo distinguishes two types of faith: anthropological and religious. Anthropological faith expresses the basic human capacity to make an unconditional commitment to ultimate meaning and value.[9] Because it commits itself to ultimates, faith interprets and judges reality accordingly. Faith, therefore, guides personal choices. Persons come to faith by committing themselves to certain values on the basis of the testimony of others ("referential witnesses") who have shown by their own lives the goodness or rightness of certain ways of living. Individuals believe something to be good and worthwhile on the testimony of another. Because faith claims absolute value for a person, it subordinates every ideology to the ultimate, whether the ideology be an economic system, an ecclesiology, or an ethics. Faith also ranks a person's values, thus helping individuals to make choices. Paradoxically, faith, which places ideologies in proper perspective, needs ideologies to express itself. Even though faith possesses a transcendent dimension that surmounts experimental verification (e.g., the truth that God is love), it requires human concepts and symbols that only inadequately express its full meaning.[10]

Religious faith builds on anthropological faith. The former comes into being when an individual moves from the level of entrusting oneself to a reliable human witness (or to a meaning structure) to a more profound level in which the individual perceives that God stands behind the reliable witnesses and meaning structure.[11] In making this leap of faith, the believer does not abandon the human witnesses and trust only in God as the only reliable witness. Continuing to trust in human witnesses, the person now recognizes that what was believed to be merely human meaning and value possesses a transcendent dimension grounded in God.[12]

Subjectively considered, faith is unconditional trust; objectively considered, faith is a "deutero-learning" process in which persons learn how to create

8. Ibid., 300–301.
9. Ibid., 15–16.
10. Ibid., 73–74.
11. Juan Luis Segundo, *The Liberation of Theology*, trans. John Drury (Maryknoll, N.Y.: Orbis Books, 1976), 179.
12. Segundo, *Faith and Ideologies*, 63–64.

new meaning systems or ideologies by immersing themselves both in the stories
of the Bible and in the experiences of people. For Segundo, working through
the hermeneutic circle constitutes an expression of faith because participants
dedicate their life to the goal of creating meaning and value. Divine revelation
as the object of faith does not provide the religious believer with a prefabricated
doctrine or a morality, but instead directs people toward the construction of
a theology and a morality.[13]

In opposition to traditional Christian theology, which regards its doctrine
as transcending ideologies, Segundo's theology (and liberation theology generally) maintains that no theology exists in an incubator unaffected by cultural
conditions.[14] Demonic elements within cultures can negatively influence the
church and its theology even as the church seeks to transform that culture
through evangelization. The Catholic church, for example, has tried to influence the state by developing ideologies to support its own missionary objectives, including laws banning divorce, ensuring Catholic education for all, and
aiding the poor. In cooperating with the Catholic church in these matters, the
state in turn has created its own ideologies. Compromises made between these
two institutions have often produced negative ideologies, such as the church
softening its prophetic voice against institutions that exploit the poor in order
to ensure support of its teaching and its parochial schools. The hermeneutic
circle addresses these kinds of ideologies infesting theology and pastoral practice
in Latin America.

Praxis Challenges Ideology

The hermeneutic circle functions as Segundo's theological method of
interpreting the Bible in light of an ever-changing reality. He defines his hermeneutic circle as "the continuing change in our interpretation of the Bible
which is dictated by the continuing changes in our present-day reality, both
individual and societal."[15] In general terms, this method consists of an open
dialectical system in which the social context, interpreted through praxis and
analysis, influences the reading of the biblical text, and a rereading of the
biblical text challenges the context. Hence, his method correlates in a dialectical
manner both praxis and Scripture.

The circle moves clockwise from praxis (ideological suspicion) to an
analysis of the superstructure and of theology. Next it undertakes an analysis

13. Ibid., 179–80.
14. Segundo, *Liberation of Theology*, 74.
15. Ibid., 8–9.

of the prevailing mode of interpreting Scripture (exegetical suspicion) that then leads to constructing a new way of interpreting the Bible (new hermeneutics). Finally, the new way of reading the Bible illumines the historical situation and thereby tries to create a new pastoral practice within the church.

Hermeneutic Circle

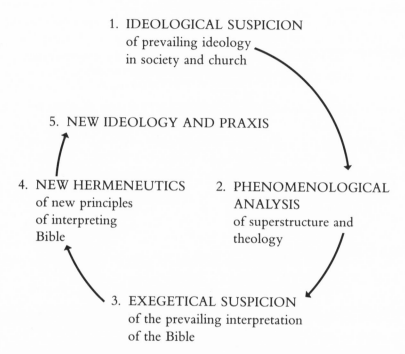

1. IDEOLOGICAL SUSPICION
   of prevailing ideology
   in society and church

5. NEW IDEOLOGY AND PRAXIS

4. NEW HERMENEUTICS   2. PHENOMENOLOGICAL
   of new principles   ANALYSIS
   of interpreting   of superstructure and
   Bible   theology

3. EXEGETICAL SUSPICION
   of the prevailing interpretation
   of the Bible

Praxis begins with an experience of an oppressive social situation, followed by a reflection on that experience. In the course of the reflection, Segundo expresses an "ideological suspicion," or an unfavorable judgment, about the ideology that justifies and thereby keeps in place the oppressive practice. He cites, for example, what many Latin Americans have observed, namely, the contradiction between the promises of development made by politicians and economists in the 1950s and the existing underdevelopment marked by hunger, high infant mortality, and illiteracy among the masses. Suspicion about the development model stimulated Latin American social scientists to undertake their own analyses, which led them to create the ideology of dependency, which they felt more accurately described the political-economic reality in Latin America.

Piggybacking on the social scientists' insight on dependency, Segundo and his colleagues began to suspect that traditional theologies and church teaching and practice reinforced the existing state of affairs and the state's model of development. His initial investigation stimulated still another hunch, an "exegetical suspicion" about the way theologians interpret biblical texts that generate conservative theology supportive of the status quo. In the final phase of Segundo's circle, he explores a new hermeneutics that will make possible the construction of new theologies that more adequately address social reality.

Praxis Challenges Ethical Language

Although Segundo does not consider himself to be a moral theologian, he does employ his method to address ethical concepts, the role of moral norms, and the nature of ethics. This section shows how he addresses ethics within his hermeneutical circle, focusing on the meaning of violence in relation to the gospel of love. From its inception, liberation theology has been attacked from many quarters, and accused of supporting Marxist class struggle and the violent upheaval of oppressive regimes. Although Segundo acknowledges the obvious fact that many Latin American nations have undergone a cataclysm over the past thirty years, he refutes the allegations that liberation theology foments class struggle as a strategy and depicts revolutionary violence as its utopian dream.[16] His major task, however, is not to defend liberation theology against such criticism but to reinterpret the meaning of violence, a necessary step in a grand project of constructing a new cultural tradition based on justice and peace.[17]

I shall show how Segundo illumines the meaning of violence by means of his hermeneutic circle, emphasizing how praxis influences the meaning of violence, ethical language, and his contextualist ethics.

Suspicion about the Meaning of Violence

Segundo's praxis (transforming theology in a revolutionary situation) arouses his suspicion that theological-ethical treatments of violence often miss the mark, as did certain theologians at the 1966 World Conference on Church and Society in Geneva. One of its participants, H. D. Wendland, argued that Christians should participate in revolution by "quiet, unarmed loving action

16. Juan Luis Segundo, *Theology and the Church: A Response to Cardinal Ratzinger and a Warning to the Whole Church*, trans. John W. Diercksmeier (Minneapolis: A Seabury Book, Winston Press, 1985), 107–38.

17. Segundo, *Faith and Ideologies*, 300.

and service." Segundo judged this theological response inadequate, because it fails to address essential questions, such as the intention of the revolutionaries—whether, for example, these agents are attempting to kill someone, defend themselves, or protect others from death.[18] Does the unarmed Christian act morally by supporting armed agents? A second participant, Jan Milic Lochman, restricted violence to the use of physical force. His definition is a negative ideology, because it gives a false picture of violence, thereby short-circuiting a constructive analysis of the mechanism of violence. Both Wendland and Lochman omitted from their discussions those conscious and unconscious mental tendencies and institutional policies that kill many more millions of people than do military arms used in guerrilla war.

Analysis of Violence in Relation to Love

Dissatisfaction with the Wendland-Lochman interpretation prompted Segundo to undertake a phenomenological analysis of violence in relation to love. He develops in his analysis the law of the economy of energy, which states that love is limited by the objective conditions of human existence: each person possesses a fixed capacity of energy available for loving others. The law therefore permits human beings to love a specific number of persons. The attempt to love beyond our capacity diminishes the quality of our love. "If we truly love a specific number of persons," Segundo says, "we cannot incorporate other people into our love . . . without taking energy away from certain areas of our love for the first group."[19] By loving person X, I make myself unavailable to love persons Y and Z. Given this human condition, each of us necessarily must adopt some mechanism to keep a whole host of people at a distance so that we can effectively love a certain group of people.

Segundo defines violence as "keeping persons at arm's length," which could mean segregating ourselves from others or dealing perfunctorily with individuals and groups. Segundo regards this mechanism as violence, because it reifies persons by treating them as though they were objects instead of subjects. Since all human beings must make choices that require treating persons perfunctorily, no one escapes committing violence, not even the most loving person such as Jesus. Human beings must necessarily treat certain persons and groups as functionaries in order to love others efficaciously.

Although Segundo may have overextended the meaning of violence, he thinks his definition more adequately expresses its core meaning. Putting others

18. Segundo, *Liberation of Theology*, 156.
19. Ibid., 157.

at arm's length lies at the heart of institutional violence, passive resistance, and all forms of armed aggression. Hence, violence, as he defines it, emerges in most ethical choices. He asks his readers to consider the case of a householder who confronts a burglar in the act of robbing his house. The dweller finds himself faced with two basic options: either treat the burglar as a person in the deepest personal sense by talking to him and by showing an interest in his situation, or deal impersonally with the thief by physically repelling him or by calling the police. Although the personal approach might at first seem more in line with the gospel command to walk the extra mile or to give up one's spare coat, other considerations, such as protecting one's own family, might urge him to do otherwise. Prior commitments of efficacious love play an important part in calculating one's store of energy or love. "Love calls for a prudent distribution of this energy if it is to be effective."[20] By relating impersonally to the burglar (e.g., calling the police or repelling him by some physical means), the householder may be loving more efficaciously even though the decision involves the use of coercion by handing the burglar over to the police.

Segundo maintains that even though all types of violence are evil, not all decisions to use violence are morally wrong. The morality of violent acts or policies depends upon the end intended. If the agent intends to love an oppressed group efficaciously, then commitment to that group, even though it involves violence to the nonoppressed, may be the more responsible act. However, should the agent commit an act of violence out of selfishness, then the action is bad. The intention of the agent (love) determines the rightness or wrongness of the action.

Although Segundo does not use the terms "premoral" and "moral" evil in his discussion, the distinction may clarify what he is saying about the morality of violent acts. Premoral evil is an act that causes harm to another, but which is either not intended by the actor, or is done for a proportionate reason such as killing an assailant in self-defense. Moral evil involves the intention of an actor to harm another for inappropriate reasons, such as killing for selfish gain.[21] For Segundo, violence always involves premoral evil because it causes harm to persons even when it is unintentional. Violence entails moral evil whenever the agent intends the harm without a sufficient or proportionate reason.

20. Ibid., 162.
21. Josef Fuchs, "The Absoluteness of Moral Terms," in *Readings in Moral Theology No. 1*, ed. Charles E. Curran and Richard A. McCormick (New York: Paulist Press, 1979), 119–22.

Because violence is always a premoral evil, Segundo formulates a corollary of his law of energy: persons should reduce "the quantum of violence required for efficacy to the lowest possible level."[22] One should minimize violence because it is better, whenever possible, to treat others as persons and not as mere functions or things. Faced with dilemmas such as the one just presented, the moral agent must consider the real alternatives, evaluate the claims that each party makes on the agent's love, and assess the foreseeable violence that might result from each alternative.

Segundo correctly demonstrates that we cannot love everyone equally or express our love to all our neighbors, but he fails to show how we should distribute our love when faced with dilemmas (e.g., according to a principle of fairness). Segundo appeals only to the virtue of prudence and the principle of preferential option for the poor as the means to guide the agent. But in situations where choices involve two or more poor groups, a standard for discerning which poor group should be given priority seems to be needed.

A weakness in his presentation of violence in relation to love is that love is restricted to action. While love without deeds is shallow and probably not love at all, love understood as willing the good of another need not be expressed in every instance by action or be thought of as nonexistent when a person cannot help a neighbor in need. Therefore, when I do not assist a person requesting my help because of a second person's more pressing need, I do not necessarily act violently toward the first person. I may continue to love the first person even though I do not help that individual here and now. Violence as reification would always seem to involve disrespecting or demeaning a person. Showing disrespect to a friend, client, or customer is quite different from treating the person perfunctorily.

Biblical Ethics and Violence

In light of his new definition of violence, Segundo reinterprets passages of the Bible that deal with conflict and violence. His praxis and analysis cast a new light on the meaning of violence found in the gospel, challenging the interpretation that says Jesus was a nonviolent man for others. The latter interpretation exempts Jesus from the basic law of the economy of energy, implying that he is not a full human being living within the limits of this law. However, if we assume that Jesus is subject to this law, then we find surprising discoveries in the gospel about his human limitations, including the necessity of his putting others at arm's length.

22. Segundo, *Liberation of Theology*, 162.

Many gospel passages demonstrate Jesus' use of violence. Jesus decides to abandon John the Baptist after the latter was arrested and incarcerated by Herod for proclaiming the same message that Jesus was proclaiming. Jesus' refusal to side with John publicly or even to come to John's rescue (Mark 1:14) constitutes, according to Segundo, an act of violence. In a second instance of violence, Jesus frequently becomes angry at the Pharisees, calling them "hypocrites" because of their refusal to deal with his question whether one could heal a person on the Sabbath (Mark 3:1-6). In a third instance, Jesus puts off the Syro-Phoenician woman who begs Jesus to cure her daughter, telling her: "Let the children be satisfied first; it is not fair to take the children's bread and throw it to the dogs" (Mark 7:27). Although Jesus finally accedes to her request, his initial response keeps her at arm's length.[23] Although all are violent acts, each action of Jesus can be justified in light of his intention to love his own people in an efficacious manner. Jesus does violence to others because he must follow the law of economy of energy; however, his actions are justified by his intention to love his own people efficaciously.

Returning to the concepts of faith and ideologies, Segundo interprets how the Bible should be used to do ethics. As we saw earlier, faith is an absolute, concerned with ultimate ends that call every human being toward humane communitarian existence and salvation. Ideologies, especially revelation, provide the concrete means for realizing the ends demanded by faith and necessary to guide persons along the path of righteousness. Although Scripture is an inspired and privileged means for illumining that path, it is a historically and culturally conditioned document. This means that Scripture can offer general guidance, but not specific prescriptions written for a particular historical audience. Specific injunctions are ideologies expressive of historical faith, but not faith itself; hence they should not be invoked as though they are absolute dictates issued by God and intended for all people throughout history. The fact that biblical imperatives sometimes contradict each other makes it evident that the Bible is a relative and historically conditioned document. For example, God through Moses commands the Israelites to slay those opposing God's plans (Deut. 7:16), but Jesus urges his followers to turn the other cheek (Matt. 5:39). The biblical commandment forbidding killing means that one must not kill another without a justifiable reason.[24]

Although Jesus commands his disciples to love their neighbor and even enemies who violate or oppress them, Segundo interprets the commands as general imperatives accentuating the unconditional character of love, which is

23. Ibid., 162–63.
24. Ibid., 166.

a demand of faith. The particular injunctions should be read as a call to live in accordance with the most efficacious love possible in the concrete situation.[25] The specification of the general command to love the enemy must be discerned within a concrete social context.

To summarize, because the specific biblical teachings about morality are ideologies that express the absolute imperative of faith for a particular people at a definite time and place in history, they cannot be used as absolute standards. Efficacious love, informed by faith, illumines the concrete goods that should be used to guide persons in their choices.

Praxis and Contextualism

Praxis enters into Segundo's method (and into the method of liberation theologians generally) through an encounter with oppression of various kinds. Oppressive institutional policies, whether economic, political, or theological, are validated by ideologies. Unless these ideologies are identified, challenged, and transformed, the oppression and the agents of oppression are impregnable. Segundo's genius lies in creating a method whereby a negative ideology—the formidable partner of oppressive practice—can be transformed.

Casting a suspicion on an ideology amounts to a denunciation or moral judgment. Unlike natural law and Kantian ethical approaches that argue to a moral conclusion guided by a standard, liberation ethics frequently intuits what is wrong or unjust by means of contrasts in the historical situation. Thus, the understanding of freedom and justice unfolds historically and contextually by recognizing what human freedom is not: it is not being reduced to silence and passivity in the work place, or being treated as a mule doing its master's every command, or being imprisoned, tortured, and executed without due juridical process. Thus, Latin Americans, faced with oppressive policies and severe repressive measures, respond with an instinctive sense for what is liberative. In contending that liberation ethics is a contextual ethics, German ethicist Dietmar Mieth says: "Reflection about praxis is replaced by reflection arising out of praxis. This means, for instance, that it is very hard to draw up general solutions to problems in advance, before they have been worked on practically."[26]

So it is with Segundo's ideological suspicion, which emerges from praxis. Segundo reaches the judgment that ideology X is inadequate or unjust on the

25. Ibid., 155.
26. Dietmar Mieth, "Autonomy or Liberation: Two Paradigms of Christian Ethics?" in *The Ethics of Liberation—The Liberation of Ethics*, ed. Dietmar Mieth and Jacques Pohier (Edinburgh: T & T Clark, 1984), 89.

basis of experiences of unjust practices or prejudicial attitudes, corroborated by an analysis of the situation, and informed by faith. In addressing the problem of violence, he draws upon general moral principles (efficacious love, economy of energy, and preferential option for the poor).

Given the general nature of these broad imperatives, critics have suggested that Segundo has constructed a radical situation ethics.[27] Addressing the criticism, Segundo rejects the type of situation ethics that confines its attention to the moment of decision alone, "because no single *moment* in itself possesses any ethical principle for defining human conduct."[28] Theology and ethics must be historically grounded; situationism by contrast is ahistorical. Segundo thinks of himself as an ethical contextualist; that is, he makes moral judgments about issues from within the historical context, illumined by social analysis and by Scripture. The absolute element of faith guides decision making, but it does not provide moral content aside from general categorical imperatives mentioned above. Faith directs moral choices first of all by reminding the persons and communities of the absolute value toward which they are striving (e.g., the kingdom of God). Thus, faith works against absolutizing a particular moral practice, such as a people's armed rebellion or a pacifist stance within a situation of revolutionary violence. Second, faith draws persons to strive after universal, communitarian values that express the ultimate value being pursued.

Segundo summarizes his ethics governing the use of violence according to the principle "the end justifies the means."[29] Faith, expressed through efficacious love, gives value or goodness to the means. This dictum does not connote that the means is merely a neutral instrument lacking value, but that it is an act deriving its value and direction from the end. In this sense, he describes his approach as a morality of ends, which means that his ethics is teleological but not utilitarian.

Commenting on Segundo's ethics, Dennis McCann suggests that Segundo is a utilitarian: "In principle there are no means that are intrinsically inappropriate to the struggle for liberation."[30] However, Segundo explicitly rejects this interpretation, pointing out that Christian morality strives toward ends that are most universal, communitarian, and generous-hearted, and therefore would antecedently oppose individualistic, self-seeking acts. The morality

27. Brian Hebblethwaite, *Christian Ethics in the Modern Age* (Philadelphia: Westminster Press, 1982), 83–100.

28. Segundo, *Liberation of Theology*, 174.

29. Ibid., 171.

30. Dennis McCann, *Christian Realism and Liberation Theology: Practical Theologies in Creative Conflict* (Maryknoll, N.Y.: Orbis Books, 1981), 225.

of human acts "stems from their relationship to an end, not from their intrinsic nature," but this does not mean that anything is justified.[31]

Segundo's law of economy of energy resembles the moral principle of proportionality in certain respects, but differs from it in others. According to proportionality, the means should be commensurate with the end. With respect to violence, the moral agent should choose the means that achieves the desired result with the least amount of violence. Similarly, the law of economy of energy subordinates means to the end and tries to minimize evil consequences. Proportionality in certain traditions (e.g., Roman Catholicism) antecedently prohibits the use of certain means, such as the intentional killing of noncombatants in war, even when the probable good consequences of that act outweigh the bad (bombing densely populated cities to end the war earlier). However, Segundo is unclear whether he would include the principle of discrimination (that protects noncombatants in war) as part of the economy-of-energy law. In an early reflection on violence (*The Liberation of Theology*, 1976), he rejects the principle that certain acts of violence are intrinsically evil. Yet in a later reflection on violence (*Faith and Ideologies*, 1984), he argues that repression that destroys the social ecology cannot be justified, suggesting that certain types of violence are to be condemned outright. Finally, Segundo's principle differs from proportionalism by its broadening the concept of violence to include any reification of persons, whether by impersonal behavior, institutional policy, or physical coercion.

Praxis Transforms the Agent

We have seen how praxis by means of the hermeneutic circle unmasks negative or one-sided ideologies that misrepresent the actual state of affairs. Negative ideologies beget and nurture a false consciousness in people by feeding them misinformation or partial explanations. As we saw in chapter 1, ideologies can also dominate the fatalistic consciousness of people like Severino, who utters with a sigh of resignation: "Some are born rich and others poor. Such is the will of God." The innovative practice of consciousness-raising developed by Paulo Freire, and appropriated with some modification by liberation theology, aimed to free persons from a fatalistic outlook so that they might assume an active control over their lives.

Consciousness-Raising as a Dimension of Conversion

Liberation theologians think of consciousness-raising as a praxis involving a growth-producing process of transformation that moves from a fatalistic and

31. Segundo, *Liberation of Theology*, 171–72.

uncritical perspective to a hopeful and critical outlook. Loosening the bonds of fatalism requires changing one's image of God from an authoritarian power who imposes suffering and preaches resignation, to a liberating God who calls a people out of bondage. The message heard from the authoritarian God is, "blessed are the poor, because while they have suffering and sorrow in this life, they'll have joy in the next life."[32] The message from the liberating God is, "blessed are the poor, because they, like Jesus, commit themselves to the crucified of this world by feeding the hungry and defending the weak and dehumanized; they will possess a life of love, solidarity, and courage."[33]

Consciousness-raising on the psychological level demands setting up conditions that allow individuals to distinguish the changeable from the unchangeable or, in Freire's terms, to recognize the difference between culture, which human beings create, and nature, which human beings receive. Once this distinction takes hold, illiterate peasants begin to see that they too can change things in their milieu. Consciousness-raising often comes about within small community settings, as within a basic community, where individuals are encouraged to identify problems encountered in their everyday lives. In dialogue with a gospel reading, men and women discuss how they can effectively address the problem, and then explore strategies for resolving it. The process seeks to instill in the participants self-awareness, social-awareness, and confidence that they can change their situation.

Liberation theologians and the Latin American conference of bishops at Medellín (CELAM II) linked consciousness-raising to evangelization and religious conversion. Gustavo Gutiérrez describes conversion as breaking with personal and social sin, and setting out on a new path. This entails changing our mental categories or attitudes that determine how we relate to God, neighbor, our cultural milieu, and social class. Conversion is the gift of God's kingdom that matures persons in profound ways, urging them to act justly toward all, especially toward those suffering.[34] Just as conversion involves growth in new awareness of who we are in relation to God and neighbor, so also does consciousness-raising involve an awakening of ourselves as creators and doers of justice. The bishops at Medellín said that justice and peace "conquer by means of a dynamic action of awakening (concientización)," which includes

32. María López Vigil, Don Lito of El Salvador, (Maryknoll, N.Y.: Orbis Books, 1990), 30–31.

33. Boff, Passion of Christ, Passion of the World, 130–32.

34. Gutiérrez, Truth Shall Make You Free; see also his Theology of Liberation, 119, and his We Drink from Our Own Wells, 95–96.

organizing the popular sectors for social change.[35] They emphasized the importance of the poor and oppressed moving from a passive state to active involvement and from resignation to critical awareness and action. As a component of conversion that heightens awareness of human beings' role in history, consciousness-raising awakens individuals and communities to become more free, less dependent, and aware of justice. All of this infuses in them a sense of responsibility, solidarity, and creativity.[36]

Being responsible subjects requires that people become aware of themselves as an oppressed social group. Awakening often happens through the experience of suffering that generates an awareness of a contradiction between what the oppressed are told they are and what they know themselves to be. Latin American women's experience of contrasts gave rise to the insight that liberation must change the patriarchal and macho culture in which they live. Working with men for many years in the liberation struggle, women became aware of the contradiction of collaborating with men for the transformation of imperialist and class dominance while experiencing male dominance within their movement. Changing the political economy was insufficient. The macho ethos and patriarchal structures also needed to be addressed.

Brazilian theologian Ana María Tepedino identified the twofold starting point for liberation theology: the existential experience of women searching for their own identity and the experience of faith lived from the underside of power and authority.[37] The search for identity, theologian Yvone Gebara says, "means working on ourselves fighting from within the false images we have acquired for ourselves."[38] Female liberation theologians include this "working on ourselves" within the wider social struggle of liberation for the poor. Woman's option for self includes an option for others.

Is Consciousness-Raising Manipulative?

Consciousness-raising has encountered criticism both in the United States and in Latin America. U.S. sociologist Peter Berger criticized the process for

35. Second General Conference of Latin American Bishops (CELAM), "Peace," in *The Church in the Present-Day Transformation of Latin America in the Light of the Council*, vol. 2: *Conclusions* (Bogotá, Colombia: General Secretariat of CELAM, 1970), par. 18.

36. Ibid., pars. 18, 21. See also Gutiérrez, *Theology of Liberation*, 57; Yvone Gebara, "Option for the Poor as an Option for the Poor Woman," in *Women, Work and Poverty*, ed. Elisabeth Schüssler Fiorenza and Anne Carr (Edinburgh: T & T Clark, 1987), 115.

37. Ana María Tepedino, "Feminist Theology as the Fruit of Passion and Compassion," in *With Passion and Compassion: Third World Women Doing Theology*, ed. Virginia Fabella and Mercy Amba Oduyoye (Maryknoll, N.Y.: Orbis Books, 1988), 165.

38. Gebara, "Option for the Poor," 111–12.

its elitist assumption about consciousness and for its exploitive practice. "Consciousness-raising," Berger argued, "implies philosophical error and political irony." The error is based on a false assumption that the illiterate peasants do not understand their own situation or what is good for them and therefore need to be enlightened. "Consciousness-raising is a project of higher-class individuals directed at lower-class populations."[39] Consciousness-raising, Berger says, erroneously assumes a hierarchy of consciousness, which moves from a semi-intransitive, fatalistic consciousness among the lower classes, to a transitive, fanaticized stage, to a third stage that is both transitive and critical. The third stage represents the fully enlightened consciousness possessed by people of a higher class. The political irony lies in the use of a consciousness-raising program by elitists from this higher class who view themselves as genuine democrats, but who fail to see that their efforts constitute a kind of "cognitive imperialism." They presume that their consciousness is more humane, more free than is the consciousness of peasants, and that they can and should raise it to a higher, more humane level. Berger concludes: "There can be no such thing [consciousness-raising] because all of us are, in principle, equally endowed when it comes to having consciousness."[40]

His contention that no one is more conscious than anyone else assumes that consciousness is an either-or phenomenon that does not admit of stages. Either people have it, or, as in the case of very young children or mentally handicapped, they do not. If they do, then the attempt by one group to "raise" the consciousness of a second group is tantamount to imposing values, perceptions, and action on those who have organized their relation to the world differently. Change of consciousness for Berger means a rearrangement of cognitive content.

Although Berger identifies problem areas in consciousness-raising, such as its proneness to becoming an elitist and manipulative structure, he distorts the meaning of the term by overemphasizing its cognitive dimension. He thinks of it as a process of acquiring knowledge and receiving a new set of values from the elite. He fails, however, to see that consciousness-raising also involves a change in a person's self-perception and critical awareness of social relationships. Consciousness is not only cognitive in the sense that the knower knows objects. It is also self-reflective, enabling the knower to know oneself as known. In reflexive knowing, the subject or knower knows oneself twice: first as a subject and then as an object. As a subject, I am aware of experiencing,

39. Peter L. Berger, "The False Consciousness of 'Consciousness Raising,'" *Worldview* (January 1975): 33–38.
40. Ibid., 38.

understanding, or creating objects; as an object, I reflect on myself to gain self-knowledge. In consciousness-raising, individuals experience themselves as subject of their action (a reflexive activity) and gain deeper insight into the world by replacing magical explanations with real causes (a cognitive activity). Both reflexive and cognitive aspects constitute consciousness-raising.

As for the danger of pastoral leaders manipulating a people, this is possible in any kind of teaching situation. However, both Freire and liberation theologians hold a profound respect for the indigenous culture, values, and experiences of a people, insisting that community leaders of a higher class must allow the lower-class people to evaluate their own attitudes and practices. Indeed, acquiring a new self-awareness can be achieved only in conditions where leaders foster the conditions of trust, mutual respect, and dialogue among participants. An oppressed consciousness attributes the explanation of certain phenomena to something outside objective reality, such as a superreality or something within themselves. This manner of perceiving and relating to the world does not change by telling people what to do, or even by value clarification. A person gains a critical consciousness through the union of action and reflection with people who share a common goal and who develop mutual respect and trust for members of that group.[41] The facilitator invites the participants to reflect upon their own world, including their own symbols, values, rituals, and everyday routines. They would then be encouraged to share perceptions of their world in an open, nonmanipulative process. The facilitator must not take over the discussion, set forth the truth, or indoctrinate. Freire and liberation theologians eschew the kind of education that imposes an alien system of values on a people. Freire calls such an imposition "cultural invasion," where the invader "reduces the people in the situation he invades to mere objects of his action."[42]

Freire and liberation theologians would concur with Berger that cognitive imperialists, like cultural invaders, should play no role in consciousness-raising. Criticism like Berger's, in the words of Chilean theologian Segundo Galilea, erroneously caricatures conscientization as "an ideological politicization marked by political impositions and cultural oppression." Consciousness-raising, Galilea says, "means moving from an uncritical, conformist outlook based on feelings of cultural inferiority to a creative outlook that is aware of its own identity and critical of all forms of cultural, ideological, and political alienation, however subtle they may be."[43]

41. Paulo Freire, *Cultural Action for Freedom*, Monograph Series (Cambridge: *Harvard Educational Review*, 1970), 32–52.
42. Ibid., 113.
43. Segundo Galilea, "Liberation Theology and New Tasks Facing Christians," in *Frontiers of Theology in Latin America*, ed. Rosino Gibellini, trans. John Drury (Maryknoll, N.Y.: Orbis Books, 1979), 173.

Radical or Reformist Awareness?

Although Berger misinterprets the meaning of consciousness-raising within liberation theology, he does identify a potential danger within conscientizing movements in which a vanguard or dogmatic leader inflicts values and strategies on the group. Brazilian philosopher Enrique Vaz, who is sympathetic to liberation theology, raised a pastoral-theological dilemma regarding the use of consciousness-raising as part of the Catholic church's task of proclaiming the gospel. Reflecting on this dilemma at the dawn of the liberation movement, he emphasized the importance of balancing local self-determination of the local basic church community and its responsibility to the larger church. Vaz pointed out that because the church in Latin America calls for religious conversion and a social awakening of the people that requires a reordering of society's interests and goals, consciousness-raising necessarily becomes ideological (in Segundo's neutral sense). Therefore, bishops and indigenous leaders must face the question: Which ideology should we embrace?[44]

In the late 1960s in Brazil, the Christian reformists and the revolutionaries debated this question. Both groups agreed that the ideology of the masses should be followed, but proposed different means for assisting the awakening of the oppressed people's spontaneous ideology for social change. In other words, these two groups clashed on the very meaning of consciousness-raising, specifically on the meaning of self-determination, political participation, and the common good.

The Christian reformists argued that the process of awakening called for integrating marginalized groups into society. For these reformists, protecting the sense of unity of society ranked as a very high, if not the highest, value. Society would not feel dangerously divided or threatened if the poor classes would lift themselves to a higher cultural and economic level through basic education. Hence, the moderates argued for assisting the poor by developing literacy programs, providing job training, and furnishing adequate housing, food, and clothing. Such assistance would lead gradually to the masses spontaneously developing their own ideology of social transformation.

The revolutionary group, represented by the Basic Education Movement (MEB), maintained that the masses of illiterate and poor people would achieve an awareness of dignity only by actively participating in a radical transformation of society. They argued that the people themselves, and not external agents, must make their own decisions. The revolutionaries encouraged education that enabled the oppressed to see their problems as intricately linked to the structural

44. Henrique C. de Luma Vaz, "The Church and Conscientização," *America* (April 27, 1968): 578–81.

problems of society and self-determination.[45] Consciousness-raising meant helping people to move forward from their fatalistic, naive ideology that confusedly struggles for liberation to a critical, mature ideology along the course that the Freire method had charted and that liberation theologians espouse.

In summary, Brazilian Christian groups engaged in the praxis of consciousness-raising found themselves differing on its meaning. The reformists, who speak of social integration of the marginalized through basic education and direct assistance programs, think that the existing social structures are basically sound. The revolutionaries insist that the political-economic structures themselves must change and that the poor themselves must lead the charge in bringing about social transformation. The first group pursues human dignity through educational programs that do not threaten the power bases of society, whereas the second think that human dignity can be achieved only through the self-determination of the oppressed themselves.

Horizon of Consciousness-Raising

Liberation theologians agree with the second interpretation that consciousness-raising should allow the poor and oppressed to set their own agenda and to go at their own pace. In addition to the principle of community self-determination, other guidelines are suggested by liberation theologians for a consciousness-raising praxis by small groups. These include maintaining a balance between local and regional or global solidarity; a policy of regularly reflecting upon indigenous cultural values in dialogue with the gospel; and a procedure for an ongoing self-evaluation.[46] Solidarity sometimes requires that a local group surrender some of its autonomy to form a regional and national project in order to achieve structural change within the state. Without such cooperation, more lasting institutional change would not be achievable. Thus, the importance of a local community cooperating with national and international groups expands the community's horizon.

Yet, the value of solidarity at the local level cautions its members against moving prematurely to levels of higher praxis before the people's conscientization program has prepared them. Liberation theologians argue for keeping these two values of self-determination and solidarity in a healthy balance. Gutiérrez warns communities against short-circuiting the process of consciousness-raising by moving too quickly to national and global issues before

45. Mainwaring, *Catholic Church and Politics in Brazil*, 66–67.
46. Galilea, "Liberation Theology and New Tasks Facing Christians," 173.

the people have achieved sufficient self-knowledge, understanding of political structures, and the spiritual motivation necessary for political action and liberating praxis.

In the church base communities in Brazil, self-confidence and dignity grew through a process of self-discovery, which has led to more critical political participation.[47] Unless the oppressed person has grown sufficiently in self-awareness and self-confidence, and has become sufficiently free from the residue of an oppressive consciousness, he or she may be thrown off course and return to a passive role by participating in a larger movement. Participants must be able to see the connection between the growth of consciousness and liberation within their own group and the larger liberation struggle. The higher "helicopter" view of the political process on a national or a continental level demands adequate preparation at the grass-roots level. Without this preparation at the base, Gutiérrez says, a higher level of praxis may lead to "self-defeating superficiality and ultimate cynicism."[48]

Clodovis Boff, in defense of solidarity with the larger movement, argues from the opposite perspective, urging small groups and the church base communities not to exaggerate the importance of local popular consciousness: "The fear of interfering in the development of popular consciousness cannot be justified on the pretense of respect. The question is not whether to influence the people. It is rather how to influence them."[49] Boff, of course, respects popular consciousness and the right of small groups to set their own agenda and pace. Yet he thinks that the needs and concerns must be genuine and not a cover for the attitude called *basismo*. The term refers to a naive belief by a neighborhood organization or a church base community (CEB) in its ability to handle its own problems without intellectuals, political parties, and other outside support.[50]

Scott Mainwaring, in agreement with Boff, argues against what he calls a "veneration of the popular consciousness," which he thinks can discourage pastoral agents from helping people develop a critical consciousness. Popular classes under immediate threat of losing their water supply or being removed from the land have no difficulty organizing themselves. The problem arises in trying to sustain this resistance and in linking up with other groups. Mainwaring shows that, historically, this has always involved outside agents. Here

47. Mainwaring, *Catholic Church and Politics in Brazil*, 212.

48. Curt Cadorette, *From the Heart of the People: The Theology of Gustavo Gutiérrez* (Oak Park, Ill.: Meyer Stone Books, 1988), 47.

49. Clodovis Boff, "Agente de Pastoral," 225. Quoted from Mainwaring, *Catholic Church and Politics in Brazil*, 222.

50. Mainwaring, *Catholic Church and Politics in Brazil*, 206.

is where Berger's fear of outside intrusion eventuating in a "cognitive imperialism" may be apposite. But cognitive imperialism or vanguardism is endemic, in my view, to all kinds of coalition building.

In this dilemma of expanding a community's awareness to include national and global concerns, theologians Clodovis Boff, Segundo Galilea, and Yvone Gebara have suggested guidelines for discerning the pace of consciousness-raising. All would agree that indigenous and outside leaders must respect the organic development of the popular classes. Among other ways, they do this by not prematurely moving to regional and international issues, even though analysis of the political situation may urge grass-roots organizations to collaborate before they are ready. Yvone Gebara, Ana María Tepedino, and other women theologians have recognized the urgency of raising the issue of patriarchy and macho attitudes in international conferences of women as well as in their local communities. Liberation theologians suggest avoiding two extreme tendencies: a *basismo* that rejects outside expert help and focuses only on local issues; and a vanguardism, in which regional leaders not only determine strategies and tactics but also may steer the base communities into directions the latter are unprepared to go.

Praxis Identifies the Human

Liberation theologians use praxis not only as the starting point and end point of their reflection. They hold that praxis constitutes the very grounding and precondition for all knowledge and theory. Hence, a people's historical context shapes liberation ethics, imbuing it with characteristics that distinguish it from other ethical systems. Although the theologians define praxis in various ways, a commonly agreed upon definition is "transformative activity motivated by love and guided by faith." The faith dimension sets it apart from materialist notions and at the same time gives praxis an eschatological quality. As a consequence, praxis, guided by faith, directs itself toward the reign of God as its ultimate end and moral standard. As a positive guide, faith illumines who the neighbor is, inspires persons to love compassionately and efficaciously, and moves them to work for justice in solidarity with the poor. As a negative guide, faith criticizes all types of praxis that are self-focused or too narrowly focused (*basismo*) and ideologies that obstruct the pathway to justice and solidarity. It cautions those working toward liberation for the oppressed against totally identifying their historical project as the definitive announcement of the reign of God.

The praxis of Segundo, that of ideology critique, responds to negative experiences by a tentative judgment of suspicion, a judgment that implies convictions about what is normatively human. Segundo and his colleagues identify the central and permanent values involved in such judgments, including compassionate love, solidarity with the poor, and basic human rights. The judgment or ideological suspicion does not flow from moral reasoning, as in a natural law or deontological argument, but from a moral intuition based on experience of negative or oppressive situations. These suspicions must be tested, however, to confirm whether one's intuitive judgment is supported by evidence.

Further evidence is provided by social analysis, which uncovers empirical data and deeper explanations, and by Scripture, which serves as the privileged summary of faith. The strength of the hermeneutic circle is its method of corroborating the insight gained from praxis by social analysis and a critical reading of Scripture. A limitation in Segundo's method is the absence of moral reasoning as an explicit step in the process.

Segundo creatively challenges traditional and contemporary biblical interpretations of themes, as we saw in his discussion of violence in relation to love. Thus, his praxis breaks open new ways of understanding Scripture. But while his praxis challenges his and other theologians' interpretations of the Bible, it is not evident whether the Bible challenges his own ideological suspicions. His colleague Gustavo Gutiérrez insists upon the importance of the reciprocal movement. We read the Bible, he says, and the Bible reads us.

Feminist theologians from the United States, who share with liberation theologians the starting point of theology (human experience), the end point (social transformation), and a type of analysis (ideological critique), fault their Latin American colleagues for failing to examine critically the Bible's ideologies.[51] Elisabeth Schüssler Fiorenza criticizes Segundo for not analyzing the social context of the biblical text as a necessary step toward identifying those biblical ideologies based on a false consciousness. To use Scripture more effectively, she suggests, Segundo should examine what praxis the biblical ideologies support. In other words, Schüssler Fiorenza urges Segundo to do an ideology critique of the text itself as well as an ideology critique of interpretations of the text. This entails doing a social analysis of the biblical context, including the Jewish and Greco-Roman worlds in which the biblical work was written. Applying ideology critique to the Bible, feminist theologians have shown how pervasively patriarchal and sexist the text is.[52] Liberation theologians would enrich their own investigations by applying their own method to the Bible, especially in areas related to patriarchy and to the use of violence.

51. Sandra M. Schneiders, *The Revelatory Text: Interpreting the New Testament as Sacred Scripture* (New York: HarperCollins, 1991), 181–82.
52. Schneiders, *Revelatory Text*, 120, 182.

The praxis of consciousness-raising is an effective vehicle for change, as the relatively short history of the liberation theology movement has demonstrated. Process theologian Charles Hartshorne, in the context of discussing how God can positively influence human beings, says that if you want to change someone, change the person's awareness. God alters us, Hartshorne says, by altering Godself.[53] Liberation theologians try to transform the poor by presenting to them an alternative image of God as a liberator who requires the people's active participation in the struggle.

Changing a person's or a group's awareness, however, can be exploitive, as Berger and Vaz note; or precipitous, as Gutiérrez points out; or too narrowly focused on local issues or a male agenda, as Clodovis Boff and Yvone Gebara indicate. Implied in the discussion about who raises whose consciousness, or who sets the agenda, or who regulates the pace of consciousness-raising is another issue: What constitutes the common good of the poor and oppressed? The concept of the common good in relation to preferential option for the poor needs to be addressed in liberation ethics. Liberation theologians, in my judgment, are dealing responsibly and creatively with problems that have historically risen in a consciousness-raising praxis.

---

53. Charles Hartshorne, *The Divine Relativity: A Social Conception of God* (New Haven: Yale University Press, 1948), 139.

4

Social Analysis and Ethics

The last two chapters have shown how praxis provides religious groups, popular organizations, and theologians with a new awareness of their social situation. Social analysis builds on praxis by deepening the individual's and the group's grasp of their reality. It does this by systematically studying the institution, breaking up the whole into its components in order to understand its nature, proportion, relationship, and function in society.[1] Liberation theologians concentrate on institutions because they are the means by which society meets its basic needs.

People often think of institutions as intimidating behemoths, like General Motors and Exxon. But as sociologist Robert Bellah and his colleagues point out, institutions vary, from the simple, welcoming custom of a handshake to the complex, not so welcoming tax laws. Bellah defines an institution as "a pattern of expected action of individuals or groups enforced by social sanctions, both positive and negative."[2] As this definition implies, institutions embody a moral element. We are expected to offer our hand to the outstretched hand of the welcomer and to pay taxes. If we do not, we are penalized.

Liberation theologians analyze institutions for the purpose of understanding precisely how an institution's values, policies, and sanctions help or hinder the poor. Like Bellah, these theologians recognize that institutions can be both enabling and restraining or liberating and oppressive. Although theologians study institutions in a variety of ways, they tend to concentrate on that mode of analysis called ideology critique, which examines doctrine and ideals that integrate, legitimate, and guide institutional behavior.

1. Joe Holland and Peter Henriot, *Social Analysis: Linking Faith and Justice* (Washington, D.C.: Center of Concern, 1980), 6.
2. Robert N. Bellah et al., *The Good Society* (New York: Alfred A. Knopf, 1991), 10–11.

According to cultural anthropologist Clifford Geertz, ideologies are "maps of problematic social reality and matrices for the creation of collective conscience."[3] In simpler terms, the maps consist of an organized body of concepts, values, and metaphors that explain human relationships and social structures, especially in areas where ambiguity and tension exist. Ideologies, or maps, justify theories of development and dependency, national security and self-determination, private and social property. Taken in this wide sense, ideology is a nonevaluative concept. To call a perspective an ideology does not necessarily imply that it is good or bad or erroneous. As Juan Luis Segundo rightly points out, every institution embodies a cluster of ideologies necessary for pursuing its goals. Yet certain ideologies distort reality by presuming to express for all what are really the goals of the few. Such ideologies take on a second, negative meaning: they disguise the true situation for the benefit of certain interests.[4]

This chapter pursues two objectives. First, it explains what certain representative liberation theologians mean by social analysis and how they actually do it. Second, it evaluates how well they do it. I have chosen to investigate three concrete social analyses: first, Leonardo and Clodovis Boff's critique of the U. S. bishops' analysis of the economy, selected because this analysis gives North American readers a flavor of how two important liberation theologians view the U. S. economic system; second, José Comblin's exposition of national security doctrine, picked because it has been frequently used to justify terrible repression of Latin Americans and the church; third, Ignacio Ellacuría's analysis of agrarian property in El Salvador, chosen because land rights, more than any other issue, divide the rich and the poor throughout Latin America.

Each case follows a four-part sequence organized by the following questions: (1) Why do liberation theologians use social analysis? (2) How do they analyze (which method)? (3) On what issues do they concentrate? (4) How well do they achieve their objective? In short, the chapter asks of each analysis: Why? How? What? How well? The chapter concludes with a general assessment and summarizes the contributions that these liberation theologians make to liberation ethics through their analyses.

3. Clifford Geertz, *The Interpretation of Cultures* (New York: Basic Books, 1973), 220.

4. Paul Ricoeur, *Lectures on Ideology and Utopia* (New York: Columbia University Press, 1986), 254–55. Ricoeur identifies three historical uses of the concept of ideology: (1) the Marxist notion as distortion due to class interest; (2) the Weberian notion as a claim to legitimacy; (3) Geertz's notion of ideology as integration. Segundo's general definition of ideology ("a systematic aggregate of ideas used to attain some goal") approximates Geertz's definition, and Segundo's negative notion encompasses the Marxist meaning.

The fourth question evaluates whether theologians have achieved their objective of satisfactorily analyzing the institution. What constitutes satisfactory analysis? In agreement with liberation theologians and many social scientists, I hold that social scientific investigators can never avoid taking sides.[5] Social analysis, however, should meet the standards of good scientific work. Such work requires at a minimum that social analysts represent the opposing position fairly and that they state the limits of their own investigation.

The first criterion, sometimes called impartiality, entails giving a fair account of the opposing viewpoint, sifting the data, and acting on the basis of the findings.[6] The second criterion, stating limits, means making what sociologist Howard Becker calls a "sociological disclaimer." It informs the reader of the perspective from which the study is being made. The authors do well to state, for example, "we have studied the prison through the eyes of the inmates and not through the eyes of the guards."[7] Even though the disclaimer does not remove the bias from the study, it alerts readers to the social location and loyalties of the investigators, thereby allowing readers to see the limits of the conclusions reached. Keeping these criteria in mind, let us see how four liberation theologians analyze a church document, a state doctrine, and private property.

Boffs' Critique of Bishops' Analysis

Leonardo and Clodovis Boff, both Roman Catholic theologians from Brazil, collaborate closely in their theological investigations. They have co-authored three books and in 1987 published a critique of the pastoral letter by the U.S. Bishops, *Economic Justice for All*.[8] Their critique, "The Church and

5. For a discussion on value-free sociology, see W. H. Werkmeister, "Social Science and the Problem of Value," in *Scientism and Values*, ed. Helmut Schoeck and James W. Wiggins (Princeton, N.J.: Van Nostrand Company, 1960), 1–21; Howard S. Becker, "Whose Side Are We On?" *Social Problems* 14 (Winter 1967); Alvin W. Gouldner, *For Sociology: Renewal and Critique in Sociology Today* (New York: Basic Books, 1973), chap. 1; Míguez Bonino, *Toward a Christian Political Ethics*, 46; Robert N. Bellah, "The Ethical Aims of Social Inquiry," in *Social Science as Moral Inquiry*, ed. Norma Haan et al. (New York: Columbia University Press, 1983), chap. 16.

6. James Rachels, *The Elements of Moral Philosophy* (New York: Random House, 1986), 7–11.

7. Becker, "Whose Side Are We On?" 30–31.

8. The three books coauthored by Leonardo Boff and Clodovis Boff are *Salvation and Liberation*, trans. Robert Barr (Maryknoll, N.Y.: Orbis Books, 1984); *Liberation Theology*; *Introducing Liberation Theology*, trans. Paul Burns (Maryknoll, N.Y.: Orbis Books, 1987).

the Economy of the United States," provides the subject matter for the first case analysis.[9]

Why Analysis?

The Boffs examine five specific areas in the pastoral letter: the bishops' description of the U.S. social reality; the bishops' moral demands on capitalism; their understanding of the poor; their viewpoint of U.S.–Third World relations; and their social proposal. Encouraged by the bishops' public invitation to dialogue, the Boffs undertake their analysis in order to identify and to examine critically certain presuppositions implied in the letter. These presuppositions, they maintain, influence what the bishops teach about economic justice.[10] The set of presuppositions constitutes for the Boffs an ideology that has negative consequences. To illustrate, the pastoral letter erroneously presupposes that capitalism is fundamentally a good system, though in need of reform. Consequently, the bishops adopt a mode of analysis (which the Boffs label "functionalist") that lacks the capacity to grapple with systemic problems and issues of a macroeconomic scale. Their use of functionalist analysis influences how the bishops interpret employment, poverty, food and agriculture, and the relation of the U.S. economy to developing nations; it also shapes the action that the bishops take.[11]

Which Analysis?

In the most general terms, the Boffs call their method "socioanalytic mediation." By "mediation" they mean an interpretative source that relates God's reign to the political world and, conversely, the world to God. Socioanalytic mediation uses the social sciences to explain the institutional causes of poverty and oppression, and to indicate alternative institutions that may foster just and humane living conditions. This scientific knowledge helps theologians to understand the social problem, which they then can address in light of another mediation, divine revelation.[12]

9. Clodovis Boff and Leonardo Boff, "A Igreja Perante a Economia nos EUA: Um Olhar a Partir da Periferia," *Revista Eclesiástica Brasileira* 47 (June 1987): 356–77. See the edited English version, "The Church and the Economy of the United States: A Look from the Point of View of the Periphery," trans. Joseph Rozansky, *National Catholic Reporter* (August 28, 1987): 14, 23–24.

10. Boff and Boff, "A Igreja Perante a Economia nos EUA," 358.

11. National Conference of Catholic Bishops (NCCB), *Economic Justice for All: Pastoral Letter on Catholic Social Teaching and the U.S. Economy* (Washington, D.C.: United States Catholic Conference, 1986), pars. 131–32.

12. Boff and Boff, *Introducing Liberation Theology*, 24.

The Boffs reduce all social analysis to either functionalist or dialectical types. *Functionalist* analysis assumes society to be an organic whole having complementary parts. Consistent with the metaphor of organism, analysis gives a primacy to order, harmony, and equilibrium. It interprets problems as dysfunctions (high unemployment) and deviations (crime) in an otherwise healthy system. On the global level, functionalist analysis describes the poverty of nations as economic and social backwardness.[13]

The Boffs associate the functionalist approach with the liberal tradition that assumes an integration between various structures within a nation and interdependent relationships among nations. Interdependence implies cooperation and power sharing among nations. Functionalist analysis does not challenge the power structure, because it assumes that social transformation can be realized within the system. Hence, it reinforces the status quo as it gathers information and makes its recommendations.

Rooted in the functionalist tradition, liberal economists address problems of employment and poverty by reforming existing structures and by changing human practices of saving and consuming. They suggest that poor nations modernize their economies through programs of development, assisted by foreign loans and technological assistance. The poor are viewed as marginal members of society who can be integrated into the system with the help of others. This tradition regards the state as an institution possessing legitimate authority within defined borders. The state uses its authority to impose taxes, to regulate the practices of multinational corporations operating within its jurisdiction, to settle conflicts, and to maintain the security of the nation. The Boffs point out that, though inequalities and tensions exist within nation states and between nations, functionalism does not address structural patterns of domination and dependence.[14]

In sharp contrast to functionalist analysis, *dialectical* analysis interprets society as a complex whole within which structural problems, or contradictions, emerge. The contradictions underlie the daily battles between the wealthy elite and the poor majority, and between wealthy and poor nations. The dialectical school regards conflicts between classes, races, and sexes as symptoms of structural and systemic problems, which at different moments in history call for revolutionary change. Its adherents relate poverty to oppression and perceive the poor as people exploited by the economic and political arrangements of society. Dialectical analysts acknowledge that their explanations, critiques, and judgments about what can be done are not value-free. Indeed,

13. Ibid., 26.
14. Boff and Boff, "A Igreja Perante a Economia nos EUA," 362–63.

they deny that social scientific analysis can be neutral.[15] The neo-Marxists within this dialectical tradition look on the state as an instrument of the dominant or ruling class (guarantor of capitalist profits) and, therefore, not as a partner helping citizens to eradicate poverty.[16]

The Boffs themselves opt for a dialectical analysis and within this generic model analyze institutions according to principles of dependency theory.[17] They choose this dialectical-dependency theory type for three reasons. First, dialectical-dependency analysis explains the problems of poverty and oppression better than does functionalism. Second, it responds more adequately to human values, including justice, participation in the economy and in politics, and freedom. Third, it offers guidance for resolving basic problems through structural and systemic change.[18]

Dependency marks the relationship between rich center nations and poor periphery nations. The subtitle of the Boffs' critique, "A Look from the Point of View of the Periphery," assumes that people in the periphery can see the world better than those in the center. The peripheral viewers see better because, as they stand knee-deep in stagnant poverty, they are able to observe the luxurious estates and actually experience exploitation at the hands of the wealthy landowners. Since the poor have the more comprehensive global picture, the Boffs speak of their view from the periphery as an "epistemological privilege." The periphery always sees the center, but the center does not always see the periphery.[19]

Dependency analysis was born in response to economic theories of development in the early 1960s.[20] Latin American economists, seeking to explain why capitalism in the Third World failed to develop and "take off" as development theorists predicted it would, presented a counterhypothesis called dependency.[21] It holds that economies of Third World nations are integral parts

15. Boff and Boff, *Introducing Liberation Theology*, 27.

16. Arthur F. McGovern, *Marxism: An American Christian Perspective* (Maryknoll, N.Y.: Orbis Books, 1980), 140.

17. Clodovis Boff, *Theology and Praxis: Epistemological Foundations*, trans. Robert R. Barr (Maryknoll, N.Y.: Orbis Books, 1987), 262 n. 35.

18. Ibid., 57–60; Leonardo Boff, *God's Witnesses in the Heart of the World*, trans. and ed. Robert Fath (Chicago: Claret Center for Resources in Spirituality), 210; Boff and Boff, "A Igreja Perante a Economia nos EUA," 362.

19. Boff and Boff, "A Igreja Perante a Economia nos EUA," 371.

20. Enrique Dussel, *A History of the Church in Latin America: Colonialism to Liberalism (1492–1979)* (Grand Rapids, Mich.: William B. Eerdmans, 1981), 326–27; Gutiérrez, *Theology of Liberation*, 84–88.

21. W. W. Rostow, "The Takeoff into Self-Sustained Growth," *Economic Journal* 66 (1956), no. 261: 25–48. Rostow's metaphor, "take off," likens Third World devel-

of the world capitalist system, but that they are limited in their growth by structural conditions imposed by outside centers of domination.

Dependency analysis focuses on the interaction between the internal structures of the periphery (mining, agriculture, tourism) and the external structures of the center (industry, international banks, transnational corporations). Proponents of this analysis maintain that the multinational corporations deplete the periphery's raw materials, capital, and foreign exchange without making just compensation. Once a subsidiary of a parent corporation has been established in the host country, it borrows money from banks or sells bonds on the host country's capital markets in order to expand its operations. This drains the country's pool of capital and makes it impossible for the local companies (which lack prestigious names) to obtain capital. The subsidiary purchases foreign exchange in order to pay dividends to the parent corporation in the home country. The export of dividends exceeds by a large amount the foreign exchange that was initially invested in the country, thus depleting Third World nations of their limited resources.[22] In their critique of the bishops' pastoral letter, the Boffs cite statistics showing that foreign corporations draw a disproportionate percentage of every dollar invested in the host country.[23]

The Boffs incorporate into their dependency analysis certain Marxist analytic categories. They speak of contradictions (e.g., large pockets of poverty in the world's wealthiest nation), socioeconomic differences between classes, and ideology critique.[24] However, it should be noted that they are not Marxists, and in fact are critical of the Marxist vision, strategy, and tactics.

Although dependency theorists agree on certain fundamentals, including those described above, they differ among themselves on their presuppositions and methods of analyzing First World and Third World relationships. Economists have identified three differing viewpoints within the school.[25] Although

---

opment to an airplane that must gain sufficient energy on the runway before it can "take off"; that is, it must move through stages of economic growth before it can achieve the level of productivity of First World nations.

22. Everett E. Hagen, *The Economics of Development* (Homewood, Ill.: Richard D. Irwin, 1980), 18–27.

23. Boff and Boff, "A Igreja Perante a Economia nos EUA," 374.

24. Boff and Boff, *Introducing Liberation Theology*, 28. The Boffs use certain categories from Marxist analysis, but take a critical stance toward Marxism, especially toward its materialistic and atheistic presuppositions.

25. Gabriel Palma, "Dependency and Development: A Critical Overview," in Dudley Seers, ed., *Dependency Theory: A Critical Assessment* (London: Frances Pinter, 1981), 42–43. Palma identifies three schools within dependency analysis: first, dependency as a theory of underdevelopment (André Gunder Frank and Teotônio Dos Santos); second, dependency as a critique of the obstacles to national development (Oswaldo

the Boffs lean toward a radical type of dependency analysis, they are eclectic in constructing their own model, drawing upon the works of both mainline and radical dependency theorists. In an earlier work, Leonardo Boff referred favorably to a school of Brazilian dependency economists—Furtado, Cardoso, Fernandes, and Ianni—all of whom analyze dependency within a capitalist framework. They are moderate in their recommendations. Although he speaks approvingly of these economists, Leonardo Boff develops his model of dependency not on the theories of these Brazilian economists, but along the lines of radical theorist André Gunder Frank.

Following Frank's line of analysis, Leonardo Boff says that underdevelopment cannot be explained as a technological lag in a society because of outmoded, premodern structures of production and consumption. Instead, underdevelopment arises from the capitalist system itself wherein a center (wealthy nations, banks, and corporations) grows in science, technology, and social well-being at the expense of peripheral areas from which cheap labor and raw materials are extracted. The periphery assumes a dependent status in all sectors of its life.[26]

The Boffs, in their critique of the bishops, borrow from Frank both his concepts and his principles of analyzing international relations. They say, as Frank holds, that underdevelopment in the periphery is inversely related to development in the center. Using Frank's expression, they maintain that capitalism of the center and of the periphery constitute "two sides of the same coin." As the economies soar in the United States and Germany, they plummet in Peru and Brazil. According to Frank, periphery and center reflect "the real dependence of the satellite or tributary nations on the great metropolitan centers." International and national capitalism historically produced underdevelopment in Latin America since colonial times and continue to generate it in the present.[27] Nothing short of a socialist revolution will allow sustained development.[28] The Boffs, like Frank, argue that capitalism will always dominate

---

Sunkel and Celso Furtado); third, analysis of concrete situations of dependency (Fernando Cardoso and Enzo Faletto). The first approach argues that the solution demands a radical change of the capitalist system. The second and third types analyze structures of dependency within the structure of capitalism. See also Ronald H. Chilcote, *Theories of Development and Underdevelopment* (Boulder, Colo.: Westview Press, 1984), chap. 3.

26. L. Boff, *God's Witnesses*, 212.

27. André Gunder Frank, *Capitalism and Underdevelopment in Latin America: Historical Studies of Chile and Brazil*, revised and enlarged (New York: Monthly Review Press, 1969), xi, xvii.

28. André Gunder Frank, *Dependent Accumulation and Underdevelopment* (New York: Monthly Review Press, 1979). For an excellent study of Frank's study, see Palma,

the periphery and that systemic change is necessary to bring true development to Latin America.

Consequently, the Boffs endorse a causal analysis, which goes to the roots of economic exploitation. Although they do not analyze international captalism in their critique of the bishops, they explore the causes behind the bishops' interpretations and recommendations. For instance, they identify in the letter a functionalist vision and analysis, which they think conditions the bishops' treatment of poverty, their perspective of the poor, and their view of multinational corporations in Latin America.[29] The Boffs suspect an ideology at work in these presuppositions, and like Juan Luis Segundo, they undertake an ideology critique. They suspect that the bishops' interpretations and recommendations are conditioned by their social location in the center.[30] Consequently, the bishops cover up, albeit unconsciously, the contradictions within the U.S. economy.

Ideologies can be of two types: the first ideology is an error that occurs under the appearance of truth—an illusion like Marx's false consciousness. The second ideology is a moral wrong or lie in which the agent consciously deceives in order to promote self-interest.[31] The Boffs do not accuse the bishops of conscious deception (second ideology), but challenge their lack of awareness

---

"Dependency and Development," 44ff. Palma distinguishes three dimensions in Frank's model of dependency: (1) peripheral economies of Latin America have been incorporated into the world economy since the sixteenth century; (2) the international economy transforms peripheral economies immediately and necessarily into the capitalist system; and (3) the world economy integrates peripheral economies into the international capitalist system by means of a chain, hierarchically arranged from metropolis to satellite. The metropolises, such as Lisbon, London, or New York, control their international satellites within underdeveloped nations, such as São Paulo and Santiago. These satellites in turn become metropolises for provincial satellites, like Recife and Belo Horizonte. The latter act as centers for regional and local satellites. Thus, the European–U.S. centers control the life of the interior of Brazil or Chile through a long chain of metropolises and satellites. Surplus capital generated at each stage is successively siphoned from the satellite by the center. Frank maintains that underdevelopment in Latin America persists as long as the capitalist economy is in place. The way out of underdevelopment involves nothing less than overturning the metropolis-satellite structure by means of a revolution.

29. NCCB, *Economic Justice for All*, par. 12.

30. Rebecca S. Chopp, *The Praxis of Suffering: An Interpretation of Liberation and Political Theologies* (Maryknoll, N.Y.: Orbis Books, 1986), 136–37, 142. Chopp distinguishes two modes of analytical interpretation: social analysis, which employs sociopolitical instruments and categories to investigate structures, ideologies, and power alignments; ideology critique, which examines systematic distortions or false ideologies embodied in laws and beliefs of a society.

31. C. Boff, *Theology and Praxis*, 42.

or naiveté (first ideology). The theologians argue that the presuppositions influence how the bishops interpret socioeconomic reality.

What Issues?

The Boffs identify and criticize four major presuppositions in the letter: (1) its functionalist vision of society; (2) a morality of individual acts rather than a morality of structures; (3) a descriptive understanding of the poor as marginalized but as potential beneficiaries of the system; (4) a harmonious worldview in which nations have an interdependent relationship.[32]

Functionalist vision   Rejecting the bishops' declaration that their pastoral letter embraces no particular socioeconomic theory, the Boffs think that the letter presupposes a functionalist vision, evident in the bishops' approach to employment, poverty, and helping developing nations.[33] Functionalism limits the bishops' vision. It does not allow them to see the cause and effect relationship of wealth to poverty. Although the bishops perceive serious problems, such as the great disparity of income and wealth between rich and poor, they interpret the problems as dysfunctions that can be repaired within the system. Their recommendations follow a descriptive analysis of unemployment and poverty. They urge the federal government to coordinate fiscal and monetary policies of the nation to bring about full employment; and they call upon private businesses, labor unions, and state agencies to expand job-training and apprenticeship programs.[34]

As the Boffs see it, such recommendations fall short of dealing with the deeper structural problems within the capitalist system. The contradiction of wealth and poverty coexisting in the richest nation in the world requires systemic causal analysis. Mere description of the negative consequences of the system and palliative measures to deal with them do not adequately address the problem.[35] Adopting the sociological categories of Frank, the Boffs view the relationship of rich and poor classes within the United States and the relationship between the United States and Latin American nations as one of dependency. Capitalism in the United States expands its wealth in the powerful

32. Boff and Boff, "A Igreja Perante a Economia nos EUA," 362, 366, 369, 372. The formulation of the four propositions is mine. The Boffs identify more propositions, but because of the limits of space, I confine this study to these four.

33. Ibid., 363; see also NCCB, *Economic Justice for All*, par. 12.

34. NCCB, *Economic Justice for All*, pars. 156, 159, 196.

35. Boff and Boff, "A Igreja Perante a Economia nos EUA," 364.

center by exploiting workers in the periphery of its own nation and of developing nations.

The Boffs move beyond analysis to moral denunciation. They call capitalism, whether growing in the center or struggling in the periphery, an evil system. To support their judgment, they compare unemployment, income distribution, and concentration of land in the United States and in Brazil. Unemployment in the United States ranged between 6 and 7 percent in 1984; in Brazil, it exceeded 15 percent during the same year. Both countries have indicated a great disparity of income distribution between rich and poor; the disparity is high in both nations, but much higher in Brazil.[36] In both nations, land is concentrated in the hands of wealthy landowners; more so in Brazil, but increasingly so in the United States. Statistics provided by the pastoral letter show a long-term trend toward fewer and larger farms. In Brazil, 50 percent of farmland is concentrated in 2 percent of the population.[37] The Boffs argue that contradictions brought on by capitalist economies are fundamentally the same in both countries, even though the disparity between rich and poor is greater and more painful in Brazil and in other countries within the periphery.

The Boffs criticize the bishops' descriptive analysis because it fails to explain structurally why such gross inequalities persist. The bishops, however, say that the socioeconomic differences between groups and between nations have increased. They argue that changing fiscal and monetary policy, transforming prejudicial attitudes toward minorities and women, and increasing education and job training for the poor will reduce these inequalities.

Morality of individual acts   The second presupposition assumes that social evils for the most part come from decisions made by individuals who are the carriers of social structures. If the individual carriers are good, the structures will also be good. By "carrier" the Boffs mean a functionary, an individual responsible for the institutions (*o portador de uma função*). The bishops lack a "clear consciousness regarding the structural dimension of morality" and therefore fail to demonstrate "ethical-structural thinking."[38] Their ethics functions as a morality of acts rather than a morality of structures. By "ethical-structural thinking" the Boffs mean an ethics that gives primacy to issues of

36. Ibid., 360–61. The richest 20 percent of U.S. families received 42.9 percent of the total income, while the lowest 40 percent received 15.7 percent; in Brazil the richest 1 percent received about 13 percent of the total, a rough equivalent of what the poorest 50 percent received.

37. Ibid., 361.

38. Ibid., 366.

justice between classes and within the political-economic system. Because the
pastoral letter presupposes a functionalist vision, it interprets social concepts,
such as institutional injustice (#55), social sin (#77), and human rights (#85),
by means of an individual-act morality. "Because of this," the Boffs write,
"the letter is highly 'individual' and not very 'political.' "[39]

The Boffs imply that if the bishops had undertaken a causal analysis of
the economic system, they would have developed a solid social ethics that
linked the injustices to social laws, institutions, and mechanisms of the system
itself. Such an ethics would suggest radical structural change and not simply
reformist recommendations. In the absence of a critical social analysis, the
ethics has become moralistic, moving from description to ethical judgment
and finally to recommendations without exposing the basic problems of the
economy.[40]

A causal analysis of the U.S. economy, the Boffs suggest, would have
moved the bishops to put their weight behind changing the system instead of
reforming it. It is impossible to know what they would have done given the
people's resistance to radical change and history of antipathy toward socialism
in the United States. Although the Boffs' forecast is highly speculative and,
in my judgment doubtful, they make a good point in insisting that good ethical
judgments about social transformation require a more thorough analysis of
the U.S. economy than that undertaken by the bishops.

The bishops' failure to do a structural and systemic analysis, the Boffs
say, consigns their ethics to an individualistic morality that deals with personal
choices. Yet the bishops encourage Christian communities to commit themselves to solidarity with those suffering, to diagnose alienating situations, and
to confront attitudes and patterns of action that institutionalize injustice (#55).
Furthermore, they call for a participatory justice that reorders social institutions, guaranteeing a basic level of access to all persons (#78). Regarding human
rights (#85), the bishops remind individuals and groups of their special duties
toward the poor and marginalized. Addressing institutions, they urge corporations to make policies according to norms of love, justice, human rights,
and the basic needs of the poor (#89–90). In short, the bishops appeal to

39. Ibid., 367.

40. James Childress, "Moralism," *The Westminister Dictionary of Christian Ethics*,
ed. James F. Childress and John Macquarrie (Philadelphia: Westminster Press, 1986).
Childress defines moralism as "excessive, rigid, and inappropriate applications of morality, particularly to areas, such as art or politics, that should allegedly be governed
by other standards." The Boffs do not define the term, but the context suggests this
meaning of moralism: "an inappropriate or possibly premature application of morality
to politics."

corporations and groups, as well as to individuals, to confront unjust patterns and to urge that institutions act justly. Given these recommendations, why do the Boffs label the letter a morality of individual acts?

They do so because they think the bishops appeal to individual corporate leaders for change rather than calling for transforming power alignments and, I suspect, for not challenging the market system itself. The Boffs do not think that moral appeals to corporate managers, government officials, and labor leaders are effective, even when goodwill is present, because these leaders do not exercise control over their organization that would enable them to bring about the change that is needed. Arguing in a manner similar to that of Reinhold Niebuhr, the Boffs reject the notion that moral persuasion or appeal to influential entrepreneurs achieves anything substantive. Niebuhr argues for a rough justice achieved mainly through balancing power. The Boffs agree with the emphasis on power, but think that the poor themselves, aided by the upper classes, must organize themselves through a process of consciousness-raising and concerted action for justice.[41]

Poor as marginalized   The bishops presuppose that the poor are marginal but not exploited members of society. Using the U.S. Department of Agriculture's descriptive definition, the bishops define the poor as those who lack sufficient material resources required for a decent life.[42] In 1984 this amounted to 33 million Americans. The bishops also describe the poor as "destitute," "needy," and "vulnerable." They never refer to the poor, the Boffs point out, as the excluded or exploited.[43] Consequently, the definition does not adequately describe the poor in Latin America and perhaps not even the poor in the United States.

Defining the poor as needy and destitute but not exploited colors the bishops' thinking and recommendations for change. First, they treat the poor as potential beneficiaries of the system. Second, because they do not see the laboring poor as exploited by the system, they urge others to create conditions that would enable the poor to participate in the economic system. They mention education, job training, and self-help programs. The bishops, however, fail to encourage the poor to act as agents of their own development. They do not urge workers to bring about their own freedom by transforming the system.[44]

41. Reinhold Niebuhr, *Leaves from the Notebook of a Tamed Cynic* (Hamden, Conn.: Shoe String Press, 1956), 94.
42. NCCB, *Economic Justice for All*, par. 173 and n. 27.
43. Boff and Boff, "A Igreja Perante a Economia nos EUA," 369.
44. Ibid., 370.

In contrast, the Boffs view the poor not simply as a marginalized and excluded group who live on low income; they are the exploited and dominated, those cursed by the system. Poverty means more than deprivation. It involves issues of inequality and injustice, and it calls for the elimination of those structures that create the poverty.[45]

Interdependency   Turning to how the U.S. economy affects developing nations, the bishops describe the relationships between rich and poor countries as interdependent. Envisioning an increasingly interdependent global economy, they say: "Equity requires, even as the fact of interdependence becomes more apparent, that the quality of interdependence be improved, in order to eliminate 'the scandal of the shocking inequality between the rich and the poor.' "[46] At the same time, they recognize the existence of dependent relationships and disparities of power between the United States and developing nations (#59). The Boffs dislike calling these relationships interdependent because it implies equality and a mutuality that presently does not exist between nations of the northern and southern hemispheres. To call rich and poor nations interdependent, when they are not, cloaks over the existing unjust relationships.[47]

The bishops make a strong appeal to the moral responsibility of the United States to alleviate and to help eradicate the misery of the poor of other nations. This appeal, in effect, acknowledges international conflict and dependence, the Boffs observe. Yet the bishops interpret the dependency "within an overarching, harmonious view of interdependence."[48] The Boffs call this viewpoint ideological because it suggests an equality that does not exist. The bishops do not perceive an unjust international order marked by domination, but one characterized by backwardness. "From this point of view, it appears that the U.S. has no fault regarding the poverty of the Third World."[49]

Assessment

The Boffs' analysis leads them to conclude that the bishops' presuppositions constitute a negative ideology that conditions their interpretation of the

45. Amartya Sen, *Poverty and Famines* (Oxford: Clarendon Press, 1986), 14–15. Sen argues against the Boffs' view that "poverty is a value judgment." Describing a prevailing prescription is an act of description, not prescription. "For the person studying and measuring poverty, the conventions of society are matters of fact (What are the contemporary standards?), and not issues of morality or of subjective search (What *should be* the contemporary standards? What *should be* my values? How do I *feel* about all this?)."
46. NCCB, *Economic Justice for All*, 252.
47. Boff and Boff, "A Igreja Perante a Economia nos EUA," 372.
48. Ibid.
49. Ibid., 373.

U.S. economy and their recommendations. In short, they contend that the bishops' analysis is flawed because it masks the deeply exploitive nature of capitalism. To evaluate adequately the Boffs' ideology critique would take more space than this chapter would allow. Returning to the two criteria for assessing social analysis (stating limits and impartiality), I shall simply mention what I judge to be strengths and weaknesses in the Boffs' critique.

Strengths   The Boffs clearly state the limits of their own perspective. Regarding loyalties, they affirm their commitment to the liberation of the poor and oppressed, which includes transforming the economic arrangements of society. As for social location, they state in the title and throughout their essay that they approach capitalism from the periphery where dependent nations encounter massive poverty and exploitation. They recognize that this commitment and context give them a perspective different from that of the bishops. Moreover, the periphery, they contend, gives them a more comprehensive and therefore a more accurate view of capitalism than the bishops, who do not see how capitalism grinds down the majority of people in many other nations. Having lived, though for short stays, in Lima, Rio de Janeiro, and Guatemala, I can attest to the Boffs' point about the importance of social location. My being with the poor in miserable living conditions surrounded by thousands of poorly housed, undernourished families does afford a view of world capitalism different from what I have experienced in the north. Although some will argue against the Boffs' contention that their social location gives them an "epistemological privilege" over the bishops, the Boffs' analysis is strengthened by their forthrightness in setting forth the limits of their study.

Regarding the criterion of impartiality, the Boffs are sympathetic to the bishops for having undertaken an enormous and challenging task and try to give their letter a fair reading. They grapple with and sift the data provided by the bishops. On the whole, they accurately identify presuppositions in the letter that condition the bishops' interpretations and recommendations, notably, the letter's uncritical acceptance of capitalism, its functionalist presuppositions, and its acceptance of an interdependent world. They make a good case for showing how the bishops' presuppositions influence their recommendations. To cite one instance, the bishops think of the poor as needy, powerless, and vulnerable, but not also as exploited (pars. 173, 188). If they had considered the poor as also oppressed, the Boffs argue, they might have drawn a more enthusiastic response as well as have appealed to a larger population, including male and female laborers who are underpaid and exploited.

Furthermore, if the bishops had recognized the poor as exploited but not powerless, then they might have encouraged these groups to take greater responsibility for organizing themselves, to transform their own workplace, and to change structures within the system itself. Herein lies a problem. If the bishops had included the element of oppression in their definition of poverty, they would have had to undertake a causal analysis in order to explain the nature of the exploitation. Perhaps they had doubts about the appropriateness of bishops doing such a critique. If they had decided to do so, they would have faced the difficult decision of choosing a mode of causal analysis among the major competing ones. Instead they chose to demonstrate in a largely descriptive mode that certain social outcomes of the U.S. economy are unacceptable according to the Catholic Christian tradition.

The Boffs convincingly demonstrate that defining the poor as an exploited and excluded class more accurately describes the poor's situation than does the bishops' description. They show it to be more consistent with the biblical vision of the poor, who are both oppressed and encouraged by God to liberate themselves. Using the bishops' statistics as well as their own, the Boffs describe the poor in the United States and in the Third World as "those forced out of the system." This stance should have impelled the bishops to examine the social mechanisms that systematically force masses of people out of work through employment policies, plant closings, and exploiting nonunionized laborers. In agreement with the Boffs, I think the bishops would have done better to explain the mechanisms of oppression, showing how they contribute to poverty abroad as well as in the United States.

Yet the causes of poverty are more complex than even the Boffs seem to indicate. Gustavo Gutiérrez says that the complexity of poverty requires that we use a variety of tools to get at the deepest causes of the situation.[50] Moreover, there is a danger in reducing poverty simply to unjust institutions, as economist Amartya Sen has said: "Poverty and inequality relate closely to each other, but they are distinct concepts and neither subsumes the other."[51] Not all poverty is created by human selfishness. Yet the kind of massive poverty that the Boffs describe arises in large part from human decisions. Having made these qualifications, I would accept as an important contribution the Boffs' insistence that poverty in most situations does imply injustice. Reinhold Niebuhr's axiom—that wherever we find disproportionate power alignments, we find injustice—supports the Boffs' notion of poverty as oppression.

Finally, the Boffs disagree with the bishops that the category of interdependency captures the concrete reality of Third World nations. On the contrary, dependency describes more accurately how rich and poor nations

50. Gutiérrez, *Theology of Liberation*, xxv.
51. Sen, *Poverty and Famines*, 9–23.

relate to each other. Whose perspective is more correct? A distinction made by economists may be helpful: dependence as a *fact* and dependency as a *theory*. Dependence as a fact describes the Third World's external reliance on and indebtedness to rich nations because of loans and interest, trade, and technology assistance. Reciprocity, but not equality, characterizes these relationships. Dependency theory attempts to explain the existence of the structural condition of dependence within the political economy.[52] Dependency theory, but not the fact of dependence, has come under criticism by economists and increasingly by the theologians themselves. Gustavo Gutiérrez has written that the theory of dependency, once used so extensively in Latin America, now seems an inadequate tool for understanding the deepest causes of poverty.[53] While the structural explanations may not be adequate, the contemporary signs of dependence are unmistakable, especially regarding gigantic national debts, an imbalance of trade, U.S. military invasions of Latin American nations to protect its economic interests, and the north's concern about environmental problems that pushes aside its concern about poverty in the south.[54]

Limitations   The Boffs make many incisive observations. I see four areas that weaken their generally good analysis: (1) the analysis insufficiently accounts for the failure of the bishops' conference (NCCB) to undertake a systemic analysis of the U.S. economy; (2) the Boffian critique assumes the validity of a Frankian interpretation of dependency theory that oversimplifies the relationship between economies of the north and the south;[55] (3) it treats capitalism unhistorically and abstractly; and (4) it proposes no concrete alternative to the capitalism it denounces.

The Boffs suppose that bishops possess the socioscientific sophistication to distinguish the various modes of analysis and to undertake a systemic analysis. But they are not social scientists and find it difficult enough to think in

52. James A. Caporaso and Richard N. Zare, "An Interpretation and Evaluation of Dependency Theory," in *From Dependency to Development: Strategies to Overcome Underdevelopment and Inequality*, ed. Harold Muñoz (Boulder, Colo.: Westview Press, 1981).

53. Gutiérrez, *Theology of Liberation*, xxv.

54. Samuel L. Parmar, "Self-Reliant Development in an 'Interdependent' World," in *Beyond Dependency: The Developing World Speaks Out*, ed. Guys F. Erb and Valeriana Kallab (Washington, D.C.: Overseas Development Council, 1975), 19–22.

55. Fernando Henrique Cardoso, "The Consumption of Dependency Theory in the United States," *Latin American Research Review* 12 (1977), no. 3: 8–9; Stephen T. Leonard, *Critical Theory in Political Practice* (Princeton: Princeton University Press, 1990), 113–16.

terms of empirical research, let alone delve into causal analysis.[56] In addition, the Boffs suppose that the members of the National Conference of Catholic Bishops think alike on political and economic issues. They do not. In fact, they may mirror the spectrum of political diversity found in the United States.

Nonetheless, the bishops criticize discrimination in employment (#147), link high defense spending with poverty and unemployment (#148), and relate the problems of farmers to external factors such as high interest rates and the heavy debt burden of food-deficient countries (#223). Moreover, they analyze the foreign debt crisis (#272) and the Bretton Woods institutions, calling for substantial reform of the latter (#277). This is not systemic analysis, but it does move beyond description to explanation.

A second limitation relates to the Boffs' use of dependency theory. The Boffs borrow ideas from two schools of dependency theory that have serious differences with each other: a critical dependency school that includes Cardoso and Faletto, and a radical neo-Marxist school represented by Frank. The Boffs' eclectic type of analysis tends, like Frank's analysis, to oversimplify things, especially the relationship between developed and underdeveloped nations. They attribute the cause of poverty exclusively to the system of capitalism, especially to capitalism in the center, saying nothing about historical precedents of present-day poverty, such as exploitation by feudal oligarchs on the hacienda and oppression by military forces and the state.[57] They pay insufficient attention to contemporary domestic structures (the state and local businesses), which cooperate with international institutions.

By contrast, the analysis of Cardoso and Faletto interprets development in the center to be a dynamic process that changes significantly at different stages, influencing the periphery as it changes in ways more complex than Frank or the Boffs seem to think. Multinational corporations, for example, have substantively transformed center-periphery relationships as well as relationships between First World countries.[58] Cardoso and Faletto contend that capitalism in the periphery manifests considerable diversity. Expansions of capitalism in Bolivia, Venezuela, Mexico, and Peru, have different histories and consequences, even though connected to the drive of advanced capitalist economies. The diversity stems from many historical events: certain local classes formed alliances with foreign interests, while others clashed with them; coalitions between powerful groups within the periphery have exploited the

56. Thomas J. Reese, *Archbishop: Inside the Power Structure of the American Catholic Church* (San Francisco: Harper & Row, 1989), 312.

57. Peter B. Evans, *Dependent Development* (Princeton: Princeton University Press, 1979), chap. 2.

58. Palma, "Dependency and Development," 60.

poor; and Latin American nations organized different forms of state that have had different outcomes for the people.[59] In short, Cardoso and Faletto present a more complex view than Frank (and the Boffs). Cardoso and Faletto avoid a simplified picture that shows foreign capital to be the sole villain.[60]

A third limitation involves treating capitalism as though it were a monolithic system. The Boffs explain differences between one historical form of capitalism and another as a matter of degree. They consider all forms as inherently evil and therefore irreformable: "Capitalism is capitalism just as a wolf is a wolf."[61] In spite of reforms, they declare with absolute assurance that capitalism will always remain a devouring and exploiting beast. Even mainline dependency economists regard this perspective as unhistorical, abstract, and mechanical. I think the Boffs should have made the abstract concept of capitalism (and socialism too) more concrete by examining concrete practices. I would also like to have seen the Boffs make more explicit use of ethics to complement their socioanalytic mediation, especially to discuss the relative merits of socialism versus capitalism. Their colleagues Gustavo Gutiérrez and Juan Luis Segundo acknowledge this to be a debatable issue.[62]

Finally, the analysis of the Boffs is not sufficiently critical, because it does not do what they say an adequate analysis should do—namely, it should offer guidance for resolving the basic problems. A critical social analysis should not only disclose the mechanisms of oppressive structures that are self-perpetuating, but also ought to present, at least in outline, the possibilities for radically changing structures.[63] The Boffs do not provide an alternative vision of a new economy, though their critique suggests a preference for a socialist society. A more adequate critical analysis would indicate how an alternative set of political-economic arrangements might better address economic problems present in the United States and in Brazil. Brazilian society today is marked by a stagnant economic rate of growth, an enormous international debt, and a high inflation rate. Capitalism has struggled under tyrannical military dictatorship in Brazil

59. Fernando Henrique Cardoso and Enzo Faletto, *Dependency and Development in Latin America*, trans. Marjory Mattingly Urquidi (Berkeley: University of California Press, 1979), xvii.

60. Gutiérrez, *Theology of Liberation*, xxiv. Gutiérrez acknowledges that the theory of dependence, once used extensively by liberation theologians, is now an inadequate tool. One of its limitations, he points out, is that it failed to take sufficient account of the internal dynamics of each country.

61. Boff and Boff, "A Igreja Perante a Economia nos EUA," 364.

62. Juan Luis Segundo, "Capitalism—Socialism: A Theological Crux," *Concilium* 96, 105–23; Gutiérrez, *Theology of Liberation*, 111–12; Gutiérrez, *La verdad los hará libres: confrontaciones* (Lima: Instituto Bartolomé de Las Casas, 1986), 101–12.

63. Leonard, *Critical Theory in Political Practice*, 119.

from 1964 to 1983. Would a socialist society be any less dictatorial? Brazilian economist Helio Jaguaribe says that "a stable democracy will not be possible in Brazil until the chasm between the masses and the upper classes is significantly reduced." Sixty-five percent of Brazilian families, Jaguaribe says, live below the poverty line.[64] How will this be done without the people falling victim again to a tyrannical society?

The Boffs' criticism of the bishops' morality of individual acts versus a morality of the social raises an important issue. They think the bishops' morality is individualist, because it lacks social systemic analysis, prophetic denunciation, and liberating praxis. In criticizing the bishops' overbenign treatment of multinational corporations, the Boffs write: "[the pastoral letter] is content with morality when we expected prophecy. What we need is more of Amos and less of Moses!"[65] I agree with their call for prophecy. Yet the prophetic utterance of Amos needs the ethical argument of Moses and Jesus, and the consensus building of Paul.

Comblin on National Security

The second case analyzes national security doctrine and its relation to the church in Brazil, Argentina, and Chile. Belgian theologian and priest José Comblin examines why the church for the most part finally rejected state support of its Christian proclamation in exchange for its cooperation with the state's national security policies. He contends that both doctrine and practice of the national security state of these nations, like peripheral capitalism, have their origins in western Europe and the United States. But like capitalism, national security in Latin America differs from national security among the Western powers. Latin American states lack strong political checks and balances present in the United States, England, and West Germany. Furthermore, Latin American nations have a strong military tradition and ethos in which military forces pride themselves as the ultimate guardians of Christian values, science, and democracy. Finally, Latin American countries, such as Brazil and Argentina, suffer from high unemployment, high infant mortality, skyrocketing inflation, and a spiraling debt that fosters revolutionary movements. These realities mold national security, à la Latin America, into a unique shape.

---

64. Lawrence E. Harrison, "Brazil: Scapegoating Debt," *Washington Post*, February 9, 1989, sec. A-19.

65. Boff and Boff, "A Igreja Perante a Economia nos EUA," 364.

Why Analysis?

In general, Comblin undertakes social analysis in order to interpret and to criticize ideologies within both theology and politics. He specifically undertook analysis of the national security state to resolve this pressing dilemma: Should the church speak out against the oppressive and repressive practices of the state at the risk of losing the state's support for its mission and possibly incurring persecution and death? Or would it be better to remain silent to ensure the security of the church and its membership? He first uncovers the mechanism of institutional oppression, showing causal connections between cultural, political, and economic components. Then he develops a strategy for change, including increasing a people's participation in politics and in the economy.[66] Finally, he criticizes the ideologies of various institutions, suggesting ways to ask more probing questions of an ethical nature about traditional roles, political practices, and rules in society. In this third step, his critical analysis overlaps with social ethics.

Like the Boffian analysis, the Comblin study does an ideology critique, disclosing values, presuppositions, and evils inherent in the national security state. Comblin goes further than the Boffs by arguing on moral grounds why this ideology is wrong and therefore should be rejected by the church.[67] In the course of unmasking ideologies, Comblin sensitizes the poor, the middle class, and the church hierarchy to the manipulative teaching and practices of the state. His consciousness-raising critiques possess the power to stir a people's faith and sense of responsibility.

Which Analysis?

Comblin describes his upbringing and early education as liberal. This changed soon after he set foot on Latin American soil, where he met the poor of Brazil, Chile, and Ecuador. His new surroundings and his perception of what was going on within society led him to reject the mainline Western socioanalytic school in economics and political science. He finds this school bound too tightly to narrow ideological interests that support present power arrangements in Latin America. Modernization theory and its programs of development fail to consider human subjectivity or interior freedom. They simply

66. José Comblin, *The Church and the National Security State* (Maryknoll, N.Y.: Orbis Books, 1979), 224.

67. Gibson Winter, *Elements for a Social Ethic* (New York: Macmillan, 1966); Reinhold Niebuhr, *Moral Man and Immoral Society* (New York: Charles Scribner's Sons, 1932).

isolate, define, and relate social phenomena governing human behavior, but do not account for human freedom in explaining these laws. Like the Boffs, Comblin thinks these social scientists screen out revolutionary change and legitimate the established order. "For them, revolution can be interpreted only through the categories of anomie, anarchy, disturbance of order."[68]

Modernization theory and its analysis give social structures the appearance of universal value and truth whereas they contain a particular perspective that controls the selection of subject matter, the perception of facts, and a methodology that always includes value judgments. Because this perspective favors the dominant group in society, it is ideological. Most ideological in this Western tradition are geopolitics and strategy, upon which national security doctrine builds its ideology.

Marxist socioscientific traditions also come under his scathing attack. Unlike the Boffs and Ellacuría, Comblin criticizes Marxist analysis because of its close association with the socialist party, which uses the analysis to justify its pragmatic decisions based on nonscientific and ideological arguments. Comblin is committed to protecting human freedom, which he thinks the Marxist materialist philosophy fails to respect. Yet for all his severe criticism of Marxist analysis, he remains more open to it than to modernization theory and functionalism, because at least it offers a critique of the capitalist system and calls for revolutionary change.[69] Nonetheless, Comblin does not adopt a Marxist analysis, though he does use concepts generally associated with a Marxist analysis (praxis, ideology, and revolutionary change).

Although Comblin does not make explicit his own analytical method, his criticism of institutions suggests that his social analysis springs from dependency theory. He attacks both foreign aid and developmental programs. Foreign aid, however well intentioned, participates in "the development process of the advanced nations, the other side of the coin of domination."[70] Development programs assimilate only the upper classes into the developed nations' way of life, allowing these elite, in cooperation with the external centers of power, to dominate the dependent lower classes.[71] He concurs with the Boffs that Latin American nations relate to the United States as periphery to metropolis. Underdevelopment flows from the development of the north as its secondary and necessary effect. "The best way to explain the world condition is as a set of relationships between 'dominating' nations and 'dominated'

68. Comblin, *Church and the National Security State*, 218.
69. José Comblin, *Antropología Cristiana* (Madrid: Ediciones Paulinas, 1985), 158–65.
70. Comblin, *Church and the National Security State*, 34.
71. Ibid., 62.

nations."[72] Comblin's solution, like the Boffs', calls for radical change in structures and processes. Moreover, Comblin, with the Boffs, says that structural
change must be undertaken by people themselves.

Dependency analysis influences how Comblin approaches the national
security state. He uses center-periphery categories in showing that U.S. geopolitics and strategy direct Latin American national security states and that
these states in turn dominate their own citizens. The internal structure of the
national security system on the periphery roughly parallels the national security
system of the United States and western Europe. His analysis involves three
steps. He first does a historical overview from colonial times to the present
that highlights patterns in church-state relations. He then examines the doctrine
itself, written largely by military officers from Brazil, Chile, and Argentina.
Finally, he shows how the state has tried to entice the church to accept its
national security doctrine and why the church, for the most part, rejected the
offer.

In explaining the church's rejection of this alliance, Comblin moves from
analysis to ethics. He explains not only why the church historically refused to
cooperate with the state, but argues on moral grounds why the church should
have refused cooperation with the national security state and why it must
continue to resist its ideology. In other words, Comblin's method organically
weaves together his descriptive-causal analysis of how national security works
in practice and an ethical evaluation of its operations.

His analysis, like the Boffs', amounts to an ideology critique. Ideologies
for Comblin nearly always connote something negative because they contain
elements that are false, oppressive, and often hidden from the consciousness
of the ideologue. His analysis of ideologies not only reveals a false consciousness
(second ideology), but deliberate deception (first ideology). The truth or falsity
of theological or political doctrine depends on whether the doctrine is borne
out in concrete situations of everyday life.[73] True theory grounded in praxis
opposes ideology, which has no basis in reality.

He opposes the ideology of national security not only because it distorts
but because it intentionally does so. Its proponents intentionally mislead the
people. In opposition to the gospel, national security ideologues teach that
human nature and society suffer an illness and so develop a strategy to safeguard
the people. Since war and distress constitute the normal human condition,
everyone should seek friends for protection against enemies. As his analysis
demonstrates, the national security state takes advantage of people's fear and

72. Ibid., 34.
73. Ibid., 25.

their corresponding need for security by persuading them that national security should take precedence over basic human rights. Thus, ideology not only misrepresents the state of affairs but also stifles the exercise of freedom in society. In summary, ideologies are false because they give structures the appearance of universal value, and they are wrong because their producers use them to dominate others.[74]

Issue: State Exploiting the Church

Drawing on his personal experience of living under repressive military regimes in Brazil and Chile, José Comblin unravels the main threads of national security as it historically developed in Latin America. This new military state, first established in Brazil and then in Argentina, Bolivia, Uruguay, Chile, Peru, and Ecuador, has operated according to a specific ideology that, Comblin argues, takes its origin from the United States. The doctrine presents a comprehensive theory about the state, the citizens within society, and the church. Citizens exist, the doctrine teaches, "only within the state and by means of the state." Because persons have security as their most basic need, they need the state in order to survive.[75] The survival of the state therefore takes priority over everything else, including human rights.

Confronted with this new doctrine, the church in Latin America had to reconsider its mission and strategy, especially in relation to the state. Because the church must live and function within the state and because the state has historically influenced the mission of the church, the church had to decide how to respond to the state's new doctrine of national security and its repressive practices.

He begins his analysis of the doctrine by examining the fascist movements in Italy, Germany, and Spain prior to the Second World War and concludes that such movements had minimal impact in Latin America. Its historical roots stem from the United States government, which, through the Pentagon, CIA, and National War College, indoctrinated the new military regimes after the coups d'état in Brazil (1964), Argentina (1966), and Chile (1973).[76]

The architects of this doctrine chose geopolitics and strategy as the basic disciplines to define national security. Although geopolitics is often defined as an objective science, Comblin dismisses its claim to scientific objectivity. "Geopolitics is the use of geography to rationalize a political program."[77] It defines

74. Ibid., 66.
75. Ibid., 168.
76. Ibid., 54.
77. Ibid., 67.

every state as a center of power that strives to defend itself against all other states and to expand its power and protect its territory. Geopolitics partitions the world into two blocs: the Eastern or Communist bloc and the Western or so-called free world. Because all of Latin America, except Cuba, belongs to the Western bloc, its national security is coordinated with Western security and controlled chiefly by the United States.[78]

Strategy, in its original meaning, is the art of war. The discipline, however, has recently been redefined, becoming the comprehensive science of the principles ruling all political knowledge and synthesizing national aims. The main goal of national strategy is the survival and security of the nation. Strategy assumes that all people live in a permanent state of war, especially against communism. Peace is the continuation of war by other means—political, economic, and psychosocial war, with military force being used as a last resort. Strategy, like geopolitics, is a highly ideological discipline, because of the absolute and total claim it makes on each citizen's life.[79]

Comblin maintains that Latin American nations have copied U.S. institutions and their doctrine, especially the National Security Council and CIA. Margaret Crahan, a specialist in Latin American political science, disagrees with Comblin. She contends that transmission of geopolitical thought and national security ideology to Latin America was a more complex process than what Comblin presents, involving a longer period of time and many more actors.[80] Crahan is probably correct regarding the greater importance of the European influences on Argentina, Uruguay, and Chile. As for Brazil, Comblin may be right that the United States government played a greater role in the practical construction of Brazil's national security.[81] Chilean scholar Genaro

78. Ibid., 76.

79. Ibid., 71–72.

80. Margaret E. Crahan, "National Security Ideology and Human Rights," in *Human Rights and Basic Needs in the Americas*, ed. Margaret E. Crahan (Washington, D.C.: Georgetown University Press, 1982), 121 n. 8. Crahan cites one of the chief proponents of geopolitics in Argentina, Jorge Atencio, who claims that writings by German geopolitical theorists R. Hennig and L. Korholz were published and distributed to the Argentine army and navy by the Escuela de Guerra Naval in 1951 and were critical in spreading geopolitical thought. Crahan contends that while U.S. strategic theorists were increasingly read by the Latin American military in the post–World War II period, the sources cited by proponents of national security ideology are overwhelmingly German, French, and Latin American.

81. Sylvia Ann Hewlett, *The Cruel Dilemmas of Development: Twentieth Century Brazil* (New York: Basic Books, 1980), 68. Hewlett shows that the Escola Superior de Guerra (ESG), set up after World War II in order to formulate a doctrine of national security, worked closely with the U.S. military. "A United States advisory mission

Arriagada contends that French military literature arising out of the Algerian war was more influential than the U.S. government in shaping the doctrine of Brazilian national security.[82]

These national security states claimed they were defending Western civilization by upholding and defending science, democracy, and Christianity. Comblin cites declarations of the three most important spokesmen in the Brazilian, Argentinean, and Chilean schools of geopolitics: General Golbery do Couto e Silva, Colonel Jorge E. Atencio, and General Augusto Pinochet Ugarte. These theorists, all generals, expressed in their doctrine and strategies a firm resolve to save Western, Christian civilization from communism and to create a new society based on Christian principles.

Comblin argues that these resolutions of the state to protect democratic and Christian ideals were figments of the generals' imaginations. In actual practice, the states of Brazil, Argentina, and Chile created dictatorships not unlike the state described in Hobbes's *Leviathan*: people surrendered their freedom to the state in order to achieve security and order.[83] As Argentinean General Villegas expressed it, "national politics is to be understood and determined from the point of view of national interest and security."[84] The survival of the nation became the absolute goal. To achieve its goals, the state assumed total power.

The state defines its primary goal as upholding national security and its secondary goal as providing social harmony necessary for economic development. To achieve these ends, the state must maximize its power.[85] On the national level, exercising power requires a balance between harshly enforcing discipline and then relaxing discipline in order to get people to carry out the will of the state without rebelling. Power on the international level involves a nation's ability to get other states to do its will in order to realize its national goals.[86]

---

was invited to Brazil and remained there between 1948 and 1960, with the result that the ESG came to be modeled after the United States' National War College both in organization and in focus. Indeed, some of the distinctive characteristics of post-1964 military governments in Brazil (pro-Americanism, anticommunism, a favorable attitude toward foreign capital, and a distaste for 'excessive' nationalism) can be directly traced to this early collaboration between the military establishments of the two countries."

82. Genaro Arriagada, "Ideology and Politics in the South American Military (Argentina, Brazil, Chile, and Uruguay)," paper presented at the Woodrow Wilson International Center for Scholars, Washington, D.C., March 21, 1979: 22–24.

83. Comblin, *Church and the National Security State*, 77.

84. Ibid., 72.

85. Ibid., 73. Comblin defines power as the capacity of the state to make its own will reality.

86. Ibid., 69.

Comblin labels this doctrine "idolatry" because its military proponents assume absolute power in the name of the state. Listen to General Golbery, chief theorist of Brazil:

> To be nationalist is to be always ready to give up any doctrine, any theory, any ideology, feelings, passions, ideals and values, as soon as they appear as incompatible with the supreme loyalty, which is due to the nation above everything else. Nationalism is, must be, and cannot be other than an Absolute One in itself.[87]

The Christian God for these military dictatorships was only a cultural symbol. Their real god was the security of the state.

After analyzing the ideology of the national security state, Comblin examines how the state tried to gain the church's support. The church for the most part refused to cooperate with the state, resisting the state's rhetoric that its own goals were identical with those of the church. Both church and state, the ideologues argued, strive to make life secure for people and to save Christian civilization from communism. The church was vulnerable to such pleas. "According to the national security theory," Comblin writes, "the armed forces and the church agree in rejecting the traditional underdeveloped anarchical, corrupt, sinful society." The military leaders often referred to achieving a regenerated society, free from corruption and based on national values, family, common good, natural law, and private property. In using a conservative and outdated version of Catholic social thought, national security doctrine presented a hierarchically organized society that seemed on the surface to be compatible with Christian principles.[88] Political and military leaders adopted clerical language and quoted selectively from papal encyclicals. More importantly, they offered the church privileges that it had lost and never recovered: the right to teach religion in public schools, financial aid to private schools, state censorship of publications contrary to the church's teaching, and defense of church laws against divorce and remarriage, and birth control.

Seeing the ploy, the majority of the Latin American church leaders pulled back.[89] They recognized that the state was appealing to a cultural Christianity, a peripheral social and psychological structure—traditions, rites, customs, and

---

87. Ibid., 78.

88. Ibid., 80.

89. Ibid., 81, 83, 232 n. 4. Comblin mentions certain church organizations, such as the integrist movements (Tradition-Family-Property), Opus Dei, and the Cursillos, that accepted the national security doctrine and developed a geopolitical version of church mission by trying to increase the prestige and power of the church. These groups, consisting of a minority among the upper classes of Christians, were convinced either by the state's argument or enticed by the state's offer of certain privileges.

symbols—all of which provided the nation with a certain identity and security. Strangely, the state never invoked values from the gospel as a prophetic or creative force. On the contrary, it subordinated Christian faith to its own national security doctrine.[90] The so-called new Christian society sought by the national security state was a fixed, passive, and archaic Christianity.

Building on this analysis, Comblin reflects on the theological-moral reasons why the church historically rejected the state's proposition and why it should continue to do so. The principal reason is that the state commits the sin of idolatry by defining national security as the supreme good. Moreover, it violates Christian anthropology by instrumentalizing Christian faith and love in order to safeguard its own absolute power. Furthermore, the military's crusade to root out the atheistic tenets of communism violates freedom and human rights, because it employed coercive methods that destroyed social patterns and persons.[91] Such methods did not, nor could they, expel atheism from the hearts of human beings. On the contrary, state repression served to symbolize a practical kind of atheism.[92] Freedom forever stands opposed to the raw exercise of power that imposes its will on another. God's gift of freedom calls each person to expel the interior elements that enslave one—namely, insecurity and fear—so that one may take charge of one's own life and live a life for others.[93]

To summarize, Comblin's ethics arises from a theological-moral reflection on his analysis of a state's domination of the church. In this negative contrast experience, Comblin identifies the highest human goods that ought to guide a people's existence: faith, love, and the universal human value of freedom. These forbid the church's compromise even for the sake of securing its mission.

Assessment

José Comblin makes a forthright sociological disclaimer at the introduction of his analysis of national security. Trained as a specialist in the New Testament at the University of Louvain, he came to Latin America under the

90. Ibid., 84.
91. For historical examples of what happened to human rights in the face of national security states in Argentina and Brazil during the 1970s, see John Simpson and Jana Bennett, *The Disappeared and the Mothers of the Plaza* (New York: St. Martin's Press, 1985); *Torture in Brazil: A Report by the Archdiocese of São Paulo*, trans. Jaime Wright, ed. Joan Dassin (New York: Vintage Books, 1986).
92. Comblin, *Church and the National Security State*, 85–86.
93. Ibid., 93.

pretext of defending the people against communism. Soon after his arrival, he underwent a conversion, he says, "of my whole existence—my intellectual process, my values, my understanding of life, and especially my priorities."[94] Meeting the ordinary people, the Indians, blacks, and mestizos turned him around, imbuing him with a hunger and thirst for justice in solidarity with the oppressed people of Latin America. In short, I commend Comblin for stating clearly the background and commitment that condition his analysis.

Turning to the second criterion of impartiality, I think Comblin uses his sources well, especially his personal experience and praxis in Brazil, Chile, and Ecuador, government documents, and Scripture. Experts in national security doctrine disagree with his underemphasizing the role of European thought on Latin American ideology and with his attributing too much influence to U.S. strategic theorists. Colonel Atencio, a chief proponent of national security doctrine in Argentina, claims that works by the Germans R. Hennig and L. Korholz were critical in spreading geopolitical thought throughout the Argentine military.[95] Apart from this possibly erroneous claim, Comblin's study accurately presents and criticizes national security doctrine and its impact on the church. Other theologians, such as Argentine José Míguez Bonino, pay tribute to his excellent analysis and use his research as building blocks in their own research.[96]

Comblin does his best analysis when he draws from his own considerable experience in Latin America. His critique of national security ideology suggests a structural analysis related to the dependency school, but his analytical roots remain unclear. Both his critique of Western capitalism and his theology of revolution show close parallels with the Boffian analysis, though he criticizes Marxist analysis and the Boffs do not. His explanation of why mainline churches rejected national security ideology is masterfully developed. Although the general tenets of dependency theory shape his analysis, he supports his critique of national security with persuasive evidence. In sum, his analysis is a careful and credible investigation.

Comblin's exposition of national security has an unmistakable ethical tone of condemnation for reasons already mentioned and for theological reasons as well. National security doctrine is wrong because it presents the state as "the unqualified good" and thinks its clandestine service is "almighty and omnipresent." The main ethical issue becomes whether all Christians and the church ought to oppose it.

94. Ibid., xi.
95. Crahan, *Human Rights and Basic Needs in the Americas*, 121 n. 8.
96. Míguez Bonino, *Toward a Christian Political Ethics*, chap. 5.

In his analysis Comblin develops reasons why the church in fact rejected the national security ideology. In his ethics he shows why the church should continue to reject this teaching of the state. Whereas his analysis establishes that national security doctrine is false because it contradicts the true state of affairs, his ethics judges the doctrine to be morally wrong because it goes counter to important Christian and human values. In sum, his ideology critique of national security concludes that it fosters a false consciousness and operates out of a morally wrong conscience.

Ellacuría on Land in El Salvador

The morning after the assassination of six Jesuit priests and their two coworkers on November 16, 1989, a young man dressed in military garb drove through the streets of San Salvador announcing jubilantly: "We got Ellacuría!" Why would this soldier and the right-wing military groups rejoice over the slaughter of the university president and his companions? The military right perceived him as a powerful, outspoken supporter of the Marxist guerrillas called the Farabundo Martí National Liberation Front (FMLN). His friends said the military forces assassinated him because he spoke the truth about what he saw happening in this war-ravaged land. The record shows he spoke candidly and powerfully in favor of agrarian reform and peace negotiations between the government forces and the guerrillas. He also vigorously opposed the violation of human rights by the government.

The fundamental issue in El Salvador's agricultural economy is agrarian land reform. In 1974 agriculture comprised 26 percent of the GNP, and in 1977 it provided four-fifths of the nation's income from exports. When Ellacuría did his analysis in 1976, more than 60 percent of the population was classified as agricultural. Farmland was then and remains today of fundamental importance for all political developments.[97] A Salvadoran lawyer said in 1987, "Too little land and too many people is our national curse." Rather, Ellacuría said, the real curse lies at the doorstep of those few who monopolize the fertile farmland while millions of landless farmers struggle to survive.

In the heat of the polemical debate on land reform, this philosopher-theologian at Central American University chose to do an analysis of farmland as private property. His analysis followed in the wake of President Molina's announcing the creation of an Agrarian Transformation Institute (ISTA) and

97. Harold Jung, "Class Struggle and Civil War in El Salvador," in *El Salvador: Central America in the New Cold War*, ed. Marvin E. Gettleman et al., revised and updated (New York: Grove Press, 1986), 65.

a land-reform program, called "The First Project." The president's announcement raised great hope among the peasants and among many members of the church who supported the claim of the poor to farmland. Landowners, however, vigorously opposed agrarian reform. They created an organization called the National Association of Private Enterprise (ANEP) and launched a powerful campaign against the government's First Project. The landowners, supported by President Molina's defense minister, General Carlos Humberto Romero, successfully pressured the government to modify several measures of the reform proposal and eventually crushed it. After the proposal was defeated, government security forces and paramilitary groups repressed the peasants and persecuted members of the church.

The repression radicalized many groups within the church, especially those in rural areas. Between February and May 1977, seventeen priests were either expelled or exiled, four were jailed and tortured, and six killed "by unknown hand."[98] Father Rutilio Grande and his two assistants were assassinated on March 12, 1977. The executions, observers noted, were blatantly political. Father Grande was well known for his pastoral work among the rural poor and socially conscious peasants in Aguilares.[99] General Romero (no relation to Archbishop Romero) assumed the presidency four months later and the repression escalated. Father Ellacuría was among the forty-six Jesuits accused by the UGB (Unión Guerrera Blanca) of terrorism and given until July 20, 1977, to leave the country; otherwise, their execution would be "immediate and systematic."[100] The assassination of Ellacuría came twelve years later.

Why Analysis?

Ellacuría undertook an analysis of private property for the purpose of helping all Salvadorans to understand how the present arrangement exploits the poor and how its ideology helps keep it in place. He thinks about ideologies much the same way as the Boffs and Comblin do: as rationalizations that cover, disguise, and protect real economic interests and social status.[101] Two fundamentally opposed viewpoints, or ideologies, have divided and continue to

98. James Dunkerley, *The Long War: Dictatorship and Revolution in El Salvador* (London: Junction Books, 1982), 108–9. Dunkerley points out that repression in the rural areas was aimed primarily at Christian groups, priests in particular. The most outstanding example was the full-scale military occupation of the town of Aguilares on May 20, 1976.

99. Joe Eldridge and Cressida McKean, "Uncivil Strife in El Salvador," *Sojourners* 6 (July 1977): 26–28.

100. Dunkerley, *The Long War*, 109.

101. Ignacio Ellacuría, "La historización del concepto de propiedad como principio de desideologización" *Estudios Centroamericanos* 31 (1976): 425.

divide the people of El Salvador: the viewpoint of the landowners, who want to maintain control over their vast landholdings; and the perspective of the landless peasants seeking farmland to survive and live a better life.[102] Landowners exercise control through the government, the military, and the media. The poor, aided by church leaders, organizations within the church, and peasant labor unions, challenge that control.[103]

Ideological thinking driven by survival and self-interest can be transcended, Ellacuría maintains, if persons and groups recognize it and are willing to confront it. This requires raising the people's social consciousness about farmland, and then encouraging them in light of their new awareness to decide whether to support or reject the reform proposal. Consciousness-raising in this situation involves becoming aware, through social analysis, of the ideological meaning that rich landowners give to private property to justify their vast landholdings.

Which Analysis?

Like his colleagues (the Boffs and Comblin), Ellacuría criticizes functionalism as a mode of analysis, adopting instead an ideology critique that identifies and criticizes those distorted perspectives embodied within institutional policy and law. Social analysis, for Ellacuría, is inextricably linked to theological-ethical reflection. He states his theological convictions and viewpoint about what is going on. He perceives a perduring sense of evil in the existing social structures, which diametrically oppose the reign of God and the common good. Therefore the present system must be transformed.

Like the Boffs, Ellacuría does not perceive global society as an interdependent cluster of nations forming a harmonious organism, though he works toward that utopian society when dominant and dependent nations cease to compete with each other and work together for just and peaceful relationships. Another theological conviction that conditions his analysis is his commitment to the liberation of the poor and oppressed. He makes no apologies for a partisan analysis (done from the perspective of the poor in El Salvador), but he insists upon rigorous social inquiry based on empirical investigation.

Ellacuría makes a distinctive contribution to social analysis by developing a method that accounts for the cultural and political context. He calls his version

102. Rosanne Klass and Barbara Slavin, "El Salvador—A Profile of Terror," *New York Times*, January 28, 1979. The country has perhaps the greatest extremes of wealth and poverty in Latin America. The vast majority of its people live in a desperate situation. A large percentage is illiterate, unemployed, and landless.

103. Raymond Bonner, "The Failure of Land Reform," in *El Salvador*, 290.

of ideology critique "historicization of concepts." This critique locates concepts (human rights or freedom) within the historical context in which they are used, explaining what the concepts actually mean, what they conceal, and what consequences they have for the poor. All liberation theologians attend to social context, insisting that theory be grounded in experience. Ellacuría goes further by examining how an important concept, such as the common good or property, evolves over a long historical period and what it comes to mean in the present. If his study concludes that a certain concept's everyday operational use differs from its universally accepted meaning, he urges that it be redefined and that new social conditions be established.

A universal concept conveys a core meaning that most people in various cultural contexts would accept. A historical concept denotes the same basic reality as the universal, but acquires a different specification within changing historical contexts. "Historical concepts are operative, their truth can be measured by their results and their content goes on changing while maintaining their essential meaning."[104] A concept such as private property may take on a meaning quite different from its core meaning and may justify activity that harms society.

Oppressive ideologies thrive on expressing themselves in abstract universal concepts because abstract dress covers over their evil deeds. A repressive state that proclaims freedom of the press and the right to private property, for instance, can conceal the practice of censoring certain newspapers or denying the poor their rights. In El Salvador, Ellacuría says, human rights function differently for the rich and the poor. The real truth of a historical process lies in the objective results of the process. The idealism of intentions must be verified by the materialism of facts.[105]

Using the historicization-of-concepts approach, Ellacuría focuses on property: its historical forms, its meaning in contemporary usage, and how it might be used to help a nation to flourish. He judges the truth of the present understanding of property on its fruits. If one group claims that private property generates creative initiative and personal freedom, but in practice the institution of private property exploits the majority of workers, the claim is ideological and false. Its future use depends on what most Salvadorans want property to mean and on their willingness to establish the structural conditions that will make the new vision a reality.

104. Ellacuría, "La historización," 428.
105. Ibid., 434.

Issue: Whether "Private Property" Exploits Salvadorans

Ellacuría historicizes property in El Salvador according to a process that involves four steps: (1) historical study of the different meanings of property in El Salvador; (2) analysis of property today and its social consequences in rural El Salvador; (3) redefining property and establishing conditions for bringing about the new concept; and (4) historicizing the concept of property in the Christian tradition (from the gospel to twentieth-century social teaching), showing how the tradition illumines and challenges the notion held by the wealthy landowners and encourages the kind of social transformation the government has initiated. I shall treat only the first three points, which deal more directly with social analysis, and return to Ellacuría's ethics (point 4) in the final chapter.

History of property   Ellacuría contends that the landowning oligarchy's National Association of Private Enterprise (ANEP) has been defending an ideological form of property that emphasizes private initiative and the maximization of production. ANEP's abstract notion glosses over a history of exploitation that began with the Spanish conquest in the sixteenth century. Before the conquest, Amerindians had developed a distinctive form of communal property on which they lived and grew crops.[106] The conquerers abolished their system, took possession of the land, and implemented a feudal system that enslaved the indigenous peasants. The agrarian reform of 1881 favored those with capital who purchased gigantic tracts of farmland. The government parceled out small, less fertile land to the majority, which proved inadequate to support a family.[107]

In the late nineteenth century, the indigenous peasants were driven off the land by private plantation owners who introduced coffee as a commodity. The owners protected their interests by new agrarian laws, which included police protection.[108] This oppressive structure brought on a communist-led peasant revolt in 1932 in which four thousand people were killed; the uprising was crushed. This was soon followed by *La Mantanza*, or massacre of four percent of the Salvadoran population by the army.[109] In summary, Ellacuría's historical sketch reveals that property has taken many forms in five hundred

106. Ellacuría refers the reader to an important work by D. Browning, *El Salvador, La Tierra y el Hombre* (San Salvador: Ministerio de Educación, 1975).

107. Ellacuría, "La historización," 429.

108. Michael McClintlock, *The American Connection*, vol. 1, *State Terror and Popular Resistance in El Salvador* (London: ZED Books, 1985), chap. 6.

109. Gettleman et al., *El Salvador*, 54, 64.

years of Salvadoran history. It also shows that its present institutionalized form evolved from illegal appropriation, maintained and defended by oppressive means.

Property today   Turning to ANEP's defense of property, Ellacuría analyzes the landowners' defense of the status quo and their attack of the government's land-reform proposal. ANEP justified private property as it operates in El Salvador today because it maintains high productivity and fosters private initiative. Productivity, ANEP argued, should be the primary criterion for deciding which land to expropriate. It urged the government to redistribute state-owned lands first, then abandoned, unused, and poorly used lands; it should not, however, expropriate large farmlands, such as those that ANEP represents, because they have maintained the highest productivity in El Salvador.

The government's agrarian transformation proposal, with its requirements for a maximum of 35 hectares and a minimum of 3 hectares per family, would decrease production, lower the standard of living, increase unemployment, erode the confidence of investors, and foment apathy. These results would increase the danger of communism within the country. ANEP said that the government's proposals for establishing cooperatives and experimenting with collectivist structures were at odds with the government's goal of achieving greater productivity.[110]

Ellacuría, using data provided by the government, challenged the landowners' assertions, showing with hard data that ANEP's claim about high productivity in the coastal areas was erroneous. The coastal zone, where the project intended to focus its efforts, was among the lowest in productivity compared to other zones of El Salvador. Land distribution within this zone was unequal: five landowners (represented by ANEP) owned 17,319 blocks (*manzanas*) of land, whereas 2,483 owners had only 5,006. Income distribution, moreover, varied greatly. Whereas each of the five landowners earned $2,479 per day, 38 percent of the landowners in the same coastal region received $.35 per day from their land. In other words, one large landowner would have the daily income of 6,968 families.[111]

110. Ibid., 429–31.
111. Ibid., 431, 450 n. 11. The author also provides these statistics for this area: "The index of illiteracy in the area is 65%, the deficit of sanitary services is 98%, that of drinking water services is 50.4%, and that of housing 35%. Unemployment in the area is up to 54.3%, so that the work expectancy for peasants is only about 141 days in the year."

Ellacuría and the government maintained that while the program proposal aimed toward higher productivity, increased productivity by itself would not solve the basic structural problem of injustice. Ellacuría argued: "El Salvador could produce twenty times more, but if the unjust economic structures—deriving mainly from the present situation of land holdings—are not corrected, a very few will not have to stand in line to eat and a great majority will not even have the opportunity to wait their turn."[112] The issue was not primarily productivity, but distribution of income. The First Project sought to enable the majority of Salvadorans to participate in a mixed economy that included private property. It opposed, however, the present structure of private property as an absolute, exclusive, and perpetual right.

The government and Ellacuría agreed in principle with the landowners' stress on increasing productivity. Yet Ellacuría pointed out the contradiction for wealthy landowners to wave triumphantly the banner of productivity and private initiative while their laborers worked the fields for low wages and under poor working conditions. Even though the major landowners have possessed limitless resources and the service of millions of Salvadoran workers for many decades, they have failed to bring about humane living standards for their workers. Furthermore, private initiative, claimed by ANEP to be so necessary for productivity, has meant nothing for the landless majority, who cannot exercise initiative without owning property. The government planned to create more private owners, thereby encouraging more personal initiative, fostering fair competition and productivity.

Ellacuría constructs three criteria that help determine whether the concept of property under study is ideological in the negative sense. First, property is suspect whenever its defenders mount an expensive campaign to defend their position. The wealthy landowners' association (ANEP) did so by its advertising and by controlling the educational structure and the communications media. Second, the concept of property is ideological whenever the dominant power remains closed to discussing the government's proposal. ANEP refused to dialogue with government representatives. Third, the concept is ideological if its proponents are unwilling to work toward the good of the whole country, demonstrated by transcending their own special interests or at least by compromising. The last criterion (the common good) serves as an important moral principle as well as a standard for determining the ideological quality of a political position.[113] Like Comblin, who evaluated the morality of the national

112. Ibid., 431–32.
113. Ignacio Ellacuría, "Human Rights in a Divided Society," in *Human Rights in the Americas: The Struggle for Consensus*, ed. Alfred Hennelly and John Langan (Washington, D.C.: Georgetown University Press, 1982), 55.

security state on the basis of freedom and human rights, Ellacuría invokes the principles of the common good and distributive justice to judge private property.

A modest proposal   After criticizing ANEP's concept of property, Ellacuría outlined what property might look like if the land reform were implemented. Until now, Ellacuría said, the untouchability of private property has served as the dogma of Salvadoran capitalism.[114] The reform program would construct a mixed economic structure in the agricultural sector, including large private corporations, medium-sized institutions, communitarian and cooperative forms of property.

The supreme arbiter and enforcer of reform would be the state. It should be noted that Ellacuría supports, perhaps more for pragmatic reasons, a Weberian (not a Marxist) notion of the state, which acts as legislator, arbiter, and executor of property rights. He calls upon the state to settle disputes between the poor majority and the rich landowners or oligarchy. He knows how, historically, the state, the military forces, and the oligarchy have cooperated in exploiting the poor of El Salvador. Yet he thought in 1976 (wrongly, as it turned out) that the state was maturing and assuming its proper role as the authoritative judge of conflicts between the bourgeoisie, the peasants, and multinational corporations. Therefore he supported the state's taking charge of dismantling the oligarchical system of landholding and redistributing the land.

Ellacuría's support of a mixed economy shows his leaning more toward socialism and away from capitalism. He envisioned workers of the land becoming owners and active agents in agrarian transformation. The product of labor must be fundamentally for the laborer. The property of the major means of production, and not simply the land, should belong to all citizens and not simply to one social class.

Assessment

Ellacuría's method of historicization of concepts resembles in some basic respects the ideology critiques of the Boffs and Comblin: all four theologians try to establish the veracity of theory using the criterion of praxis. Like Comblin, Ellacuría's attention to the historical roots of ideologies strengthens his

114. Ellacuría, "La historización," 435. Ellacuría says that the landholding oligarchy controls the armed forces as well as the legislative, judicial, and executive powers, enabling it to intervene directly in coups d'état and the nomination of presidents, advantageous laws and to block the passage of others.

critique. His distinctive method of historicizing concepts examines social and political notions in their historical situation in order to determine whether the concepts represent what the general population thinks they mean and wants them to mean. The middle phase of this process, called "deideologization," determines whether the formal contemporary understanding is verified in practice by looking at its consequences. In the third step, he reinterprets the basic or universal meaning of the term and establishes the social conditions for bringing it into being.[115]

Strengths   Like the Boffs and Comblin, Ellacuría states his commitment, which helps the reader understand the parameters of his investigation. He candidly states that his investigation seeks justice for the poor, convinced that his proposals will foster the good of the whole nation. His analysis delves more deeply into the statistics regarding landholdings, income, wages, and education. He pays attention to the power alignments that support the economic arrangements. Aided by data provided by the government, Ellacuría demonstrates that ANEP used property abstractly, thereby concealing the negative impact private property has had on the nation as a whole and the peasants in particular.[116]

Thus, Ellacuría achieves his objective of demonstrating that ANEP's concept of private property is narrowly ideological by showing that private property as institutionalized in rural El Salvador violates the common good. Landowners staunchly resisted the moderate agrarian-reform project aimed at helping landless peasants to participate in capitalist enterprises. He provides evidence supporting his contention that the predominant form of agrarian property has served the interests of a very small percentage of Salvadorans. He refutes ANEP's claim that productivity was high and that it benefited the nation more than any alternative measure could. Ellacuría points out that the economic situation of peasant laborers working in the coastal zone was desperate. The motivational factor—private initiative—meant nothing to these small farmers or workers, whose prospects for increasing their holdings were dim. In sum, Ellacuría presents a penetrating analysis of the institution of private property within a historical context.

Ellacuría's analysis of ideology improves upon the Boffs' and Comblin's approaches mainly because he sifts through vast amounts of empirical studies,

115. Thomas L. Schubeck, "The Reconstruction of Natural Law Reasoning: Liberation Theology as a Case Study," *Journal of Religious Ethics* 20, no. 1 (Spring 1992): 166–67.
116. Ellacuría, "Human Rights in a Divided Society," 432.

including the writings of his opponents, to support his own contentions. Like Comblin, he makes explicit the ethical criteria, such as the common good, that he uses to evaluate private property. He argues cogently that just distribution must qualify the economic principle of maximizing production. Ellacuría argues convincingly against ANEP's claim that increasing productivity brings a corresponding increase of benefits for all.[117]

Limitations   Although his method of historicization of property is sound, certain points of his argument need clarification. It is not clear whether he opposes private property in principle or simply its monopolistic structure in present-day El Salvador, because of its questionable productivity and poor distribution of benefits. Does he think the best arrangement would be a mixed economy that includes both social and private property, or does he envision this as a transitional stage en route to a full socialist economy? What he clearly rejects is a monopolistic and uncontrolled private property system. He leaves open the acceptance of private property. It can be justified, he wrote, "only when it is the best way of accomplishing and fulfilling the primary destiny of the goods of the earth and the solidarity of all human beings."[118] In the context of El Salvador, he favors a socialist concept of property within a mixed economy. Since production is social, its distribution must be social.[119] Moreover, social distribution of property is consonant with the essential tenets of Christian doctrine.

Critics might charge that Ellacuría's position on property within a mixed economy with its socialist bias amounts to an ideology. This critique cannot be satisfactorily answered because Ellacuría's plan was never implemented. Yet Ellacuría does spell out criteria for judging whether ideologies are distortions or "one-sided" (Segundo's term). They are distortions when the concept and practice do not represent the actual state of affairs or the consensus of the majority, and when its proponents do not work for the good of the whole nation. Whether his concept of property would have gained the consensus of the majority and would have fostered the good of the community remains an unanswered question.

A key actor in land reform is, of course, the state, which has always supported the wealthy landowners. Whether the state would possess the moral will to work for the common good and to break its long-standing allegiance to the powerful entrepreneurs is doubtful. As counterweight events both before

117. Ibid., 433.
118. Ibid., 446.
119. Ibid., 439.

and after Ellacuría's proposal showed, strong affinities between government officials and entrepreneurs have existed and continue to exist. Endowing the state with sufficient authority and power to distribute farmland may only shift the monopoly from the private sector to the state. Ellacuría was aware of that danger. But because the state had achieved a certain incipient stage of development, he was confident that it would not become totalitarian. "If the state belongs to all and stands for all, there will be no dictatorship of the state, and anyway, a dictatorship of a given social group would be worse."[120]

What Analysis Brings to Ethics

These three cases show how liberation theologians generally do social analysis as a component of ethics. All three analyses involve ideology critique, which is the predominant, though not the only, way these theologians analyze institutions. Ideology critique uncovers distortions in concepts, convictions, and laws that justify how institutions operate. For all four theologians, ideology critique involves practical reasoning that closely links explanation and evaluation. Because ideologies contain moral elements that justify institutional policy, the critique of them implies a moral judgment. The analyses of Comblin and Ellacuría present a moral argument that supports their judgment. In these three analyses, the Boffs judge capitalism to be inherently exploitive, Comblin rejects the national security state as totalitarian, and Ellacuría considers the monopolistic control of fertile farmland to be a violation of justice.

Ethicists may criticize mixing social analysis and ethical reasoning. But as sociologist Robert Bellah has demonstrated, ethical reflection is not extrinsic to the social inquiry of the most significant social thinkers.[121] Even though liberation theologians critique the validity of moral concepts and norms in terms of praxis and empirical investigation, they do not think that the experiential or empirical can ever justify what morally ought to be. As we shall see in the following chapter, revelation in dialogue with praxis discloses moral obligation. Liberation theologians do not reduce ethics to analysis.

Ethics relates to social analysis in at least three ways. First, as the Boffs state in their analysis, choosing the instrument for doing analysis involves moral criteria.[122] Second, analysis helps theologians determine how accurately they assess the mechanism, power, and ideologies of an institution. It provides sources of information about social realities that ethics alone does not have

120. Ibid.
121. Bellah, "Ethical Aims of Social Inquiry," 373.
122. See Boff, *Theology and Praxis*, 57–60; Gutiérrez, *Truth Shall Make You Free*, chap. 3.

access to, but which it needs in order to evaluate behavior or policy. Third, ethics, not analysis, determines which norms are fundamental for evaluating the institutions, as we saw in the analysis of Comblin and Ellacuría.[123]

Ideology critique raises questions about values and challenges institutional power that theologians think exploits the poor. In this way, the critique challenges social ethics, as Comblin and the Boffs said, to deal with political and economic institutions and not simply with individual decisions made by managers of these institutions.

A pitfall to be avoided is making premature moral judgments before scrutinizing the evidence and testing moral intuitions by means of careful moral argument. Ellacuría does well in testing his intuitive judgment on private property by his study of the gospel and church social teaching. Good analysis also requires openness to different modes. As Gutiérrez points out, social sciences are not neutral; they carry ideological baggage that requires discernment.[124] Hence, getting locked into one type of analysis can lead the analyst into an ideological trap.

It is not always clear in the analyses themselves whether ideology means "false consciousness" or "bad conscience," even though Segundo and Clodovis Boff carefully distinguish these two types of ideologies. The ideological cross fire between the theologians and their critics does call for more precision in the use of this term. Comblin seems to reduce ideology to an unjust doctrine. Although Ellacuría recognizes that all groups operate according to ideologies (understood in the neutral sense), he sometimes implies that ideologies simply mean conscious deception. Segundo is more careful to distinguish the neutral use of ideology from its negative uses (false consciousness and conscious deception).

123. John Langan, "Violence and Injustice in Society: Recent Catholic Teaching," *Theological Studies* 46, no. 4 (December 1985): 686.
124. Gutiérrez, *Truth Shall Make You Free*, chap. 3.

5

Scripture and Ethics

The poor and oppressed pose challenging questions when reflecting on the Bible. Gathered in a church base community, they ask whether their campaign for land has any basis in the Bible, or whether the gospel instructs them to love class enemies.[1] They also raise questions about right biblical interpretation: "One priest reads the Bible in a way which encourages the people, and another priest reads the same Bible in a way which justifies the rich. Which of the two is right?"[2] The present chapter investigates how liberation theologians, mainly Jorge Pixley and Gustavo Gutiérrez, use Scripture to speak to such urgent issues and how they join praxis to Scripture to do ethics.

Although neither theologian is an ethicist by training or by self-identification, their writings deserve this special focus for a number of reasons. First of all, both Pixley and Gutiérrez have made important contributions to the development of liberation theology. Second, they represent Protestant and Catholic theological traditions in Latin America. Third, they use Scripture in ethics in a variety of ways. Finally, they relate Scripture to nonbiblical sources, especially praxis and social analysis, in their effort to illumine moral problems and to make critical judgments.

Each theologian's use of Scripture will be examined following the same general structure developed in the last chapter: (1) Why?—the theologian's reasons for interpreting a specific biblical book or passage; (2) How?—the method of interpretation; (3) What?—the specific way each theologian uses Scripture in ethics; (4) How well?—my assessment of each theologian's use of Scripture in ethics. The chapter concludes with general comments on Pixley's

1. Ernesto Cardenal, *The Gospel in Solentiname*, vol. 2, trans. Donald D. Walsh (Maryknoll, N.Y.: Orbis Books, 1978) 2:109–11.
2. Carlos Mesters, *Defenseless Flower: A New Reading of the Bible* (Maryknoll, N.Y.: Orbis Books, 1989), 9.

and Gutiérrez's contributions and then offers some positive guidelines for using Scripture in developing a liberation ethics.

Bible, Christ, and Ethics

As William Spohn has perceptively noted, "disagreements on using Scripture stem from the different positions taken on Christ, ethics, and revelation."[3] Spohn's insight suggests that those who regard Jesus as a moral lawgiver emphasize the moral prescriptions of the gospel and think of ethics primarily as following rules (deontology). Those who think of Jesus as a liberator develop broad biblical themes, such as covenant, liberation, and concern for the poor. They construct their ethics in terms of a single goal (e.g., a new society), attending to consequences in relation to the goal. A few preliminary observations about the Bible, about Christ, and about ethics may help to identify the distinctive ways in which liberation theologians use the Bible in ethical discourse.

Bible   Liberation theologians emphasize that God addresses human beings within concrete events. The word of God is enfleshed in history in the sense that God's self-communication takes place in historical moments, of which Sacred Scripture is witness.[4] Hence, the point of departure of the biblical text is an experience of God that is gathered up in a word. The Hebrew people first undergo a radical liberation and later narrate it.

Biblical liberation theologian J. Severino Croatto says that the word interprets the event in the very act of telling the story. The word does this by giving priority to one specific experience and by closing off others. The original event, even after being set down in writing, expands its meaning by subsequent interpretations made in light of new events, such as reading Exodus in light of the Babylonian exile. Consequently, a contemporary reading of the deliverance from slavery in Egypt never repeats the meaning of the original Exodus, but taps its "reservoir of meaning" that has built up over the centuries.[5] The inexhaustibility of the meaning and inspiration of Exodus becomes apparent

3. William C. Spohn, *What Are They Saying about Scripture and Ethics?* (New York: Paulist Press, 1984), 129.

4. "Dogmatic Constitution on Divine Revelation" (*Dei Verbum*), in *The Documents of Vatican II*, ed. Walter M. Abbott (New York: Herder and Herder, 1966), no. 13; Allen Verhey, *The Great Reversal: Ethics and the New Testament* (Grand Rapids, Mich.: Eerdmans, 1984), 170.

5. J. Severino Croatto, *Biblical Hermeneutics: Toward a Theory of Reading as the Production of Meaning* (Maryknoll, N.Y.: Orbis Books, 1987), 38.

in subsequent readings by the Hebrew people, later by the Christian community, and today by people in liberation struggles.

People engaged in a praxis confer an added meaning to the text, and a faithful reading of the text gives new meaning and direction to their praxis. As Gutiérrez is fond of saying, we read Scripture from within the context of our own praxis, but Scripture also reads us by effecting change in us.[6]

Carlos Mesters, a biblical theologian who has spent a lifetime studying how ecclesial base communities in Brazil interpret the Bible, distinguishes two dimensions of the environment within which people interpret the Bible: the "pre-text" or social situation and the "context" or communitarian faith. Pre-text is the concrete world that people bring as they prepare to read the text. Context consists of people sharing their faith in community. Illumined by the pre-text and context, the text comes alive for the people gathered in prayerful reflection, giving them hope.[7] Sometimes their reading challenges the meaning of the biblical formulations. Even though the Bible expresses truths applicable for people in every age, unlettered people instinctively recognize that particular historical and cultural perspectives condition and limit the expression of these truths (e.g., the acceptance of slavery and patriarchal structures).[8] As one person expressed on behalf of the group, "The text is not to be taken literally when it doesn't fit our situation."[9]

Mesters's pre-text and context means reading the Bible critically and with eyes of faith. This approach allows the community to discover the Spirit's meaning in the text, "the meaning for us." Exegete Norbert Lohfink speaks of this transcendent dimension as the "surprising otherness" that may challenge a person's and a community's moral life and the social order by presenting an alternate vision of human relationships and community life.[10] Reading the Bible critically requires discovering its historicoliteral meaning—that is, the text's literal meaning—and the cultural context in which God's word was received.[11] Mesters relates the historicoliteral meaning and the contemporary meaning in

6. Gutiérrez, *Truth Shall Make You Free*, 47.

7. Mesters, *Defenseless Flower*, 12–22.

8. Carolyn Osiek, *What Are They Saying about the Social Setting of the New Testament?* (New York: Paulist Press, 1984), 2.

9. Ibid., 7.

10. Norbert F. Lohfink, *Option for the Poor: The Basic Principle of Liberation Theology in the Light of the Bible*, ed. Duane L. Christensen, trans. S. Linda M. Maloney (Berkeley: BIBAL Press, 1987), 51.

11. Carolyn Osiek, "The New Handmaid: The Bible and the Social Sciences," *Theological Studies* 50, no. 2 (June 1989): 265.

terms of a metaphor of a railroad track. They are like two rails that "carry the train of interpretation."[12]

Christ   Since liberation ethics is a Christian ethics, it is reasonable to expect that Jesus Christ plays an authoritative role in the writings of liberation theologians. Christians, however, interpret Jesus as the Christ in various ways: as moral teacher, as prophet, as savior, or as liberator. These interpretations on the meaning of Christ affect the way Christians interpret the Bible.

A related question asks whether Jesus serves as the hermeneutical key for interpreting the Old Testament writings, or whether liberation theologians use another hermeneutical principle to interpret them. Do liberation theologians interpret the Old Testament in light of the New? Does Pixley interpret the book of Exodus and Gutiérrez the book of Job in light of the Jesus story?

Ethics   The majority of Christian churches and Christian ethicists would endorse the view that Scripture is normative for Christian ethics in a significant, though not in a fully autonomous, sense. This means that Scripture, as the primary witness to the word of God, plays a central role in forming the moral identity of Christians and informing their moral decisions. But few Christian theologians think Scripture alone provides a fully self-sufficient morality because they recognize that the specific moral questions and answers in the Bible do not directly apply to contemporary situations. Liberation theologians would share this consensus. For the latter, Scripture enjoys a primacy in their theology and ethics, but it must be interpreted by today's Christian community in light of the Christian tradition and the contemporary situation.

This chapter explores hermeneutics, specifically how two important liberation theologians interpret Scripture in their thinking about ethics. Jorge Pixley and Gustavo Gutiérrez reflect on how God's word interfaces with people's praxis. Since neither theologian is an ethicist, it should not be expected that they would undertake a systematic study of how Scripture illumines ethical issues. However, they may give clues about how Scripture relates to ethics in the course of their theological reflections.

Christians have used Scripture in many ways to do ethics.[13] First, certain groups have appealed to injunctions or imperatives in the Bible as moral

12. Mesters, *Defenseless Flower*, 20–21.

13. James M. Gustafson, *Theology and Christian Ethics* (Philadelphia: Pilgrim Press, 1974), 121–45. I follow with some adaptation three of the four main uses of Scripture in ethics developed by Gustafson: (1) formal commands; (2) moral ideals; (3) analogy; (4) great variety of values, norms, and principles. I add three other uses, developed first by philosopher Henry David Aiken, and adopted by Christian ethicists. See Verhey, *The Great Reversal*, 187–97; Bruce C. Birch and Larry L. Rasmussen, *Bible and Ethics in the Christian Life*, rev. ed. (Minneapolis: Augsburg, 1989), 111–13.

standards for Christian living, such as the Decalogue (Exod. 20:1-17) or Paul's practical rules (1 Cor. 10:14-31). Ethicists call this a formal-rules approach or "deontology." It says that certain actions are obligatory, right or wrong because of a prior command or duty (God commands it, or reason demands it) and not because of foreseeable consequences of the act.[14]

Second, a person might appeal to the moral ideals in Scripture, such as justice expressed in the covenant or as love through service of the needy (Matt. 25:31-45). Such ideals serve as goals toward which all Christians should strive and according to which their behavior will be judged. Ethics functions as a teleology in which an ultimate value (telos) serves as the standard for judging the goodness of a human act.

A third use tries to evaluate behavior or strategy based on an analogy between a contemporary event and a biblical event. The biblical narrative, such as Exodus, serves as an authoritative precedent for evaluating present practices or future strategies, such as those that Latin Americans become engaged in as they struggle for freedom and justice. The analogical use may overlap with other types discussed above. For example, the interpreter may also attend to the commands within the Exodus account, using them to evaluate specific actions, such as the use of physical force to advance the liberation movement.

A fourth use relates the Bible as a potential source for inspiring conversion, changing the moral character of an individual person or community. In this way, Scripture indirectly influences moral decisions by changing the moral character of the decision maker. Hence, this ethics is called an ethics of character or virtue.

A fifth use involves scriptural perspectives and values as normative for criticizing ethical systems themselves, such as utilitarianism or an ethics based on merit.

A sixth use provides the ultimate reasons for being moral, or the ground of moral principles. Scripture establishes how God or Christ is the ultimate basis of moral commands.

These last three uses of Scripture address ethics on levels different from the moral-decision types of the first three. All six types provide a general guide for identifying how liberation theologians, especially Pixley and Gutiérrez, use Scripture in ethics.

14. John Macquarrie, "Deontology," *The Westminster Dictionary of Christian Ethics*, ed. James F. Childress and John Macquarrie (Philadelphia: Westminster Press, 1986), 151.

Exodus and Kingdom of God: Pixley

Liberation theology draws upon certain themes from the Bible that serve as paradigms for its theological reflection. Jorge Pixley has written books about two of these paradigmatic themes: the exodus and the kingdom of God. An examination of them may reveal the way he uses the Bible in thinking about what Nicaraguans and others should do within their revolutionary situation. It may also manifest how Pixley sees God's word interfacing with political praxis. I should like to begin first with his commentary *On Exodus*, and then examine an earlier work, *God's Kingdom*.

Objectives

Pixley, an ordained Baptist minister and a biblical scholar, presents both an "evangelical" and a "popular" reading of the book of Exodus. By evangelical he means two things: first, the Bible carries the highest authority for believers, more authoritative than official church and scientific authorities;[15] second, it means "good news" for anyone seeking God's plan for freeing oppressed persons and groups. Therefore, an evangelical reading interprets the Bible through the perspective of the oppressed.

Searching for God's liberating plan in the Bible implies that God directs human behavior through Scripture. Pixley's emphasis on God's command revealed in Scripture is a trademark of his evangelical tradition. However, he provides a distinctively new quality to traditional evangelical ethics by his use of nonbiblical sources, including social analysis and the perspective of the poor.[16]

His second objective—doing a "popular" reading of Exodus—does not mean writing a popularized account but providing an interpretation that is of the people. Biblical concepts, such as the exodus and the kingdom of God, must be read in terms of the historical, political struggles of communities, and must never be used as abstract concepts.[17] Pixley's own biblical interpretations start from the people and return to the people.

His book *God's Kingdom* pursues the same general aims as does his work *On Exodus*. He contends that the kingdom of God in certain historical moments

---

15. Jorge V. Pixley, *On Exodus: A Liberation Perspective* (Maryknoll, N.Y.: Orbis Books, 1987), xiv. In addition to social sciences, Pixley uses other nonbiblical disciplines (philology, philosophy) to clarify passages in the text.

16. Carl Henry, "Evangelical Ethics," *The Westminster Dictionary of Christian Ethics*, 212–13.

17. Jorge V. Pixley, *God's Kingdom: A Guide for Biblical Study* (Maryknoll, N.Y.: Orbis Books, 1981), 20.

guided the people toward a free and egalitarian society, whereas at other moments it dominated them.[18] Pixley hopes both his books help Latin Americans discover whether God's kingdom and Exodus generate good news for them by helping them to realize freedom and justice.

Pixley's objectives—doing an evangelical and a popular reading of Exodus and God's kingdom—state succinctly his understanding of Scripture. The Bible is the most authoritative organ of truth for the faith of a people because it reveals who God is, what God does in history, and what God invites people to do. Pixley's emphasis on God's plan and God's will for people implies his strong interest in the ethical dimensions of Scripture.

Method

Like Segundo, Mesters, and Severino Croatto, Pixley interprets Scripture dialectically by allowing biblical and contemporary context to illumine the text, and by suggesting how the Bible casts light on contemporary events in Latin America. His interpretation of Scripture challenges men and women involved in today's struggle for liberation to read again how God takes part in the movement toward freedom.[19]

Using the standard literary-critical methods (including form- and redaction-criticism), he interprets Exodus within the larger literary whole of the Pentateuch and not from the perspective of the Jesus event. He studies the kingdom from its origins as the revolutionary project of the peasants in the Canaanite hills, through the Davidic monarchy, the exile, the Jesus movement, and then under the leadership of Paul.

With most exegetes, Pixley holds that the present text of the Pentateuch is an amalgamation of three narrative traditions: the Yahwist, the Elohist, and the Priestly. These traditions, together with the work of the Deuteronomist and Deuteronomic history, were pulled together in the text we have today by unknown redactors sometime in the postexilic period.[20] The unique characteristics of each tradition and data from sociohistorical studies help identify four sociopolitical contexts of the narrative.

The first level is the original production of the story told by those who actually experienced the exodus. This account cannot be identified in today's text. Pixley identifies the people as a heterogeneous group of peasants in Egypt along with immigrants from the East, who collectively came to be known as

18. Ibid., 3.
19. Pixley, *On Exodus*, 120–21.
20. Ibid., xvi.

"the Levites." Guided by Moses, they rebelled against the Egyptian pharaoh and fled into the wilderness of Sinai.

The second level of the account was produced by an alliance of rural tribes known as "Israel" in the land of Canaan sometime between the fourteenth and the eleventh centuries B.C.E. Pixley, following the social analysis of Norman Gottwald, describes the situation in which the oppressed Hebrews, freed by Yahweh, organized with peasant bands in Canaan to revolt against an oppressive Canaanite monarchy and formed an egalitarian society.[21] These tribes reinterpreted the original exodus as a class struggle, providing an ideological support for their own struggle against the kings of the cities of Canaan who demanded tribute and submission.[22] This level, like the first, is largely obliterated from the text.

The third level of the Exodus account was created during Israel's battles with the Philistines, which led to Israel's establishing a monarchy and organizing a professional army. This representation of the exodus interpreted the first exodus as a national liberation struggle between two peoples: Israel and Egypt. The account is narrated by the Yahwist and Elohist traditions.

Finally, the fourth level of the exodus account—the text we have today—interprets the liberation event as the act of God to demonstrate Yahweh's divinity. Critical-literary analysis identifies this totally religious interpretation as the work of the Priestly tradition.[23]

Pixley understands the book of Exodus (and the Bible generally) as both a religious and a political document. He does not define religion or politics, but his discussion of these two key concepts suggests the following definitions: religion refers to the relationship between God and humans; politics unveils the network of power relations between individuals and groups in society. According to this definition, politics refers to Moses' negotiations with the pharaoh and with his people, to the organizational structures within the various Egyptian, Hebrew, and Canaanite societies, and to the nature of the conflict between groups. Although he distinguishes between the religious and the political dimensions within the exodus event, he insists upon their inextricable linkage. They who interpret Exodus solely as a religious account misread the text. His emphasis on the political-religious realities of the Bible resembles the

21. Pixley, On Exodus, xviii–xix; Norman K. Gottwald, The Tribes of Yahweh: A Sociology of the Religion of Liberated Israel, 1250–1050 B.C. (Maryknoll, N.Y.: Orbis Books, 1979), 389–434.

22. Pixley, On Exodus, xix. Pixley acknowledges the influence of Gottwald's Tribes of Yahweh on his own thinking.

23. Ibid., xx.

approaches of many other Latin American biblical scholars, including Carlos Mesters, José Severino Croatto, and José Porfirio Miranda.[24]

Uses of Scripture

Pixley's commentary on Exodus and his historical study of God's kingdom reveal four distinct, though related, ways of using Scripture in ethics: (1) as analogy, (2) as a source for transforming people, (3) as witness that God's will grounds moral law (metaethics), and (4) as a source of moral content (normative ethics).

Analogy   Just as the prophets and Jesus drew inspiration and enlightenment from Exodus, so also the oppressed in Latin America call upon this same source, reinterpreted in light of the present-day situation, to give them strength and guidance in their struggle for liberation. What God accomplished in the exodus establishes an authoritative precedent for liberation movements today. Many similarities between the exodus then and liberation today warrant using the biblical event as an analogy or paradigm. These similarities include, first of all, a movement from oppression marked by a class struggle: in the first case, a struggle between the enslaved Hebrews and the tributary state of the Egyptians; in the second case, between the oppressed Latin Americans and the military-entrepreneurial wealthy class within a global capitalist system. Furthermore, both oppressed peoples do battle with powerful regimes that exploit religion in order to justify the prevailing order and to crush the resistance of the poor.[25] Moreover, participants from both movements become enmeshed in a revolutionary-counterrevolutionary dynamic within an overall stride toward greater social awareness and freedom.[26] Finally, both groups accept the same God as their liberator.

Regarding this last similarity, Pixley challenges those Latin American revolutionaries who might be skeptical of the role that religion and God play in the revolution, asking them whether Latin American revolutionaries believe that God guides them in their own liberation movement, as the Hebrew people

---

24. The following works demonstrate how important biblical theologians in Latin America relate Scripture to the social situation: Mesters, *Defenseless Flower*; José P. Miranda, *Marx and the Bible: A Critique of the Philosophy of Oppression* (Maryknoll, N.Y.: Orbis Books, 1973); J. Severino Croatto, *Exodus: A Hermeneutics of Freedom*, trans. Salvator Attanasio (Maryknoll, N.Y.: Orbis Books, 1981).

25. Jorge V. Pixley, "Divine Judgment in History," in *The Idols of Death and the God of Life: A Theology*, ed. Pablo Richard et al., trans. Barbara E. Campbell and Bonnie Shepard (Maryknoll, N.Y.: Orbis Books, 1983), 54.

26. Pixley, *On Exodus*, 21–35, 81–84.

believed God guided their emancipation from slavery.[27] Pixley plants the question but respectfully gives no answer, convinced that only those struggling for freedom have the prerogative to respond. The revolutionaries, not the biblical scholar, must judge whether the analogy of their struggle with the exodus rings true. If it does, then the account may illuminate, even inspire today's liberation movement. There is no doubt in the reader's mind, however, that Pixley sees a close fit of today's liberation with yesterday's exodus.

Turning to the kingdom metaphor, he tries in a similar manner to help Latin Americans determine whether God's reign symbolizes good news for them. His historical overview shows that certain communities within the Jewish-Christian traditions exploited God's kingdom as an ideology of domination.[28] During the exodus and Jesus' mission, however, the kingdom inspired freedom, solidarity with the poor, and a movement toward an egalitarian society. Jesus and his followers incorporated the best elements of this metaphor by preaching and living the egalitarian principles and by preaching good news to the poor. Jesus rejected the prevailing class structure by attacking the system of trade and taxes collected in the temple and the system of privileges for the priests.[29] Yet Jesus was unable to achieve sufficient popular support to realize the project.

Pixley's use of exodus and God's kingdom as moral analogies raises an important question of control—namely, whether the biblical event or the contemporary event functions as the primary analogue.[30] If the biblical paradigm is given higher authority, the interpreter reads today's happenings in light of the biblical events. If today's liberation event takes on higher authority, then the interpreter attends to those aspects of exodus and God's kingdom that correspond to the contemporary event. The latter runs the risk of prooftexting and thereby exploiting the Bible for ideological purposes.

Pixley's use of Marxist concepts (e.g., class struggle and classless society) suggests that the contemporary event functions as the control, though the case is not so clear when one considers other evidence. Pixley does a careful analysis of the text, interpreting it in light of its historical development and not in light of contemporary events in Latin America. This suggests that the exodus event is in control. I see him trying to steer a middle course by allowing both the biblical and contemporary events to illumine each other. Modern concepts, such as solidarity with the oppressed, class analysis, revolution, and counter-revolution, all color his interpretation of Exodus. On the other hand, he tries

27. Ibid, 101.
28. Pixley, *God's Kingdom*, 54.
29. Ibid, 75.
30. Gustafson, *Theology and Christian Ethics*, 133–34.

to remain faithful to his conviction that the Bible possesses the highest authority by challenging liberation projects. He asserts, for example, that true and lasting revolutions must be in conformity with the will of God.[31] He casts suspicion on revolutionary projects fought only in the name of a human leader, whether that leader be Moses, Lenin, or Castro. Biblical scholar Jon Levinson, however, charges that Pixley imposes a Marxist perspective on the text that significantly distorts Exodus.

Personal transformation   Pixley appears to direct his work *On Exodus* primarily to two groups: those Christians already involved in liberating the oppressed and those Christians who stand apart from this movement as spectators. He hopes his exegesis may encourage liberationists and even set a fire under spectators. I read his biblical interpretations as his own praxis intended to deepen or transform his reader's social and religious awareness of God's liberating action. In effect, he interprets Scripture for the sake of transforming or awakening the consciousness of his people.

He does this first by contending that Exodus and other biblical books are political as well as religious documents, and second by convincing others that God helps rather than hinders people in the struggle for liberation. God deepens a people's self-determination by calling them to venture forth into the unknown and by guiding them through the trials of the desert. Thus, Pixley's writings serve as an awakening process by interpreting the exodus as a call to assume greater responsibility by following the plan of God. Like Gutiérrez, he consistently demonstrates how God instigates movement within the oppressed toward freedom. Unlike Gutiérrez, he does not describe the liberating process as religious conversion that changes its participants; but it is a political activity congruent with God's will.

Pixley's lack of interest in discussing personal conversion as a dimension of the liberation process might be rooted in his Calvinistic, predestinarian presuppositions. The Calvinist focuses attention on doing God's just will in a universe where spiritual growth is frosting on an already fixed cake. Catholic liberation theologians, however, hold that a person's destiny is judged on the basis of conversion to the neighbor, as we shall see in examining Gutiérrez's theology. For Pixley, transformation of persons involves perceiving the necessary connection between God's will and human participation in the political liberation struggle. Grasping this link may be related to a new form of Calvinistic certitude about one's destiny. The sign of being elected, I suggest, is that one struggles for liberation in solidarity with the oppressed.

31. Pixley, *On Exodus*, 101.

Pixley singles out two unenlightened groups of Latin America, both of them loath to speak of God's involvement in political movements, but for different reasons. The revolutionaries, who often choose antireligious or non-religious theory to guide their liberation movement, reject God-talk either because God does not exist or, if alive, seems to support the oppressors. They consider the Bible, including Exodus, irrelevant to their fight for freedom. The second unenlightened group consists of believing Christians who divorce politics from religion. They believe in God's saving power but read the exodus account simply as a vertical relationship in which God redeems the Israelites in spite of or apart from what happens in the sociopolitical sphere. For these religionists the exodus does not present an experience of authentic revolution in which a self-determined people, guided by Yahweh, takes into its own hands the historical destiny that had been snatched from it by oppressive rulers.[32]

Rejecting both positions, Pixley tries to persuade the politically involved nonbelievers and the nonpolitical believers that Exodus is at once a religious and a political document. It narrates the experience of the Hebrews' belief in a God who delivers the people from a concrete sociopolitical and economic enslavement, leads them through trials in the wilderness, and helps them organize into a totally new kind of classless and egalitarian type of society. Yahweh inspires the people and they, under the leadership of Moses, organize themselves. Therefore, both God and Moses have liberated Israel.

Pixley also seeks to convince his readers that God's taking the initiative in freedom movements does not eviscerate human freedom; on the contrary, God's involvement encourages freedom and responsibility. Pixley speaks about human freedom as a divine and a human construction. God accompanies the Hebrews throughout their struggle as Moses and the Israelites participate as agents of their own history. The deliverance unfolds as an act of divine salvation and human revolution. Knowing and trusting God gives the enslaved people a vision of liberation and the courage to pursue it. God initiates the movement and Moses executes, not as a slave or a puppet but as a responsible leader who, before taking action, must first become convinced of the worthwhileness of the project, work through personal fears, and clear up foreseen problems.[33]

The Yahwist-Elohist literary traditions reflect the historical experience of the original exodus by their holding in skillful balance God's initiative and Moses' active cooperation. This account corresponds with liberation theology's emphasis on integral liberation, or growth in freedom within the realms of

32. Ibid, 121.
33. Ibid., 20.

the sociopolitical, human, and religious. Pixley downplays the Priestly tradition because it stresses the omnipotence of God and the impotence of humanity.[34]

The heart of the matter for Pixley is freedom. Following the philosophy of Alfred North Whitehead, he describes God's role as the "universal instigator of the new and the better." By actualizing the maximum potential of human beings, God brings about newness and greater freedom. He summarizes the role played by God and human actors in the liberation project of Exodus: "God does nothing—if by 'do' we mean God is the exclusive agent of anything. On the other hand, God does everything—if by 'do' we mean that God is present in every event, prompting it to the realization of its fullest and best potential. God is the co-creator of everything new that emerges in this historical world."[35] God inspires the human person, who chooses to cooperate with God's initiative. Following Martin Buber, Pixley interprets the miraculous events (the plagues) as the activity of the prophet Moses, who interprets these natural portents as God's judgment on the oppressive king who refuses to release slaves so that they could celebrate a religious festival. "It may be," Pixley says, "that the massacre of the exodus night was a terrorist action—inspired by God."[36]

To summarize, freedom in Exodus involves God's encouraging presence strengthening human beings to venture forth by engaging in a worthwhile social project. Pixley sees the book of Exodus as an inspiring and enlightening source for awakening, encouraging, and guiding people in the liberation movement.

God as the ground of morality   In the fourth part of his commentary on Exodus, Pixley discusses covenantal law as the basis for a new egalitarian society.[37] The source of the law is Yahweh, the liberator God. Covenantal law, like freedom, has a human and political dimension. Law arises from within a social structure consisting of tribes of small farmers in a classless and stateless

34. The Yahwist tradition describes God's accomplishing liberation by human means supported by extraordinary signs. These signs, mediated by Moses, are intended to bend the will of the pharaoh. In contrast, the Priestly account employs signs and wonders as a means to harden the pharaoh's heart, thereby requiring that God perform even more miraculous phenomena. Whereas the Yahwist author narrates Moses' negotiating with the oppressive ruler, the Priestly author narrates God's punishing the recalcitrant pharaoh directly without the aid of Moses.

35. Pixley, *On Exodus*, 80.

36. Ibid. See also Martin Buber, *Moses: The Revelation and the Covenant* (New York: Harper), 1958.

37. Pixley, *On Exodus*, 118–19.

society without kings, priests, police, judges, and jails.[38] In the absence of a state to lay down and enforce laws, the tribes of premonarchic Israel developed traditional norms adapted to their situation. Authority for the law was invested in the people themselves, who corporately assumed responsibility for imposing penalties. Hence, these norms grew out of the legal wisdom of the people.

Covenantal law also has a divine origin. Before the exodus, the people did not know God by name.[39] They came to know Yahweh in the wilderness as a liberator who freed them from their oppression. No longer simply known as the God of their ancestors, God becomes known as "Yahweh your God who brought you out of the land of Egypt, out of the house of slavery" (Exod. 20:1-2).

God's self-disclosure as the people's liberator established a new relationship marked by a distinctive set of moral demands. Because God brings freedom, so must the people respect freedom: their own, God's, and their neighbor's. Pixley interprets the Decalogue as a set of formulations intended to safeguard these freedoms.

The first commandment—"You shall have no gods except me" (Exod. 20:3)—involved a decisive choice between Baal, who symbolizes oppression, and Yahweh, who represents freedom. The covenant relationship forbade divided loyalties and therefore prohibited the worship of any god alongside Yahweh.

Underlying this law, Pixley maintains, is "the social reality of the class struggle." Not only does Yahweh free the people from class domination, but it is God's nature to keep them free from future dominators, whether the oppressor be the pharaoh in Egypt, the oppressive kings in Canaan, or tyrannical kings in monarchical Israel. Worshiping the gods of their oppressors would be a compromise of Israelite freedom. Consequently, the Israelite and Canaanite societies were irreconcilable.

Another primary command of the covenant defends the freedom and dignity of marginal members of Israelite society: "You must not molest the stranger or oppress him. . . . You must not be harsh with the widow, or with the orphan" (Exod. 22:21-24). The prohibitions against exploitation of the defenseless are expressed in the same kind of formulation as the fundamental prohibitions of the Decalogue, thus giving them the highest authority.

In this manner, Pixley grounds the ethic of the covenant in the people's experiential knowledge of God. By demonstrating the intimate link between covenantal laws and God's liberating nature, Pixley suggests that these same

38. Ibid., 165–67.
39. Pixley, "Divine Judgment in History," 47.

commands have relevance for guiding revolutionary social change today. Knowing this liberating God means that the oppressed people in Latin America must resist exploitation and oppression, and work to create just relationships.

In accenting the religious and political origins of law, Pixley rejects interpretations that speak of the Decalogue dropping out of heaven, as later redactors of the biblical narrative themselves present the origin of Israelite law. God inspires the creation of laws by revealing God as Yahweh, who frees them and assists them in their basic human needs. Hence, law, like freedom, is a divine and human creation. Yet Pixley is inconsistent. He also speaks of God as imposing norms on the people, as though God has a blueprint for what the egalitarian society must look like.

Option for the poor   The fourth and last use of Scripture in ethics involves using the primary commandments to evaluate situations today. Although Pixley says the people themselves must make such application, he applies one primary command, the option for the poor, in his interpretation of the morality of Moses' use of violence.

The expression "option for the poor" arose only in recent times within the context of Latin American liberation theology.[40] Within this context, it means a basic commitment to serve the poor and oppressed by joining them in their struggle for freedom.[41] Liberation theologians also speak of the option as a principle that helps interpret the applicability of certain moral norms. Although this expression is new, the reality behind the term is not. Pixley and other exegetes have shown that it existed in many ancient Near Eastern societies, especially in premonarchic Israel, in the nation of Israel, and in societies surrounding Israel.[42]

As we have seen, God's preferential option for this enslaved people stamped a distinctive quality on the moral demands that arose from knowing Yahweh. God's people were enjoined to assist the poor and oppressed in their society—the widow, the orphan, and the stranger—because their knowing Yahweh demanded it. Exploiting the weak is the sign of abandoning God.[43]

40. For a history of its origin and meaning, see Madeleine Adriance, *Opting for the Poor: Brazilian Catholicism in Transition* (Kansas City, Mo.: Sheed and Ward, 1986), 11–15; Donal Dorr, *Spirituality and Justice* (Maryknoll, N.Y.: Orbis Books, 1984), 74–86; Leonardo Boff and Virgil Elizondo, eds., *Option for the Poor: Challenge to the Rich Countries*, trans. Marcus Lefebure *Concilium* 187 (Edinburgh: T & T Clark, 1986).

41. Boff, *When Theology Listens to the Poor*, 10.

42. Jorge V. Pixley and Clodovis Boff, *Opção pelos pobres* (Petrópolis, Brazil: Editora Vozes, 1986); chap. 1; Lohfink, *Option for the Poor*, chap. 1.

43. Pixley, "Divine Judgment in History," 46ff.

This option served as the touchstone of justice in Israelite society. First, it established the basis for the prohibition against coveting the neighbor's goods, a law intended to protect the poor. Second, the option demanded accountability from the community on how well it met the vital needs of the poor. Third, it subordinated the right to own property to the right to use basic goods.[44]

Pixley uses option for the poor as a moral principle to qualify more specific norms, especially the norm prohibiting homicide. A specific instance is Pixley's applying the option as a principle to interpret Moses' defense of a kinsman by slaying an Egyptian. In this defense of a fellow Hebrew (Exod. 2:11-14), Moses serves as the human model of solidarity with the poor and oppressed. This action leads to Moses' exile from a comfortable palace life. Later, under God's inspiration and guidance, he becomes the leader of an oppressed people and the mouthpiece for Yahweh against the pharaoh.

Even though Moses had not yet known Yahweh at the time he took the Egyptian's life for striking the Hebrew, Moses had already intuited what he would later learn from Yahweh; namely, that it would be necessary to kill under threat of extermination implicit in the Egyptian class system. Although the fifth commandment—thou shall not kill—is categorical, it has certain qualifications: it permits capital punishment and killing enemies in war. It forbids intentional homicide under the penalty of death. Oppressing the poor, in Pixley's view, further qualifies the prohibition against taking human life. Does the biblical text justify Moses' violent defense of a Hebrew slave?

Pixley does not give an explicit answer, but his comments imply an affirmative response. He justifies Moses' violent act on the basis of the option for the poor. He does not invoke the authority of certain New Testament texts that justify Moses' action, such as the Letter to the Hebrews (11:24-28) and the Acts of the Apostles (7:23-38). Nor does he contrast Jesus' approach to violence with Moses' approach. In his book *God's Kingdom* he maintains that the Gospels do not present Jesus as categorically rejecting physical violence.[45] Rather, Pixley supports his interpretation of Moses' deed on the basis of the text of Exodus, illuminated by the sociohistorical context.

The context manifests severe oppression of the Hebrews, peasant uprisings, and a class struggle. Moses, a Hebrew reared in the palace court of the Egyptian ruling class, committed an act of class betrayal by killing the Egyptian in defense of a lower-class Hebrew. Moses thus cast his lot with the oppressed class. His action is "defensive" in the sense of defending life, but it is not based on any religious motivation, because Moses does not yet know God. His

44. Pixley, *On Exodus*, 179–80.
45. Pixley, *God's Kingdom*, 82.

motive, Pixley says, is love for justice and life, especially the life of the weakest.[46]

Pixley reads the text (Exod. 2:11-15) as "a simple case of capital punishment"[47] (or, in Spanish, *ajusticiamiento*). The Egyptians had put the Hebrew slaves under hard labor in order to reduce their number and to deplete their strength. Seeing an Egyptian beating one of his own people, Moses killed (*nakah*) the Egyptian.[48]

The Hebrew verb *nakah*, often used in the context of war, is an exception to the general prohibition against taking human life. Just as Moses struck (*nakah*) a mortal blow against the Egyptian, so God struck (*nakah*) the Egyptians with a final plague involving the death of the firstborn (Exod. 12:29).[49] The following day, Moses tries to prevent one Hebrew from beating another. The chastened Hebrew replies to Moses: "Do you mean to kill me (*lehorgueni*) as you killed the Egyptian?" The verb used in this sentence *lehorgueni* literally means "to murder me." Similarly, the pharaoh seeks to "kill"—that is, to murder—Moses (*leharog*) rather than execute him for a capital offense. The author implies by the switch of verbs, Pixley argues, that Moses' action is not murder, but justifiable homicide.[50]

Moses pays the price for his solidarity with a kinsman. Losing his social status and fleeing to exile, he becomes one of the oppressed. God makes a self-presentation to Moses, the exiled rebel. Pixley interprets God's invitation to Moses as justification of his use of violence. Indeed, Moses has acted as God will soon act: taking the life of others in defense of the poor and oppressed.

Pixley's interpretation has an important bearing on situations in Latin America today. The practice of summary executions without a fair trial, euphemistically called *ajusticimiento*, is carried out today and defended both by guerrillas and government forces in Central and South America. It raises an important issue regarding the establishment of objective and universal standards of justice governing the use of violence and just procedural rules.

His evaluation of Moses' killing the Egyptian involved two ethical demands: the prohibition against murder and the option for the poor. The option principle qualifies the prohibition. Accordingly, Pixley judges Moses' violent

---

46. Pixley, *On Exodus*, 9.

47. Ibid, 8.

48. Jorge V. Pixley, *Éxodo, una lectura evangélica y popular* (Mexico City: Casa Unida, 1983), 30. I am following the original Spanish text in this section. The English edition uses another word for "kill," *rayach*.

49. Frederick C. Holmgren, "Violence: God's Will on the Edge: Exodus 2:11–25," *Science and Religion* 16:425–29.

50. Pixley, *On Exodus*, 8.

act not as murder but as a defense of life akin to capital punishment. One difficulty with Pixley's interpretation is that the text itself does not explicitly moralize about the goodness or badness of Moses' action.[51] He seems to be confusing the author's descriptive level (narrating what happened) with the interpretive level (what God commanded or justified as good). Moreover, the narration suggests moral ambiguity that the author does not resolve. Moses feels righteous about slaying the oppressor, but he also recognizes that he possesses no authority to execute the Egyptian, evidenced by his secrecy and cover-up. Does looking over his shoulder before killing the Egyptian and feeling apprehensive after the deed suggest moral guilt or fear of retribution? The text does not tell us. Pixley rests his case on the fact that Yahweh called Moses after he had slain the oppresser to lead the people to freedom, which would involve the use of militant means. We can only speculate about the meaning of God's silence on Moses' summary execution of the Egyptian and about God's choosing him to lead the people: whether God tacitly approved the deed, or whether God chose Moses in spite of his sinful act.

The passage is morally ambiguous and probably not resolvable. Pixley's interpretation, however, demonstrates his deontological use of Scripture in doing normative ethics. The a priori norm operating here is that human life of those unjustly treated must be defended—even by violent means, if necessary—because God is the defender of the oppressed. Hence Yahweh, both a liberator and a warrior, is the ultimate standard of goodness and judge of what is just. God becomes angry with Moses because of his frequent objection to the plan for liberation (Exod. 4:13-17). God becomes infuriated with those who stand in the way of Israel's liberation plans and mercilessly exterminates Canaanite kings who oppress the tribes of Israel.

Pixley makes a rare application to situations in Latin America. Like Yahweh, the oppressed in Latin America have the right to become angry with and to use force against those who deprive them of their right to life. "If Yahweh can become angry with resistance to liberation plans, who can deny the same right to those who suffer oppression?"[52] Pixley argues, in effect, that the Bible justifies the use of violence in certain situations. The major difficulty with this kind of argument is that it assumes a discernment process capable of answering important questions such as, Under what conditions and with what kind of force ought a community take up arms to fight the oppressor? Pixley does not address such questions.

51. Brevard S. Childs, *The Book of Exodus: A Critical, Theological Commentary* (Philadelphia: Westminster Press, 1974), 44–45.

52. Pixley, *On Exodus*, 26.

Assessment

This last section evaluates how well Pixley uses Scripture in ethics by raising issues related to his understanding of the Bible, the role played by Jesus, and the nature of ethics.

The Bible as Good News   Pixley understands the Bible as good news because it reveals God's involvement in liberating the poor and because it reveals Jesus' solidarity with those who suffer injustice. His interpretation of the Bible, expecially his commentary on Exodus, tries to steer a middle course between an overtranscendent-individualistic and an overhistorical-social interpretation. His use of form-critical analysis enables him to make a strong case—against a whole tradition of interpretation—for establishing the political-ethical importance of Exodus.

Does Pixley achieve his objective of balancing the religious and political dimensions in his interpretations? Or does his use of social analysis, which includes Marxian analytical concepts, give an ideological reading of the Bible? Pixley thinks that all biblical interpretations necessarily imply an ideology understood as a culturally conditioned perspective. Adequate interpretations must not distort the meaning of Scripture to support a special interest. The criteria for testing for an ideological reading in the latter sense rest finally on their compatibility with the writings of the Israelite and Christian apostolic communities. He depends on fellow exegetes to evaluate his work on this basis.[53]

Inasmuch as Pixley uses social analysis to understand the historical situation behind the text, a complete evaluation of his work would examine his use of this nonbiblical source, asking questions regarding the objectivity of his method and whether it is reductionistic or deterministic.[54] Doing a full evaluation of his analysis and his exegesis would go beyond the objective of this overview. A few general observations must suffice.

First of all, Pixley is successful in integrating a careful exegesis of the whole text of Exodus with a contemporary social analysis of the biblical context. Gottwald's class analysis, upon which Pixley partly relies, is generally regarded as hypothetical and not without its problems.[55] Yet Pixley provides

53. Jorge V. Pixley, interview with the author, Managua, April 9, 1988.
54. Osiek, "New Handmaid," 275–76.
55. For reviews of Gottwald's *Tribes of Yahweh*, see Robert Wilson, *Sociological Approaches to the Old Testament* (Philadelphia: Fortress Press, 1984), 35–36; George E. Mendenhall, "Ancient Israel's Hyphenated History," in *Palestine in Transition: The Emergence of Ancient Israel*, ed. David Noel Freedman and David Frank Graf (Sheffield, England: Almond Press, 1983).

textual evidence from the Pentateuch supporting the existence of a stratified society in which the lower class, consisting almost entirely of Hebrews, was exploited by the dominating class of Egyptians.[56] The existence of a particular kind of class struggle may well have been a social force at work, though it seems likely that other forces, such as rebellion against ethnic, racial, and religious oppression, would also have been operative.

In reading Exodus as a movement toward a classless society, Pixley interprets God's commands as mandating a socialist egalitarian society, which seems to go beyond the biblical evidence in the Pentateuch. His assertion that "Moses is the mediator of the norms that Yahweh dictates for life in the classless society" makes God's imperatives more specific than the text warrants.[57] Assuming that a classless, nonhierarchic society was God's will for the Israelites, we would have to conclude that the stratified Israelite societies within the Davidic monarchy and in later Israelite societies were living in opposition to God's plan. However, the prophets never include this charge among the many sins of infidelity committed by the people.

Even with these qualifications and questions, Pixley's primary thesis that exodus was an authentic revolution achieved by a deeply religious people under the inspiration of God is based on solid textual evidence. Moreover, other scholarly works support the general lines of this thesis.[58] He integrates very well the book's transcendent and sociohistorical dimensions. In this respect, his book on Exodus achieves a far better balance than did his earlier work, *God's Kingdom*, which overemphasized the sociopolitical forces at work.

Pixley's integration of the religious and political dimensions in Exodus would be improved if he were to bring out how God's liberating activity moved the people and elicited from them a grateful response. In his efforts to demythologize the solely transcendent emphasis of the Priestly narrative, Pixley seems to lose the wondrous, astonishing elements present in Exodus. Old Testament scholar Norbert Lohfink expresses the uniqueness of this astonishing, miraculous event: "Nowhere else in the ancient Near East have I encountered in the context of divine aid to the poor even the remotest suggestion that a god might physically remove the poor who cry to him or her from the world that oppresses them as human beings."[59] Lohfink, who applauds liberation theologians for recognizing the exodus from Egypt as decisive, feels that neither they nor their critics have understood the fullness of the Exodus

---

56. Pixley, *On Exodus*, 30–35. See also Lohfink, *Option for the Poor*, 38.
57. Pixley, *On Exodus*, 119.
58. Michael Walzer, *Exodus and Revolution* (New York: Basic Books, 1985); Lohfink, *Option for the Poor*.
59. Lohfink, *Option for the Poor*, 39.

statement in "its surprising otherness, an otherness which remains astonishing for us as well."[60]

Pixley does emphasize God's initiative and the people's undivided loyalty and obedience as key elements in Exodus, but does not capture the people's sense of astonishment, surprise, and gratitude that gave rise to that strong loyalty and obedience. Showing the connection between God's liberating action and the people's grateful response might enable Pixley to explain how God inspires human beings to create law. In his commentary on Exodus, he speaks both of a God *moving/inspiring* the people to create norms and of a God *imposing* norms on the people. His interpretation of God as the lawgiver who imposes injunctions does not fit with his fine interpretation of God as liberator who encourages risking and taking responsibility. More compatible with the liberator image are divine initiatives that invite, inspire, and motivate the people of Exodus. Law that arises from a grateful, free response to God's offer of liberation is not imposed law.

Pixley's giving greater authority to the Yahwist-Elohist over the Priestly tradition in Exodus raises another issue of the selective use of Scripture. Does his emphasis on the Yahwist-Elohist over the Priestly tradition mean that the former has more authority and that the latter should be disregarded?[61] Pixley holds that some books (Proverbs, Revelation) and literary traditions (Priestly) in the biblical canon are less authoritative. He insists, however, that the more marginal books and passages should be respected as part of the inspired canon.[62] The Yahwist-Elohist traditions illuminate human experience more comprehensively and, hence, more fully and adequately, without thereby obviating the need for the emphasis provided by the Priestly source.

Role of Jesus   Pixley interprets New Testament themes as a historical development from the Old Testament, especially from Exodus. The latter serves as the fundamental paradigm and principle of organization of the Bible.

60. Ibid, 51.

61. J. Severino Croatto, "The Socio-Historical and Hermeneutical Relevance of the Exodus," trans. P. Burns, in *Exodus: A Lasting Paradigm*, ed. Bas van Iersel and Anton Weiler, *Concilium* 189 (Edinburgh: T & T Clark, 1987), 128. Croatto, like Pixley, acknowledges the importance of the liberation–exodus paradigm for liberation theologians. He justifies the selective use of the Bible on two counts: first, the diverse traditions found in the Old Testament demand different interpretations; second, the Christian tradition has always read the Bible by giving greater attention to certain passages and books. Readers of Scripture should be more suspicious of the kind of selectivity that ignores its sociohistorical dimension.

62. Based on an interview with Pixley in Managua, April 9, 1988.

Pixley locates the earliest origins of God's kingdom in the exodus story. In tracing the development of the kingdom from premonarchic Israel to the Palestinian movement of Jesus, Pixley shows that Jesus' proclamation fits with the best elements of that metaphor—namely, a reaffirmation of the principles of an egalitarian society based on justice and freedom.[63]

Does the Jesus story add anything distinctive to Pixley's theological ethics? In some important areas, it does not. The death and resurrection of Jesus do not seem to add any new development either to the exodus or to the kingdom of God in the Old Testament.[64] Nor does Jesus' teaching present anything different regarding the treatment of enemies and the use of violence. He interprets Jesus' sayings on forgiveness (Matt. 18:21-22) as demands made upon those within the movement for the sake of internal peace.[65] Pixley interprets Jesus' teaching on reconciliation and nonviolence (Matt. 5:38-45) as the way in which the Jesus movement separated its strategy from that of the Zealots. Jesus opposed the Zealot option to resist Roman authorities, not because they used military power, but because he saw as the principal oppressor the domination of the temple by the priests. In a word, Jesus adds nothing distinctive to the original paradigms of Exodus and God's kingdom, or to the norms and values rooted in the paradigms.

The importance of Jesus lies in his upholding the best elements of the exodus-kingdom tradition and in his proclaiming it with the highest authority. Like the God of the exodus, Jesus as liberator or the messiah of the poor[66] leads his followers to the God of the exodus.[67] He requires them to engage in a praxis of solidarity, service, and sacrifice.[68] Jesus is not a moral teacher, but a liberator-prophet who announces the good news to the poor, defends their right to life, and pays for this solidarity by his blood. Jesus is declared by God the just one, and through his resurrection he is appointed judge over those who condemned him.

63. Pixley, *God's Kingdom*, 77.

64. Pixley does not relate the exodus to the life, death, and resurrection of Jesus. As for God's kingdom, Jesus and his followers embody its egalitarian principles in their communal living and preaching. Pixley makes the hypothesis that Jesus' proclamation of the kingdom was a denial of the class structure that gave special privileges to the priests. But shortly after the death of Jesus, the kingdom takes on a spiritual and individualistic meaning, as seen in the letters of John, Paul, and Hebrews. Thus, in Pixley's writings, the death and resurrection do not seem to advance the social and egalitarian dimensions of the Kingdom. See *God's Kingdom*, 77–78.

65. Ibid., 82.

66. Pixley, "Divine Judgment in History," 54.

67. Clodovis Boff and Jorge V. Pixley, *The Bible, the Church and the Poor*, trans. Paul Burns (Maryknoll, N.Y.: Orbis Books, 1989), 92.

68. Ibid, 112.

Nature of ethics   We have seen the varied ways in which Pixley uses Scripture as a source in ethics: as moral analogy, as the ground for moral norms, as a source for the norms themselves, and as a source for transforming the moral agent. Underlying all these uses by Pixley are two implicit assumptions: that ethics is both deontological and theological. His ethics is deontological because the rightness of acts is determined by prior obligations. It is theological because the obligations are based on knowing God and Jesus Christ. The ultimate reason for striving for freedom and working for justice is that God desires it.

The original exodus serves as an archetype for understanding the whole Bible, as well as the paradigm for interpreting moral behavior and strategy. As an archetype, exodus is a repeatable event, but it assumes a new meaning as it is reenacted historically. Yet the original exodus epitomizes the best features of a classless, egalitarian society marked by justice and freedom. Contemporary liberation movements return again and again to the original expression.

This raises the question whether the archetype of exodus can be transformed or whether it is merely reproduced. As Pixley sees it, the so-called egalitarian classless society was patriarchal in its laws and customs. Women were regarded as inferior to men. Elisabeth Schüssler Fiorenza argues that Scripture is not archetype but "prototype"; that is, a historically concrete model that undergoes change rather than continually repeating itself.[69] Within Latin America today, women liberation theologians have criticized an overemphasis on class analysis that overlooks structural patterns of discrimination against women.

As noted earlier, Pixley uses the demands of the covenant to illuminate, not to prescribe, solutions to problems facing Latin Americans today. He wisely recognizes that local communities must discern whether certain structures are morally wrong or whether they should adopt a strategy based on certain biblical values. As an exegete, Pixley does not present a method of discernment, though he sketches a general ethical process that includes drawing insights from praxis, analysis, and from Scripture to resolve moral issues or to plan strategy.

Gutiérrez's Use of Scripture

Gutiérrez's theological questions nearly always have ethical implications. The primary question he raised in his first major work, *The Theology of Liberation*, shows his double interest in theological issues and ethical concerns. He

69. Elisabeth Schüssler Fiorenza, *In Memory of Her: A Feminist Theological Reconstruction of Christian Origins* (New York: Crossroad, 1983), 33–34.

asks, "How do we relate the work of building a just society to the absolute value of the Kingdom?"[70] On the theological level, he wants to show how God is present in the world, especially in human relationships. On the moral level, he seeks greater clarity on how God's presence motivates the human heart and converts unjust social structures. His overall consuming interest is that of elucidating the meaning of faith from the perspective of the poor and oppressed. He pursues this interest by developing a spirituality of liberation, which for him constitutes the core of a liberation ethics.[71]

Objectives

Gutiérrez's question about how to correlate a just society with the kingdom of God reveals one of his fundamental presuppositions: justice is rooted in God's revelation articulated, most authoritatively, in the Bible. In this respect he concurs with Pixley that the Bible speaks with the highest authority in theological and moral matters. Neither theologian bases moral norms in natural law. But his theology, in contrast to Pixley's, does contain an aspect of natural law, an issue that the following section on method will address.

He breaks down his primary question into a subset of questions, chief of which are two. First, how is Christ related to the neighbor? He searches for an answer to this question in the parable of the Last Judgment (Matt. 25:31-45). Second, how should we speak about God to those suffering terrible injustices in Latin America? He looks to the book of Job for enlightenment on this question. Both questions probe God's presence in the sociopolitical world and examine the meaning of love in relation to justice. In pursuing these two objectives, Gutiérrez reveals how he uses the Bible in ethics.

Method

Theology, Gutiérrez says, "is a critical reflection from within and on historical praxis of liberation in confrontation with the Word of the Lord lived and accepted in faith."[72] In less technical language, this means that Gutiérrez lives with the poor, talking, working, and worshiping with them. Aided by socioscientific studies, he analyzes certain structural patterns that burden his people. Finally, he reflects on their questions in light of the analysis and

---

70. Gutiérrez, *Theology of Liberation*, 74.
71. Gustavo Gutiérrez, interview with author, Lima, Peru, February 26, 1988.
72. Gustavo Gutiérrez, "Liberation, Theology and Proclamation," in *The Mystical and Political Dimension of the Christian Faith*, ed. Claude Geffré and Gustavo Gutiérrez, *Concilium* 96, 70.

Scripture. His theological method also addresses ethical questions, such as whether and to what extent international economic policies exploit consumers and workers in Latin America and how victims should respond to victimizers.

Scripture may illumine such problems, but it works in concert with other sources. Gutiérrez emphasizes the imagination and critical reason as key resources for relating Scripture to political issues. The exercise of the creative-critical powers comprises a dimension of liberation called "human-utopian." These human faculties interpret and relate empirical information to revelation. All three dimensions—the empirical, the human, the faith—represent aspects of a person's and a community's reflective activity, and work interdependently toward the single goal of integral liberation.

The first dimension contributes to this goal through social analysis and praxis. The second builds on the analysis and on praxis. It explores how values of freedom, justice, and love can be embodied in relationships that are qualitatively different. The third, or faith, dimension provides insight into alienation brought about through selfishness. This religious dimension sets in sharp relief the goal of God's kingdom and the means for realizing this goal. This level reflects on and responds to the word of God in Scripture.

The human dimension, more than the other two, deals with normative ethics. Critical reason evaluates institutional practices, and imagination proposes new alternatives for making human existence more humane and just.[73] Evaluative judgments encompass the social-scientific findings from the first dimension and the values from divine revelation. In summary, Gutiérrez's ethics consists of a spirituality that calls persons to undergo a conversion to God and neighbor, and of a normative structure that makes judgments about unjust institutions and makes proposals for alternative structures. The distinctive intellectual faculties are critical reason and creative imagination.

This normative ethics functions especially within a church or community of faith, where members of a prayer-discussion-action group carry on dialogue about their common concerns. In light of their shared experiences and reflections on pertinent biblical passages, group members may come to a greater sense of solidarity, freedom, and even insight into what practical steps to take in order to improve the quality of their lives. Gutiérrez cautions communities against directly applying biblical norms to the political situation. A direct application fails to respect the complexities of politics and the nature of the

73. Gutiérrez, *La verdad*, 188–93. Even though Gutiérrez distinguishes these dimensions of liberation, he points out that in practice they are inseparable in a truly liberating process. Gutiérrez also added in the personal interview that ethical values, while distinctive of the second level, operate on the other two levels as well. See Ismael García, *Justice in Latin American Theology of Liberation* (Atlanta: John Knox Press, 1987).

Bible. Misuses lead to a kind of fundamentalism called "politico-religious messianism."[74]

Gutiérrez correlates these three dimensions within his hermeneutical method. His hermeneutical circle consists of a sequence of steps that begins with (1) *historical praxis*, (2) *social analysis* of praxis that presents (3) *questions*, which (4) the *Bible* illumines; this leads to (5) *insight* and *judgment*, which then guide (6) a *new praxis*, which completes the circle.[75]

Hermeneutical Circle

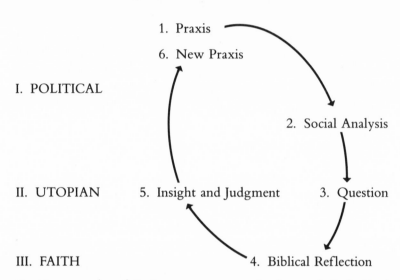

1. Praxis

6. New Praxis

I. POLITICAL

2. Social Analysis

II. UTOPIAN   5. Insight and Judgment   3. Question

III. FAITH   4. Biblical Reflection

Gutiérrez speaks of Scripture as a two-edged sword. Individuals and communities read the Bible, asking questions from within the context of their own situation. The Bible also reads them, challenging their lack of hope, presuppositions, and values. Gutiérrez employs this hermeneutical circle in his interpreting the Matthean parable and the book of Job.

Uses of Scripture

Like Pixley, Gutiérrez uses Scripture in ethics in similar ways: to transform the moral agent, to provide general guidelines for action, and to provide a biblical basis for the ethics. Gutiérrez uses Scripture in another way, as a critique of certain ethical systems. I shall develop these uses mainly from two of his most important books: *A Theology of Liberation* and *On Job*.

74. Gutiérrez, *Theology of Liberation*, 138.
75. C. Boff, *Theology and Praxis*, 133.

Transformation of agent   Gutiérrez's first and primary use shows how Scripture calls persons to change by means of a process he calls conversion. He calls this transformation "conversion to the neighbor," a process that allows a person to encounter others fully, and through the others to encounter God. He shows the intimate link between loving one's neighbor and loving God by means of stories and parables that invite, inspire, and guide persons to a life of loving service, especially to the liberation of the poor. This commitment to the most needy persons involves a fundamental ethical choice that finds its most profound motivation in the gospel.[76] For Gutiérrez, opting for the poor is a moral choice; that is, it is a free decision to do something and at the same time a choice that all persons must make. "The poor also have to opt for the poor."[77]

The gospel account of the final judgment, sometimes called the parable of the sheep and the goats, epitomizes for Gutiérrez the gospel teaching about God's identification with the poor neighbor through Christ.[78] Gutiérrez identifies the controversial verses of the passage, presents different interpretations, states his own position, and then develops three theses based on the parable. Unlike Pixley, he does not do an exegesis of this biblical text. Rather, he interprets the parable thematically, calling upon other pertinent biblical passages to clarify his interpretation.[79]

The principal controversy in the final judgment passage involves two questions. The first asks who is to be included in "all the nations" being judged by the Son of Man. "When the Son of Man comes in his glory, and all the angels with him, then he will sit on his glorious throne. Before him will be gathered all the nations, and he will separate them one from another as a shepherd separates the sheep from the goats" (Matt. 25:31-32). The Son of Man, also called the king, rewards the sheep for meeting his basic needs: food, drink, hospitality, clothing, and the consolation of a visit while sick and incarcerated. He condemns the goats for refusing to care for his needs. The obvious question on the lips of all those gathered is, "When did we see you and act thus toward you in such situations?" "And the King will answer them [the righteous], 'Truly, I say to you, as you did it to one of the least of these my brethren, you did it to me.' . . . Then he will answer them [the cursed], 'Truly, I say to you, as you did it not to one of the least of these, you did it

76. Rosino Gibellini, *The Liberation Theology Debate*, trans. John Bowden (Maryknoll, N.Y.: Orbis Books, 1988), 9.

77. Mev Puleo, "How Do You Tell the Poor God Loves You? An Interview with Gustavo Gutiérrez," *St. Anthony Messenger* 96, no. 9 (February 1989).

78. Gutiérrez, *Theology of Liberation*, 112.

79. Gutiérrez, *La verdad*, 66–67.

not to me' " (Matt. 25:40, 45). The parable astonishes its listeners because the Son of man identifies himself with "the least." This prompts them to ask about the identity of "the least of these": Do the least refer to all needy people? To all Christians?

Gutiérrez presents three different answers given by biblical scholars to the questions about the identity of "all the nations" and "the least of these my brethren." The first position holds that the Son of man judges all persons on the basis of their love for all neighbors in need. The second states that all Christian peoples are judged on the basis of their love shown to disadvantaged members of the Christian community. The third maintains that all pagan nations are judged on the basis of their actions toward all Christians.

Gutiérrez supports the first and most universalist interpretation, because this parable in particular and the gospel in general emphasize the universality of the judgment and the universal, gratuitous character of charity.[80] Verse 32 states unambiguously that all nations are to be judged.[81] The phrase "the least of my brethren" (vv. 40 and 45) is less clear. Gutiérrez contends that it refers to all persons lacking basic necessities of livelihood because charity, both in Matthew's account and in other New Testament writings, has an inclusive, universal character. Writing in 1971, he correctly observed that the majority of exegetes then supported this universalist position. Since that time, biblical scholars have amassed a great deal of evidence supporting the second position; namely, that "the least" refer to Christians, either missionaries or suffering members of the community. What was once a consensus has evolved into an impasse within the circle of biblical scholars.[82] Solid reasons support both positions.[83]

80. Gutiérrez, *A Theology of Liberation*, 112.

81. Ibid. Gutiérrez cites the works of Wolfgang Trilling, *Das wahre Israel: Studien zur Theologie des Matthäus Evangeliums* (1964), 26; Heribert Mühlen, *L'Esprit dans l'Eglise*, vol. 1 trans. (from German) A. Liefooghe et al. (Paris: Les Editions du Cerf, 1969), 149.

82. John R. Donahue, "The 'Parable' of the Sheep and the Goats: A Challenge to Christian Ethics," *Theological Studies* 47, no. 1 (March 1986): 4–8; Sherman W. Gray, *The Least of My Brothers: Matthew 25:31-46: A History of Interpretation* (Atlanta: Scholars Press, 1989).

83. Recent Roman Catholic magisterial teaching follows the universalistic position. The Second Vatican Council, in its "Pastoral Constitution on the Church in the Modern World" (*Gaudium et Spes* in *The Documents of Vatican II*, ed. Walter M. Abbott [New York: Herder and Herder, 1966]), interpreted the neighbor in Matthew 25 as "absolutely every person" (no. 27). Popes Paul VI and John Paul II, citing this very paragraph of *Gaudium et Spes*, have reiterated the universalistic interpretation. The Latin American bishops at Puebla identified the faces of all those who suffer with the suffering

The debate about whether "the least" refers to all human beings or only to Christians focuses mainly on the meaning of the Greek phrase, "the least of these my brothers and sisters" (*eni toutōn tōn adelphōn mou tōn elachistōn*). The Greek term *adelphōs* (brothers and sisters, too) refers to siblings, compatriots, and coreligionists, but never refers to an unconverted Gentile. On two occasions, Matthew states that Jesus' disciples are his brothers (12:49, 28:10). The Greek "the least" (*tōn elachistōn*) refers to the vulnerable Christians. Together the phrase "the least of these my brothers" seems to refer to the Christians most in need. This interpretation is supported by other passages in Matthew where there exists a striking similarity between "the least" (25:40, 45) and "these little ones" (10:42, 18:6,10,14). The expression "these little ones" clearly refers to Jesus' disciples.[84]

The universalist position, held by Gutiérrez, raises a few difficulties with the foregoing interpretation. First, Matthew always uses the phrase "these little ones" (*tōn mikrōn toutōn*) and never any variant to describe Jesus' disciples (Matt. 10:42; 11:11; 18:6,10,14). The particularist interpretation does not explain why Matthew would use another expression, "the least" (*tōn elachistōn*), to refer to Jesus' disciples in the final judgment scene.[85] Second, the good works mentioned in chapter 25 are a classic list used by rabbis that describes basic care for all people. The first Christian disciples were rejected, persecuted, and imprisoned, and probably sick, but we do not hear of starving, thirsty, and naked missionaries of Jesus.[86]

Gutiérrez argues for the first interpretation on the basis of the universalist and gratuitous character of charity. Love of neighbor in Matthew, as well as in Luke (the Good Samaritan parable), the first letter of John (4:7-8), and Paul's letter to the Galatians (4:6), shows that all human beings are destined to total communion with God and neighbor. Love expressed in service of others should be carried out without distinction as to friend or foe, male or female, Christian, Jew, or Gentile. Loving the neighbor for the sake of drawing close to God

---

features of Christ (nos. 31–39). In a similar vein, the U.S. bishops, in their pastoral letter *Economic Justice for All*, interpret "the least" as "the poor, the outcast, and the oppressed" (no. 44).

84. Donahue, "The 'Parable' of the Sheep and the Goats": 11–13. Donahue argues that "the least" refers to the disciples in Matthew (and hence the early Christian missionaries). However, the passage focuses on the works of justice. What is done to the missionaries provides the criterion by which any person may be called just. While the missionaries provide the occasion for doing the works of justice, the passage does not mean that these works should be done to them alone.

85. Eduard Schweizer, *Good News According to Matthew*, trans. David E. Green (Atlanta: John Knox Press, 1975), 479.

86. Miranda, *Marx and the Bible*.

may instrumentalize the neighbor. Therefore, love for God must include a genuine love for the neighbors because of who they are in themselves.[87] This love freely given to others is a gift received from experiencing God's love.[88]

Gutiérrez develops three theses from the parable of the last judgment and from pertinent New Testament texts. These theses collectively imply an eschatological ethic. The first thesis states the ultimate goal, or promise: total communion with God and the fullest brotherly/sisterly relationships with all human beings. The second and third theses talk about charity as the means necessary to realize the goal. The second thesis says that supernatural charity exists only in concrete deeds. The third states that love for God is unavoidably expressed through the love for neighbor.[89]

Traditional Roman Catholic teaching speaks about the final end of human persons as salvation and the final state as the beatific vision. Salvation centers on the supreme happiness of a soul seeing God face to face in a contemplative union.[90] For Gutiérrez salvation means total communion with God and neighbor in fully loving relationships. Matthew's surprise that loving the neighbor means loving Christ has a reciprocal side: loving Christ carries a mandate to love neighbor. Anyone who says with the Spirit, "Abba, Father" (Gal. 4:6), participates in God's love. This acceptance of God as Father/Mother is the foundation of all communion among human persons.

For Gutiérrez the opposite of communion is alienation, or sin. According to Matthew's parable, sin is the refusal to serve God by failing to serve the least. The first thesis emphasizes the profound nature of this love. It is *total* communion of the *fullest* kind of loving relationship. Gutiérrez speaks of it as trinitarian love—loving as God loves. Love expresses itself through active service of others. The neighbor is the person we actively seek. "The neighbor was the Samaritan who *approached* the wounded man and *made him his neighbor*."[91] Gutiérrez adds emphasis to the active verbs to stress the active commitment involved in going out of one's way in order to serve the poor.

Gutiérrez's second thesis states that charity exists only in concrete actions, such as feeding the hungry, sheltering the homeless, and visiting the imprisoned. Charity expressed in service forms the core of his understanding of

87. Gutiérrez, *Theology of Liberation*, 116.
88. Ibid., 119.
89. Ibid., 113–16.
90. Avery Dulles, "The Meaning of Faith Considered in Relationship to Justice," in *The Faith That Does Justice*, ed. John C. Haughey (New York: Paulist Press, 1977), 16.
91. Gutiérrez, *Theology of Liberation*, 113; see also his *Power of the Poor in History*, trans. Robert R. Barr (Maryknoll, N.Y.: Orbis Books, 1983), 44.

praxis. This charity embodies fully the nature of God's love, a love expressed concretely by meeting the needs of others. Charity is not fleshless charity that responds dutifully or out of self-interest.

Gutiérrez's third thesis states that love for God is mediated *through* love of one's neighbor: "As you did it (did it not) to one of the least, you did it (did it not) to me." Loving one's neighbor is an act of love toward God. God is revealed in history present in humanity. This means that no supernatural charity exists apart from concrete human love, and no authentic human love exists apart from supernatural charity.[92] He develops this third thesis with the aid of another metaphor—Christ as the temple of God. In tracing the development of this metaphor from the historical books and prophets to the Gospels, Gutiérrez shows that the image of temple reflects more and more both the universal divine presence (God embraces all who love Christ) and the integral divine presence (God embraces the whole person).[93] This twofold development culminates in the incarnation. Christ is not a private individual but the savior who incorporates all people into his body. Therefore, the imperative to love Christ through the least transcends cultic and church boundaries. Every human being who welcomes the word of God into his or her heart becomes a temple of God.[94]

Ethical criterion   In addition to motivating persons to commit themselves to the poor neighbor, Matthew's parable also serves as the ethical criterion for judging the goodness or badness of human decisions. For liberation theologians and for Gutiérrez, this criterion—the obligation to serve the basic needs of the neighbor—establishes an authoritative basis for the preferential option for the poor. As a formal principle, it serves as a general directive. Gutiérrez specifies it first by extending its application to the social level, and second by relating it to a concrete norm, or middle axiom, within the Latin American context.[95]

Matthew's parable does not distinguish between caring for individual needs and needs of groups. Gutiérrez develops the social interpretation of the

92. Gustavo Gutiérrez, *Lineas Pastorales de la Iglesia en América Latina* (Lima, Peru: Centro de estudios y publicaciones, 1970), 55.

93. Gutiérrez, *Theology of Liberation*, 106–10.

94. Ibid., 109, 115.

95. Eschatological ethics is teleological in the sense that the ultimate end (total communion with God and neighbor) is a future promise that influences the present, historical situation. For Gutiérrez, the promise or ultimate end transforms the political sphere by means of people, in communion with God, creating new personal and structural relationships. See Gutiérrez, *Theology of Liberation*, 122.

parable in light of praxis, social analysis, and contemporary Christian thought. Praxis and analysis give causal explanations for the existence of widespread and severe hunger, thirst, sickness, and nakedness. Gutiérrez credits theologian Marie Dominique Chenu, Pope Pius XII, and other theologians for expanding the social meaning of neighbor and charity. Chenu talks about the masses as our neighbor. Pius XII refers to charity as "political charity." These contemporary insights lead Gutiérrez to understand caring for the poor as a social and political action. The hungry, naked, and imprisoned in Matthew's parable are not simply individuals; they are groups. Consequently, serving their needs involves more than ministering to their individual wants; it urgently calls for transforming the structures of society that create situations of hunger, nakedness, and imprisonment.[96] Thus, Gutiérrez specifies the general eschatological imperative from loving all needy people to transforming the political-economic structures that benefit the few at the expense of the many.

He goes one more step by translating the mandate for structural transformation into a middle axiom that links the biblical imperative with the political realities of Peru.[97] The axiom, Gutiérrez says, should involve radical transformation of the infrastructure—that is, changing private ownership of the means of production.[98]

Returning to Gutiérrez's hermeneutical circle, we can now retrace the theologian's methodological steps that outline his ethics. First, he begins with the problem in which the majority of Latin Americans experience widespread exploitation and repression. Second, he reflects on structural causes of the problem, aided by the analysis of social scientists. Third, in light of the analysis, Gutiérrez raises a question that has ethical implications: How is God present in the neighbor, especially in the poor and oppressed neighbor? Fourth, he addresses the question in light of the last judgment, which reveals that we become one with God and neighbor by loving human beings who lack basic human needs. Although the imperative to love the least is not restricted to the poor, this commitment is a necessary condition for salvation. Fifth, theological-ethical reflection on the parable leads to a middle axiom that calls for serving the poor by radically transforming social structures. In summary, Gutiérrez's

96. Ibid., 116, 230 n. 43.
97. A middle axiom is a concrete action guide for social policy or social change that builds upon a theological-moral principle and empirical evidence. See Ronald Preston, "Middle Axioms," *Westminster Dictionary of Christian Ethics*; Carol Robb, "Ethical Procedures of Gutiérrez and Alves," *Society of Christian Ethics: 1979 Selected Papers*, 80–81.
98. Gutiérrez, *Theology of Liberation*, 116.

eschatological ethics demonstrates how the future promises articulated by the gospel help shape specific norms in today's Latin American society.

Critique of ethical systems   Gutiérrez's commentary on the book of Job illustrates how Scripture can be used, first, to criticize a theological-ethical system, and second, to give a theological grounding to human goods. His commentary, entitled *On Job*, written fourteen years after *Theology of Liberation*, is perhaps Gutiérrez's best work. In a recent interview, he said, "You have not asked me any questions about my book on Job. That is closer to me than *A Theology of Liberation*."[99]

Although he follows the basic methodology, he adapts it in this work by emphasizing more the contemplative, prayerful aspect of praxis. In *Theology of Liberation*, praxis means loving activity: "real charity, action, and commitment to the service of others."[100] In his commentary on Job, he speaks of praxis as contemplation and practice. Together they comprise faith experience, or lived faith. Theology becomes a reflection on faith experience. He also replaces utopian language found in his earlier work with prophetic language. However, the basic reality underlying these new terms (prophetic language and faith experience) has the same essential meaning as the old (utopian language and praxis).

Gutiérrez's commentary moves dialectically from the human word to the word of God and from the word of God to the human word.[101] The human word may express truth, but it seeks deeper insight from God's word. Job's human word of complaint against unjust suffering and, analogously, the protesting word of Latin Americans against poverty and oppression need divine guidance. Gutiérrez relates a story by Peruvian author José María Arguedas about deep and endless suffering of the Amerindians in Peru. The character Ernesto in the novel *Deep Rivers* speaks about the mourning of the people, symbolized by the ringing of the cathedral bell called "María Angola." This bell was constructed with gold and by the slave labor of the workers:

> Afterwards, when my father rescued me and I wandered with him through the towns, I found that people everywhere suffered. Perhaps the María Angola mourned for all of them, here in Cuzco. I had never seen anyone more humiliated than the Old Man's pongo [unpaid Amerindian servant]. At every stroke the bell became more mournful and its sound penetrated everything.[102]

99. National Catholic News Service, July 13, 1988: 6.

100. Gutiérrez, *Theology of Liberation*, 9.

101. Gutiérrez, *Power of the Poor in History*, 61.

102. Gustavo Gutiérrez, *On Job: God-Talk and the Suffering of the Innocent*, trans. Matthew J. O'Connell (Maryknoll, N.Y.: Orbis, 1987), xv–xvi.

How is it possible, asks Gutiérrez, to bring to the people's innocent suffering a new memory, the joy of the risen Christ? How does the word of God speak salvifically to the Jobs living in Latin America today?

Satan raises the theological question: "Does Job fear God for naught?" (1:9). Gutiérrez, looking at the faces of oppressed Peruvians as he contemplates Job's physical and mental anguish, asks a parallel question: "Are human beings capable, in the midst of unjust suffering, of continuing to assert their faith in God and speak of God without expecting a return?"[103] God's response to the innocent Job and to the innocent Peruvians challenges them to expand their horizons, to refine their thinking about justice, and to learn something new about God.

Gutiérrez structures his theological reflection about Job's God-talk into three parts: first, the wager; second, Job's prophetic language; third, the development of his contemplative language. Job's prophetic language protests against injustice and against an erroneous theory of justice. He uses contemplative language to express his silent wonder before God, the recognition that everything comes from God's gratuitous love, and his surrender to this love.[104] The two languages converge and mutually enrich each other.

First, the wager. Satan bets that Job will curse God when misfortune falls; God accepts the challenge. Satan's challenge does not contest that Job was living a good life, but that his motives for doing so were less than ideal. Satan gambles on the suspicion that Job lived the good life and praised God because he knew only blessing and never misfortune.

Gutiérrez extends Satan's wager to all human beings who resemble Job after misfortune struck: those millions of dispossessed, yet innocent people, who sit on the garbage heap in Lima or São Paulo confused about God's role in their misfortunes. Can those people continue to place their trust in God? This question plumbs the depths of religion, asking whether human persons have the capacity to love God unconditionally. It also poses a hard question for ethical systems. Are systems of justice constructed on a standard of punishment and reward valid?

Job passes the first test. Bereft of family and fortune and suffering great misery, he refuses to curse God. The meeting between Job and his friends Eliphaz, Bildad, and Zophar begins with a week of silence. Neither he nor his comforters are able to speak. Gutiérrez asks how Job—and, indeed, how

103. Ibid., 1.
104. Gustavo Gutiérrez, "Speaking about God," *Different Theologies, Common Responsibility: Babylon Pentecost?* eds. Claude Geffré etal, *Concilium* Edinburgh: T & T Clark, 1984): 30.

anyone who has suffered severe injustice—can find words to address God. Equally difficult, how do those living in solidarity with the oppressed in Latin America proclaim the reign of love and justice to those who live in miserable situations that contradict such a reign?[105] Gutiérrez's question resembles Pixley's: Is God's kingdom good news for the oppressed?

Job's friends explain that he suffers for sins committed and therefore should repent. Eliphaz questions Job: "Can you recall anyone guiltless that perished?" (4:7). Job's own sense of justice and faith in God help him recognize that the doctrine of retribution underlying Eliphaz's question is false. God does not reward and punish people on the basis of their behavior.

Gutiérrez translates Job's dilemma as a choice between two theologies: "between a religion that sets conditions for the action of God and applies a calculus to it, and a faith that acknowledges the free initiative at work in God's love."[106] Job rejects the first theological system but is tentative about the second. Before he can fully embrace God's action as gratuitous love, he must see his personal suffering as connected with the suffering of others, and he must expand his understanding of justice.

Gutiérrez perceptively observes that the doctrine of retribution is an individualistic ethics, similar to the kind of individualism present in capitalist ideology today. This individualistic ethics interprets the possession of wealth, privilege, and health as the reward for an individual's honesty and hard work; it interprets poverty and sickness as God's punishment for being lazy and sinful.[107]

As Job rejects this ethical doctrine, he undergoes a change in his own thinking. The breakthrough occurs after his friends' charge that he suffers because of his past injustices to the poor. Job did in fact care for the poor. "Uprightness (*sedaqah*) I wore as a garment, fair judgment (*mishpat*) was my cloak and my turban. I was eyes for the blind and feet for the lame. Who but me was father of the poor?" (29:14-16). Then it dawns on Job that the real issue is not the suffering of one isolated person that is at stake, but the suffering of all the poor. His misery is a social, not simply an individual problem. Realizing this, Job comes to feel a solidarity with them.

Lived communitarian experience plays a prominent role in Gutiérrez's interpretation in this work. Job's faith and his human relationships convince him of his innocence and illuminate the errors of his friends' ethics of retribution. The friends, in sharp contrast, rely on ideas learned in the past "instead

105. Gutiérrez, *On Job*, 13.
106. Ibid., 15.
107. Ibid., 22–23.

of turning to the concrete lives of living persons, asking questions, and in this way opening themselves to a better understanding of God and God's word."[108]

Biblical basis of justice   Gutierrez's commentary on Job manifests a fourth use of Scripture; it provides the theological basis of moral value, specifically the values of love and justice. Whereas Pixley establishes God's nature (what God wills and does) as the ultimate source of moral obligation, Gutiérrez identifies God's gratuitous love as the basis of moral good. Moral goods, such as loving the poor and respecting others as equals, come into being because human beings first experience God's love and justice. Experiencing God's gift carries an obligation to love and serve the neighbor.[109]

Using Job as an exemplar, Gutiérrez shows how his love and justice expressed in prophetic language and deeds undergo further transformation due to his experiencing God's gratuitous love. Job's speech manifests this change by gradually switching from prophetic to contemplative language. Using prophetic language, he denounces his friends' ideas as erroneous, maintains his own innocence, expresses solidarity with other innocent sufferers, and questions the way God governs the world, and even reproaches God for "laughing at the plight of the innocent" (9:23). God seems unjust. And so Job takes his case to court, a procedure that requires an arbiter, a witness, and a defender.

Job's plea for a defender/avenger (*go'el*) follows upon his angry complaint and protest against both his friends and God: "Why do you, like God, pursue me? Why are you not satisfied with my flesh?" (19:22). Then the prophet's righteous anger switches into the contemplative's trust in the defender. "I know that I have a living avenger (*go'el*) and that at the end he will rise above the dust. After they pull my flesh from me, and I am without my flesh, I shall see God; I myself shall see him, and not as a stranger, my own eyes will see him. My heart is burning within my breast" (19:25-27). Who is the *go'el* in whom Job trusts, God or a third party who serves as Job's advocate against God? Gutiérrez, aware of the controversy on this question, holds that the defender/advocate is God.[110] Job, he says, splits God in two, as it were, producing "a God who judges him and a God who will defend him at that supreme

108. Ibid., 27.

109. Gutiérrez, *La verdad*, 53.

110. Gutiérrez follows the position of Robert Gordis, *The Book of God and Man: A Study of Job* (Chicago: University of Chicago Press, 1965). On the identity of the *go'el*, Gordis writes: "Actually, the problem arises only because of the tendency to apply Western categories of logic to the Oriental spirit. The sharp delimitation of personality is foreign to biblical thought. In all these passages, Job is affirming his faith that behind the God of violence, so tragically manifest in the world, stands the God of righteousness

moment; a God whom he experiences as almost an enemy but whom he knows at the same time to be truly a friend."[111]

These two images of God form the basis of two types of justice: God as just judge corresponds to Job's prophetic and solidaristic justice that rails against oppression of the innocent and the poor. God as defender corresponds to Job's plea for justice tempered by mercy. Job has an incipient awareness even before God responds to him that God's justice can be understood only in the context of a prior and gratuitous love for himself and others.

God does not crush Job but speaks to him of a creative freedom that profoundly respects human freedom. Job had questioned the plan of God in his rejection of his friends' interpretation of God's justice. Now God asks, "Who is this that darkens counsel by words without knowledge?" (38:2). God challenges Job's presuppositions, going back to the source of all existing things and asking him where he was when God set up the pillars of creation. Job lacks understanding, but gradually learns from God that Yahweh is a generous, even an extravagant, creator who can send rain "on lands where no one lives" (38:26). God's creation from the beginning expressed a free, generous love. Job will come to reject definitively the doctrine of retribution when he understands this love.

In his first response to God's revelation, Job humbly expresses his "littleness." He abandons his anthropocentrism, but continues to focus on himself: "I feel my littleness; I had better lay my hand over my mouth" (40:4-5). Yet he expresses no repentance for wrongdoing that would have deserved punishment.

God speaks a second time to Job, revealing another dimension of divine justice. God so profoundly respects human freedom that God will not forcefully bring justice about. "Have you an arm like God, and can you thunder with a voice like his? . . . Look on every one that is proud and bring him low; and

---

and love—and they are not two but one" (527). Gutiérrez disagrees with Norman Habel's position against Gordis—namely, that interpreting God as the *go'el* would mean reversing the pattern of Job's previous thought about God as a judge—an idea that persists after Job's famous cry of hope. Habel says: "Job has portrayed God consistently as his attacker not his defender, his enemy not his friend, his adversary at law not his advocate." Norman C. Habel, *The Book of Job: A Commentary* (Philadelphia: Westminster Press, 1985), 306.

111. Gutiérrez, *On Job*, 65. Gutiérrez supports his interpretation with an earlier passage in chapter 14 that Job had appealed to God against God: "If only you would keep me safe in the abyss and shelter me there till your anger is past, and you appoint a place for reconciliation with me!" (14:13). He also supports his split-God image with a story about Latin American writer César Vallejo, whom Gutiérrez credits for helping him understand the book of Job.

tread down the wicked where they stand." Job cannot do what is impossible for God to do, namely, to enforce justice while respecting human freedom (40:14). God's power to bring about justice is restricted by God's respect for human freedom.[112]

Job undergoes further transformation as he silently contemplates this new revelation. His second response expresses a remarkable change. First, he moves from a self-focus to a God-focus in an act of faith: "I know that you are all-powerful and there is no plan you cannot carry out" (42:2). Second, he recognizes the plan of God's boundless and freely given love. Finally, Job acknowledges humbly and joyfully his meeting with God that has changed his life: "I once knew you only by hearsay, now my eyes have seen you" (42:5).

Justice expressed in prophetic language does not have the final say about how God's people should speak about God. Grace gives justice its full meaning. When God's freedom and divine justice mold human justice, the latter becomes a giving freely what one has freely received.

Prophetic language works together with contemplative language. The former protests against human exploitation of people, especially of the poor. Contemplative language complements prophetic justice by helping people to understand God's predilection for the poor.[113] God favors the poor, says Gutiérrez, not because they are necessarily better than anyone else, but because they are living in an inhuman situation contrary to God's desire for any human being. Contemplative language expresses the unconditional nature of God's love; prophetic language expresses concretely the demands this love makes. Yet contemplative language challenges prophetic language to incorporate a higher viewpoint and a more generous, merciful response. Justice should not constrict, but ought to move people to greater freedom. Contemplative language moves Job from a self-focus to solidarity with the poor; from an anthropocentrism to a theocentrism.

Gutiérrez's commentary begins and ends with Jesus. Job is a prefigure of Jesus. Jesus, like Job, also used the twofold language of prophecy and contemplation, though in a less hesitating manner than Job. Jesus, the innocent and suffering servant, protested vigorously in solidarity with the poor against unjust treatment by religious and civil officials. He proclaimed a message of universal love and preference for the poor. "This radical communion with the suffering of human beings brought him down to the deepest level of history at the very moment when his life was ending."[114] By his life and by his death,

112. Ibid., 77.
113. Ibid., 88.
114. Ibid., 100.

the Son of God showed that contemplation of God must be realized through the cross.

Returning to his original question—"How is it possible to talk of God in the midst of unjust suffering?"—Gutiérrez answers: follow Jesus by embracing the cross in life and in death. However, the followers must read the Bible anew in light of their own situation. Speaking from within the context of Ayacucho, Peru, where terrorist and counterterrorist activity has brought massive deaths, torture, disappearances, and exile, he asks: "How are we to do theology while Ayacucho lasts? How are we to speak of the God of life when cruel murder on a massive scale goes on in Ayacucho?" Job and Jesus give the fundamental directives by their vigorous protests, by their concrete commitment to the poor, and by their self-surrender to God's gratuitous love in darkness and loneliness. Although he remains silent on the matter of using counterviolence in the context of Ayacucho, Gutiérrez's commentary seems to take a position that the gospel stands as the last outpost against brutal violence. The God of Job and Jesus is not a warrior God. The God of Job does not bring justice about by means of coercion. Jesus surrenders in protest, but nonviolently to the sentence of the cross. Hope in God replaces feelings of abandonment.

Job and especially Jesus are exemplars for Latin Americans living through suffering marked by injustice and violence. Gutiérrez stops short of giving more specific directives for strategies in such violent contexts. Followers of Christ must find their own specific way of protesting against the injustices and of responding to God's love.

Assessment

This section evaluates how well Gutiérrez uses Scripture in ethics. Like the assessment of Pixley's method, this section will relate Gutiérrez's use of Scripture to his understanding of the Bible, the role of Christ, and the nature of ethics.

Bible as the book of life   Gutiérrez refers to the Bible as "the book of life" because it is the source for shaping Christian identity, spirituality, and morality in all dimensions of human existence: the material and the spiritual, the individual and the social, the present and the future.[115] It is the highest authority and has the last word in theological matters.[116] Like Pixley, Gutiérrez

115. Gutiérrez, "Speaking about God," 31.
116. Gutiérrez, *Theology of Liberation*, 180 n. 34, 181 n. 40.

insists that biblical themes, parables, and narratives must be reconsidered in light of praxis and in light of historical-cultural realities different from the situations in which the Bible was written.[117] Praxis and Scripture relate dialectically in Gutiérrez's system, mutually challenging and illuminating each other. Gutiérrez's own reading of Scripture itself becomes challenged and transformed by Scripture. His lifetime commitment to the poor enabled him to discover how Job's awareness of solidarity with those suffering unjustly led Job to experience God's gratuitous love in silent contemplation. Job came to recognize that he did not understand everything about social justice and so needed to hear God's word at a more profound level. Gutiérrez's insight from Job—the intimate relationship between prophecy and contemplation—challenges and enriches his own understanding of praxis. In his early works, praxis connotes a dynamic activity, prophetic proclamation, or word concretized in gesture.[118]

Without diminishing the importance of the active, prophetic aspect of praxis, Gutiérrez emphasizes, in his book *On Job* and in his later writings, the contemplative aspect of praxis. Loving and serving the poor requires receiving God's love through the poor. This dynamic of giving and receiving, of prophetic activity and contemplative receptivity, establishes the theological basis for mutuality as an essential element of social justice. Other liberation theologians, especially women, have emphasized mutuality as an essential element of pastoral practice and justice.[119]

Like Pixley, Gutiérrez regards the Bible as the inspired word of God that has social and political significance. His strength lies in developing the transcendent dimension of the word of God while never losing focus on how God's face watches over human events. He does this in at least three ways. First, he brings out a sense of wonder, such as astonishment about God's justice that does not coercively impose itself on human freedom, even on the self-determination of evildoers. Second, he emphasizes the understanding of things beyond themselves, such as perceiving life sprouting from Job's garbage heap. Third, he stresses the total personal engagement and transformation that an encounter with the word of God invokes, such as commitment to serving

---

117. Ibid., 21.

118. Gutiérrez, *Power of the Poor in History*, 37.

119. Ivone Gebara, "Women Doing Theology in Latin America," 126–27, and Ana María Tepedino, "Feminist Theology as the Fruit of Passion and Compassion," 165–72, both in *With Passion and Compassion: Third World Women Doing Theology*, ed. Virginia Fabella and Mercy Amba Oduyoye (Maryknoll, N.Y.: Orbis Books, 1988). See also Jon Sobrino and Juan Hernández Pico, *Theology of Christian Solidarity*, trans. Phillip Berryman (Maryknoll, N.Y.: Orbis Books, 1985), 19.

others who live on the garbage heap in Latin America. Gutiérrez's genius lies in his ability to relate these revelations of God's promise to the Latin American experience.

Unlike Pixley, he does not develop the sociopolitical context in which the biblical works were written. He moves from today's world to the biblical text and then back to the contemporary situation. This limitation is somewhat mitigated by his expressing deeply human concerns in Latin America as questions for Scripture, such as how to proclaim the reign of God to those who live in a reign of terror and exploitation. He does not demand from the Bible answers to inappropriate questions, such as biblical guidelines for governing guerrilla warfare.

In recent years Gutiérrez has developed a method of using the Bible in an integral and coherent manner. His early writings emphasized Old Testament themes more than New Testament themes, and failed to integrate sufficiently the distinctive witness of Jesus.[120] His later writings achieve this integration better, as seen in his commentary on Job. This commentary also demonstrates an advance in his comprehensive method of dealing with specific biblical books. He treats the book of Job as a literary whole, unlike his early writings, which failed to distinguish differences between literary forms and the intention of the author.

He strives for coherence by trying to make sense of apparently contradictory images of God in the Bible. In Job, Gutiérrez tries to reconcile the just avenger with the merciful defender by means of his split image of God. He differs from Pixley in giving primacy to the image of God as a nonviolent defender and liberator of the oppressed.

Role of Christ   Jesus Christ continues the liberating work of the God of Exodus and the God of Job. Through his life, death, and resurrection Jesus becomes the radical and efficacious way by which all persons may be joined in communion with God in the kingdom. Belief in Jesus requires entering into the kingdom, the heart of which involves proclaiming the liberating news to the poor and accepting God's love through the poor. Jesus' message calls people to conversion. It is not a moral code, though in its general directives the proclamation presents a vision of justice.

Gutiérrez calls Jesus Christ the hermeneutical principle of faith, by which he means that people come to know God through Christ. He implies that

120. Spohn, *What Are They Saying about Scripture and Ethics?* 64. Spohn's observation is made on the basis of Gutiérrez's first major work, *Theology of Liberation* (1973). The later writings of Gutiérrez would include *We Drink from Our Own Wells*, (1984) and *On Job* (1987).

Christ is also the hermeneutical key to understanding Old Testament books. Gutiérrez, much more so than Pixley, relates Exodus, Job, and Psalms to the death and resurrection of Jesus. In doing so, Gutiérrez does not spiritualize or privatize the political and religious dimensions.

Nature of ethics   Ethics for Gutiérrez is fundamentally teleological because a twofold goal—communion with God and solidarity with neighbor—serves as the ethical standard. More specifically, his type of teleology is an eschatological ethics in which the future promise of total communion, while beyond history, is fulfilled within history through the love commands.

The eschatological dimension characterizes his various uses of Scripture in ethics. As a source of personal transformation, or conversion, the living word calls persons to new life by breaking with mental categories, attitudes, and ways of relating to neighbor and to God. It especially urges persons to open themselves to those who suffer injustice and to commit themselves to the oppressed. This commitment conditions all subsequent moral decisions affecting persons, property, and human rights. On the level of moral content, Gutiérrez uses Scripture appropriately by developing a general principle of option for the poor from the Matthean and other biblical texts. Consistent with his theological method, he does not move directly from this biblically based principle to politics, but enters politics by way of a historical-utopian level in which he constructs middle axioms. His method lacks ethical reasoning supporting his conclusions, as for example that a socialist political economy would be more just than the present system. His recommendation that social change in Latin America move toward socialism reflects the judgment of many social analysts and participants in the struggle. Recently, however, Gutiérrez has qualified his views on socialism versus capitalism.[121]

In developing his positions on issues, Gutiérrez does not distinguish between theological and ethical arguments but presents a position based on values and principles based on faith (option for the poor), on human values (freedom to speak, the right to participate), and social analysis (dependent capitalism).[122] He does not engage in ethical reasoning that might support the biblically based option for the poor. For example, he could relate the preferential

121. Gutiérrez, *Theology of Liberation*, 16–17, 49–54; *La verdad*, 220–21. In an interview in Maryknoll, New York, July 12, 1988, Gutiérrez said that he thought some form of social ownership of the means of production was needed in the form of coooperatives, not necessarily in the form of state ownership. "We must try to combine social property and private property."

122. Marciano Vidal, "Is Morality Based on Autonomy Compatible with the Ethics of Liberation?" 83.

option for the poor to the common good, arguing that only by systematically addressing the needs of the poor and exploited groups on a global level can the good of the international community be realized.

The preferential option for the poor is a general norm and therefore cannot guide strategy for change or evaluate concrete problems. Concrete moral norms are needed to specify this option in areas such as equitable interest rates, repayment of debts, and land redistribution.

In general, Gutiérrez uses Scripture effectively and appropriately, especially as a source for consciousness-raising involving personal conversion and for grounding justice in God's gratuitous love. Probably, he does not think of his work as a kind of metaethics that forms a theological basis for ethical norms. Yet his consistent emphasis on the experience of God's gratuitousness as the basis for the virtue of justice might be effectively used as the ground for principles of justice.

On a pastoral level, Gutiérrez's prophetic-contemplative spirituality serves as a solid spirituality for addressing people in Christian base communities who struggle for years against great forces to liberate themselves and others. Participants in these communities can grow discouraged by slow efforts to bring about changes. The trial of Job, illuminated by the trial of Jesus, does speak to these participants who ask, "What are we accomplishing? Things are no better." Gutiérrez's reflections on Job and Jesus provide a framework for encouraging people to continue in the face of setbacks, frustration, and failure.

How Liberation Theologians Read Scripture

Summarizing how liberation theologians read Scripture, especially in relation to issues of justice, is a risky venture and perhaps an impossible task. Yet a pattern begins to emerge not only from analyzing the works of Pixley, Gutiérrez, Mesters, and Croatto, but also from the writings of Segundo, the Boffs, and Comblin, studied earlier. I shall limit my summary to five statements: (1) liberation theologians read the Bible as the book of life; (2) they relate the word of God to praxis in a dialectical process; (3) they read it from the perspective of the poor and oppressed; (4) they focus on eschatology that serves as the general framework for their ethics; and (5) they use Scripture in a variety of ways, but primarily as a source to transform others into free and just human beings.

Book of life   For a community of faith, the Bible shapes all aspects of life. The people read Scripture, Carlos Mesters says, not to interpret the Bible, but to interpret life with the help of the Bible. As a witness of God's presence in events, the Bible can, if opened up, bring freedom and life to a hopeless or trapped people. For the Bible to release its meaning, people must themselves experience their own captivity and struggle, their own death and resurrection. Croatto says that the memory of biblical events, such as the exodus, will have meaning for us only if we are in some way involved in a process of liberation. "Oppressors," he says, "cannot celebrate the Passover."[123]

Word and praxis   As the book of life, Scripture holds word and event in a unity that gives identity and a sense of purpose to a people. Pixley, in his work on Exodus, shows how the political and religious dimensions connect. Gutiérrez recognizes a unity in the two languages of contemplation and prophecy in Job, each of which inspires its own praxis. The Bible is created first by experiencing God's presence in event; then the event is told and retold until it takes hold in the written word. Each subsequent remembering and celebrating of the original event contributes to the reservoir of meaning. Contemporary praxis taps this reservoir and contributes its own meaning. Contemporary assertions of the dignity of the poor, resistance to male domination, and contemplation of the earth from its own satellite break open deeper meaning in Scripture, which in turn casts light on contemporary praxis.

Perspective of the poor   Although all liberation theologians interpret Scripture from the viewpoint of the wretched of the earth, certain ones like Gustavo Gutiérrez, Yvone Gebara, and Clodovis Boff try to live with the poor in order to better understand their perspective. With this perspective, the theologians' reflections on exodus and freedom, the meaning of death and resurrection, church, and Eucharist take on new symbolic value and speak more powerfully to the people's own praxis.

Eschatological ethics   The word of God not only inspires and gives strength to those pursuing freedom; it guides them in making difficult choices. For Pixley, obligation arises from the experience of who God is, what God wills, and what God does in history. The obligation to live in solidarity with the poor arises in obedience to God's word. For Gutiérrez, the same commitment to the poor originates in the experience of God's gratuitous love. Both theologians discern obligation from within an eschatological framework wherein God addresses the hearers of the word. Eschatology shapes liberation

123. J. Severino Croatto, *Exodus: A Hermeneutics of Freedom*, trans. Salvator Attanasio (Maryknoll, N.Y.: Orbis Books, 1981), 23.

ethics by establishing love and service of God and neighbor as its basis. It also gives perspective by showing that a people's specific project does not encompass the definitive plan of God's kingdom. Moral discernment is done communally within a faith context where a variety of experiences are brought to bear upon the text.

Knowing God in relation to the neighbor   Liberation theologians do not use concrete ethical commands as prescriptions for what we ought to do today. Most often the theologians, such as Gutiérrez and Jon Sobrino, focus upon a spirituality of liberation, rooted in Scripture, that strengthens and challenges people to commit themselves to the reign of God. Thus, liberation ethics concentrates on the commitment and freedom of the moral decision makers, not on the norms for making decisions. The heart of the matter involves coming to know God and Jesus in relation to the neighbor, especially those who are considered outcasts in society.

Part
Three

MODELS
of Ethics

6

Ethics of Discipleship

Many liberation theologians—Gutiérrez, the Boffs, Pixley, and Sobrino—approach ethics through discipleship.[1] They maintain that persons act faithfully and justly by reproducing the Spirit of Jesus in proclaiming the kingdom of God. Discipleship involves a call to personal conversion and, at the same time, a movement toward establishing a community of worship in which disciples engage in corporate moral discernment and the promotion of justice for the poor. Hence, discipleship for all these theologians attends to both the subjective and objective dimensions—the subjective aspect focusing on the agent's motives, freedom, and commitment, and the objective aspect examining values, norms, and method.

Gustavo Gutiérrez considers conversion the central element of discipleship. Persons must first experience God's justice, he says, before they can know true justice and be capable of promoting it. Moreover, the experience of God's gratuitous justice creates in the hearts of disciples great desire to serve others, and spontaneous joy in the very act of service.[2]

Discipleship for Leonardo Boff means proclaiming the utopia of the kingdom of God and translating it into practice.[3] Utopia, translated into earthly realities, calls the disciple to defend and promote the rights of the impoverished, to support a minimally decent standard of living, and to create a grass-roots church in which the people have voice and a sense of community.[4]

Clodovis Boff and Jorge Pixley in their book *The Bible, the Church, and the Poor* highlight the praxis of discipleship: solidarity, service, and sacrifice.

1. Leonardo Boff, *Jesus Christ Liberator*, trans. Patrick Hughes (Maryknoll, N.Y.: Orbis Books, 1978), 264–95; C. Boff and Pixley, *Bible, the Church, and the Poor*, 68–91; Gutiérrez, *We Drink from Our Own Wells*, 35–71.
2. Gutiérrez, *Truth Shall Make You Free*, 97.
3. L. Boff, *Jesus Christ Liberator*, 291.
4. L. Boff, *When Theology Listens to the Poor*, 88.

Jesus' action and message convey solidarity with the poor, service to the needs of the humblest, and a readiness to suffer whatever persecution such solidarity brings. Boff and Pixley regard conflict with the powerful and wealthy as the inevitable cost of discipleship.[5]

Sobrino includes many of these same ideas in his reflections on discipleship and has developed them more extensively. For this reason a concentration on his ethics of discipleship seems more than justified. Like Leonardo Boff, Sobrino writes about the promotion of human rights and sees their embodiment in human relationships as corresponding with God's kingdom. Like Gutiérrez, Sobrino places the experience of gratuitousness as the cornerstone of his ethical framework. And like Clodovis Boff and Pixley, he recognizes and reflects upon the conflictual nature of discipleship.

Sobrino not only incorporates representative elements of discipleship from the writings of these Latin American theologians, he also emphasizes certain features that, collectively, distinguish his mode of discipleship. First, discipleship means following the *historical* Jesus, which for Sobrino means the total life of Jesus of Nazareth. Second, Sobrino accents the guidance of the Holy Spirit (the Spirit of Jesus), who accompanies disciples as they proclaim the kingdom of God. Third, Sobrino sees the beatitudes as epitomizing the message and action of Jesus. These blessings, understood more as spirit than as law, inspire the praxis of disciples. Sobrino singles out one beatitude in particular as distinctive of his approach to the ethics of discipleship: "Blessed are the pure in heart, for they shall see God" (Matt. 5:8). He reads this blessing as a call to live with a basic honesty—that is, to see things as they are and to speak the truth about that which one sees. The other beatitudes—thirsting for justice, being merciful—encourage disciples to give generously without expecting any return. This unconditional and mutual love, which the beatitudes express, serves as the mainspring of Sobrino's ethics.[6]

Another important reason for considering Sobrino's work as a model is that he consciously attempts to construct from his Christology the foundations of a Christian morality. Working on this foundational level of ethics, Sobrino argues that the kingdom of God, embodied in the life of Jesus, is the ultimate good "which founds Christian morality and gives it a Christian sense."[7] In

5. C. Boff and Pixley, *Bible, the Church, and the Poor*, 68–71, 91.

6. Jon Sobrino, interview with author, Central American University of Simeon Cañas, San Salvador, April 24, 1988.

7. Jon Sobrino, *Christology at the Crossroads: A Latin American Approach*, trans. John Drury (Maryknoll, N.Y.: Orbis Books, 1978), 110. Sobrino's understanding of "fundamental" is close to what Frankena means by "metaethics." See William K. Frankena, *Ethics*, 2d ed. (Englewood Cliffs, N.J.: Prentice-Hall, 1973), 4–5. Christian

addition to the foundational level (or metaethics), Sobrino talks about morality on a second level, which ethicists call normative morality. Here he treats norms, such as the option for the poor and the method of moral discernment. Finally, he applies his moral criteria to illumine moral questions, like whether Central American University ought to commit itself to the poor of El Salvador. In short, Sobrino sketches for us an ethics that accounts for three major dimensions of ethical discourse: the foundational, normative, and applied.

Before considering these three dimensions, some criticisms raised about Sobrino's use of Scripture as a basis of ethics might be noted. Sobrino makes two claims about his ethics, both of which raise critical questions. The first relates to the adequacy of Scripture as a basis for Christian ethics, and the second to his biblical exegesis. Regarding Scripture, Sobrino claims that the kingdom of God as revealed in Christian revelation and not human nature serves as the primary foundation of Christian ethics.

Moral theologian Vincent MacNamara raises the question whether liberation theologians can claim that the interpretation of revelation can "give a specific and concrete Christian insight into what is morally required, what God is requiring and enabling us to do."[8] He concurs with liberation theologians that a theological ethics must possess Christian content. He disagrees, however, with those theologians, such as Juan Luis Segundo, Ignacio Ellacuría, and others, who use the Bible to resolve contemporary issues that are too specific. "Too specific" would include Segundo's claim that the Bible provides warrants for the choice of socialism over capitalism, or Ellacuría's apparent claim that the Bible justifies revolutionary violence.[9] MacNamara does not mention Sobrino. But because Sobrino's ethics of discipleship depends primarily on the gospel, a variation of MacNamara's question might be asked of him: whether Scripture, informed by Christian experience and by social analysis, can yield content specific enough to illumine contemporary moral problems.

Second, Sobrino claims that the historical Jesus and not the Christ of faith idealized by the biblical writers serves as the authoritative interpreter of

---

ethicists like James Gustafson make a distinction between "ethics" and "morals" that parallels Frankena's distinction between "metaethics" and "normative ethics." See James M. Gustafson, "Theology and Ethics," in *Christian Ethics and the Community* (Philadelphia: Pilgrim Press, 1971), 85–86; see also Richard M. Gula's development of the latter's distinction in *Reason Informed by Faith* (New York: Paulist Press, 1989), 10–11.

8. Vincent MacNamara, *Faith and Ethics: Recent Roman Catholicism* (Washington, D.C.: Georgetown University Press, 1985), 138.

9. Ibid., 139. MacNamara cites the following works: Juan Luis Segundo, "Capitalism Versus Socialism: *Crux Theologica*," in *Frontiers of Theology in Latin America*, ed. Gibellini, 240ff.; Ignacio Ellacuría, *Freedom Made Flesh* (Maryknoll, N.Y.: Orbis Books, 1976), 187ff.

God's kingdom. The call to discipleship summons persons to proclaim the kingdom of God, following "the historical path of Jesus."[10] Biblical theologians Michael Cook and John Meier have independently questioned Sobrino about his definition of the historical Jesus and about his criteria for determining the historicity of the gospel.

Cook says that Sobrino wants to claim too much about the historical Jesus without giving sufficient evidence. For example, Sobrino sees Jesus, as narrated by the Gospel of Mark, undergoing a kind of conversion that develops along two stages. The first stage shows Jesus using his power, struggling against oppressive laws, debating his adversaries, and healing the sick. In the second stage, Jesus is on the receiving end. He suffers the consequences for stands taken: hostile resistance, persecution, and death. Sobrino interprets these as historical stages that reveal an actual transition in Jesus' understanding of the mission and a corresponding shift in his praxis. Cook asks whether the figure upon which Sobrino builds his theology is derived from a chronological biography of Jesus or only a restatement of Mark's Gospel.[11]

Meier criticizes Sobrino's misuse of the term "historical Jesus." It does not mean the totality of Jesus' history, as Sobrino asserts, but the "Jesus reconstructed according to the canons of historical criticism."[12] He lacks evidence to support his contention that a basic historicity exists in the gospel narratives. Meier quotes Sobrino: "To anyone living and suffering history on the South American continent, it seems altogether probable that 'Jesus was like that.' "[13] Meier asks whether the total reality of Jesus of Nazareth can be known when it is no longer accessible to us by scholarly means.

In summary, MacNamara raises the methodological question about the liberation theologians' use of Scripture in moral reflection. Cook and Meier raise the exegetical and hermeneutical questions about how Sobrino interprets the meaning of the gospel texts in their original context and how he translates the texts for Latin Americans today.[14] These questions serve as a useful backdrop for looking critically at Sobrino's use of sources.

10. Sobrino, *Christology at the Crossroads*, 136–39.

11. Michael L. Cook, "Jesus from the Other Side of History: Christology in Latin America," *Theological Studies* 44 (June 1983): 273.

12. John P. Meier, "The Bible as a Source for Theology," in *Proceedings of the Catholic Theological Society of America* 43 (1988): 3–4.

13. Ibid., 7.

14. Gula, *Reason Informed by Faith*, 166–67. Gula uses Kenneth R. Himes's fine distinction of four tasks in relating Scripture and moral theology: "(1) the exegetical task: determining the meaning of the text in its original context; (2) the hermeneutical task: determining the meaning of the text for today; (3) the methodological task: using scripture in moral reflection; (4) the theological task: explaining the relationship of scripture to other sources of moral wisdom."

Foundations

In his first major work, *Christology at the Crossroads*, Sobrino investigated the foundation of the "ought" in Christian morality. He located the imperative in the moral object rather than in the nature of the subject, or human person. The moral object refers specifically to an experience with Jesus. Encountering Jesus creates both a desire and an obligation to follow Jesus toward helping him establish God's kingdom.

Although educated in the natural law tradition, Sobrino maintains that religious experience that involves a radical conversion is the more basic source for Christian morality than natural law or some other mode of philosophical reasoning.[15] The encounter with the crucified Jesus, mediated by the poor living their faith on the edge of existence, urges persons to make a fundamental decision: whether to accompany Jesus on a lifelong mission to fashion the kingdom or to reject the invitation. This decision conditions specific moral choices.

Comparison with Natural Law and Divine Command

A brief comparison of Sobrino's model of discipleship with both the divine command theory of Karl Barth and the natural law morality of St. Thomas Aquinas may hew its features more sharply. Sobrino's model includes important elements found in both systems, as well as significant differences with Aquinas and Barth. Sobrino holds with Saint Thomas and Barth that God is the ultimate source of morality, though all three relate the ultimate standard differently to human acts. For Saint Thomas natural law serves as the vehicle communicating God's law to human beings.[16] Thus, persons act morally when they make choices in response to the dictates of human reason based in eternal reason. For Barth the word of God issues God's command. Scripture provides summary statements of good and responsible human behavior—for example, the Ten Commandments, the beatitudes, and the injunctions of Saint Paul. Divine commands, however, are not restricted to what is set down in the Bible.[17] Finally, for Sobrino, the kingdom of God, understood as God's loving and just relationship with creation, conveys the ultimate design for human beings. God establishes through Jesus and his disciples a covenantal relationship with the human community that makes certain demands. It obliges

15. Sobrino, *Christology at the Crossroads*, 110–11.
16. Saint Thomas Aquinas, *Summa Theologica*, trans. Fathers of the English Dominican Province (New York: Benziger Brothers, 1947), I-II, 91.2.
17. Karl Barth, *Church Dogmatics* (Edinburgh: T & T Clark, 1960), 3/4:4.

persons to change exploitive patterns of personal relationships and dehuman-izing social structures.

To summarize, Sobrino's kingdom-of-God metaphor, which accentuates transforming unjust relationships in fidelity to God's covenantal relationship, differs from natural law, which emphasizes human reason rooted in the mind of God, and from the divine command that stresses obedience to the will of God. While each of these metaphors gives rise to distinctively different ethical systems, they all agree on this basic point: God serves as the ultimate standard of morality.

One may wonder why Sobrino casts aside natural law as the primary basis of ethics. According to natural law theory, human persons recognize within themselves a universal dictate: do the good and shun the evil. Saint Thomas identified specific expressions of this fundamental imperative. Human persons recognize the imperative to preserve and respect life, to procreate and educate their offspring, to tell the truth, and to form friendships.[18] All rational beings can know these obligations and so possess the capacity to know the will of God independently of divine revelation.

Sobrino rejects a natural law approach, because the kingdom of God, not human nature, is the fundamental meaning of reality according to which human life should be measured. Moreover, Christian ethics involves more than doing good acts and avoiding evil acts. It is primarily a matter of trans-forming the evil in order to achieve the good. Therefore, discipleship demands a praxis that natural law does not emphasize. Finally and most importantly, natural law is based on an analogy between the human and the divine, the validity of which the cross negates. The cross of Jesus, Sobrino argues, negates every human attempt to have access to God. "On the cross, we find nothing similar to what is usually regarded as divine."[19] The cross questions people about themselves and their self-interests. It probes a person's understanding of the human and gives it new meaning. The cross contradicts certain natural inclinations (e.g., saving one's life) and natural law's insistence on following the reasonable course of action.

Reason is an important, but not a sufficient, resource for ethics. People come to know and to follow God not through reason but through suffering: the suffering of Jesus, the poor, the outcasts, and the wretched of the land. "God on the cross explains nothing; he criticizes every proffered explanation."[20]

18. Gula, *Reason Informed by Faith*, 238–40. St. Thomas calls this aspect of natural law the "order of nature" and those distinctively human inclinations (truth telling and love) the "order of reason."

19. Sobrino, *Christology at the Crossroads*, 221–22.

20. Ibid., 222.

Hence, the normatively human becomes redefined in terms of a relationship with God, who is known through the suffering servant, Jesus, and the oppressed today.

Human suffering illumined by the Old and the New Testaments becomes the source for identifying the presence of God's kingdom. Persons come to know Jesus by means of solidarity with the least in society. The least, most especially those who live in misery, mediate God's truth to others. Sobrino calls this kind of knowledge of God connatural. "It is knowledge born of shared communion with the sorrow and suffering of the other person." This shared knowledge helps persons to know the good and to change the causes of suffering brought on by human decisions. Therefore, the cross of Christ, and not natural law, serves as the norm of obligation.

Sobrino does not cast off all his natural law origins. As in natural law, liberation theology uses reason to search for the truth of the situation. Sobrino searches for the truth of the situation by means of socioanalytic reasoning. Unlike natural law moralists, Sobrino does not emphasize synthetic reasoning that deduces from premises a judgment about human acts. His specific type of analysis, more historical-philosophical than social-scientific, aims to attain the truth of a certain reality—for example, investigating the structural pattern of violence in El Salvador. Using social analysis to probe into the deep causes of terrorism and repression brings one closer to the truth and thereby accomplishes one of the two essential tasks of moral reasoning in natural law.

In some respects, Sobrino's ethics of discipleship seems closer to the divine command of Karl Barth than to the natural law of Thomas Aquinas. Like Barth, he emphasizes God's divine revelation and the centrality of Jesus Christ in revelation. The imitation of Jesus helps the Christian respond faithfully and generously to God. Moral imperatives in both systems flow from a covenant of grace or gratuitousness. For Barth as well as for Sobrino, the command of God connotes gracious invitation rather than edict. Both theologians require moral discernment in specific historical contexts. Finally, Sobrino and Barth reject a natural law approach, although Sobrino reappropriates certain elements of it.[21]

21. Barth, *Church Dogmatics*, 2/2:546. Barth maintains that all human attempts, such as natural law ethics, to discover and then to carry out the law, fail. Although Barth does not deny the existence of natural law, he thinks human sinfulness darkens the mind and depraves the will, thus preventing human beings from knowing and carrying out this law. The gospel of Jesus Christ, understood more as grace, liberates people from the law and sanctifies them in a twofold act of condemning and acquitting. This divine action frees believers to act morally.

And yet Sobrino differs from Barth in two significant ways. First, Jesus' praxis and the praxis of the poor play important roles in Sobrino's ethics. The way Jesus engaged in praxis—his teaching and action on behalf of the poor—instructs disciples how to live. The concrete life of the poor helps express God's living word. Barth does not refer to the praxis of Jesus' ministry, nor does he speak of the praxis of the poor as a special source of God's word.

Second, social analysis scrutinizes the operations of powerful forces, such as the national guard and agribusinesses. Barth does not concern himself with social analysis of structures. U.S. Christian ethicist Charles West observed that Barth's Christian "rushes into political and economic judgments armed only with theological insight and limited experience, ignoring a vast body of social scientific literature."[22] Sobrino, for his part, considers this literature vital.

From Experience to Imperative

The experience of Jesus as Christ—as revelation of ultimate truth and meaning—forms the basis of Sobrino's ethics. Moral obligation flows from this experience and creates two interior movements within the disciple: urgency and gratuitousness.[23] The feeling of urgency emerges as the disciple recognizes Jesus as the Christ. Sobrino speaks of urgency as an awareness of ultimacy. The same religious experience generates a heart exceedingly grateful for being invited to accompany Jesus. These religious affections—a heightened awareness of the ultimate and a feeling of unconditional acceptance—impel one to follow Jesus.

The first disciples experienced Jesus' gratuitous love, which transcended anything they had dreamt possible. Jesus' unconditional forgiveness not only surprised his disciples, but also astonished those who formerly had rejected and persecuted him. Instead of seeking vengeance, Jesus pardoned his enemies. Even more astounding, he invited former enemies to join him as companions in the mission, to follow him and to proclaim the kingdom of God. Unconditional acceptance by Jesus roused men and women to follow him. In Sobrino's words, "The total reality of Jesus, not merely his verbal demands, makes Christian morality obligatory. It is basically the experience that Paul succinctly states: 'The love of Christ impels us' " (2 Cor. 5:14).[24]

The "total reality of Jesus" is what Sobrino means by the historical Jesus. Approaching Jesus as a historical person means understanding Jesus' own self-awareness, his praxis, conflict, and preaching in historical context rather than

22. Charles C. West, *Communism and the Theologians* (London: SCM Press, 1958), 286.
23. Sobrino, *Christology at the Crossroads*, 111.
24. Ibid., 112.

reading his life in idealistic terms.[25] Disciples today can know Jesus as the Christ only insofar as they first undergo conversion, engage in Christian practice, and struggle for justice on behalf of the poor and oppressed. The decision to follow Jesus involves reproducing Jesus' own history by historicizing the values he proclaimed: love, justice, freedom. Historicizing these values constitutes for Sobrino fashioning the kingdom on earth.

In linking obligation with the interior movements inspired by the Spirit of Jesus, Sobrino respects both the divine initiative and the autonomy of the moral agent. The Spirit of Jesus initiates the call, motivates persons to follow Jesus, and gives them the capacity to do so. At the same time, the human subject chooses to act or not act in accordance with the inspiration. Thus, Sobrino argues that the experience of Jesus' love affects the disposition, motive, and intention of the moral subject as well as the subject's freedom to act. It also inspires an imperative, though a very general one, to work toward the realization of the kingdom of God. But does this graced event contribute to specific moral content?

Normative Ethics

Sobrino asks himself whether "Christian moral life and theology end up being a formal morality without any hard content insofar as it appeals to Jesus himself."[26] He then gives a yes–and–no answer to his own question. Yes, the graced event through Jesus gives a content that remains universally valid in differing historical situations. No, Jesus is not a lawgiver but serves as the spirit of Christian morality. These positive and negative responses require further explanation.

Discipleship as a Historicizing Ethics

Jesus is normative for his disciples, but not by teaching them virtue, or handing out a set of prescriptions, or offering disciples his concrete praxis for imitation. Rather than establishing a type of fundamentalism, Jesus urges the disciples to historicize values. Sobrino follows his colleague Ignacio Ellacuría on the notion of historicization. This involves today's disciples placing ideals and values proclaimed by Jesus within their own concrete historical context.[27]

25. Ibid., xxii.
26. Ibid., 136.
27. Ignacio Ellacuría, "Human Rights in a Divided Society," in *Human Rights in the Americas*, ed. Alfred Hennelly and John Langan (Washington, D.C.: Georgetown University Press, 1982), 59.

Sobrino identifies three principles of historicizing values from the praxis of Jesus. First, Jesus approached the reconciliation of the whole of society through a particular group. He aligned himself with one class of people (the poor and outcasts), who lived in conflict with another class (the religious and political leaders). Jesus historicized his ultimate goal of universal solidarity by means of his partial solidarity with the economically poor and the outcasts. These groups opened themselves to the message of Jesus, and he shared their experiences of poverty and hostility directed at them by the powerful. Day-to-day contact reinforced and deepened his initial conviction that God's justice demanded a partiality toward the poor, the powerless, and the downtrodden.[28]

Second, Jesus historicized justice by fighting against specific injustices. The struggle brought him into conflict with the powerful. Nonetheless, he refused to retreat into a safer and abstract preaching about the ideal of justice, as though doing so would suffice to remove the oppression. The kingdom demands active struggle to overcome deeply entrenched injustices not removed simply by appealing to individual consciences. Sobrino, again contrasting his view of morality with that of natural law, says that it is not a matter of "doing good and avoiding evil," but "doing good and fighting evil to wipe it out."[29]

The third principle calls for an openness to continual conversion, and specifically openness to love as efficacious action and love as suffering. Jesus' own life demonstrated the need for continual openness to the Spirit of God, an openness that required change. Hence, Sobrino thinks of Jesus as undergoing conversions in response to the Spirit. Conversion, in this specific sense, means breaking with the past and surrendering to the new. As Jesus entered into his mission, he broke with his past, transcended his own interests, and placed his gifts in service of the kingdom. In his early Galilean ministry, he preached, healed, and changed people's ways of thinking and acting. In the later stages of his life, as he encountered mounting resistance to his ministry and even threats, his love became expressed through suffering. Following Jesus would require openness to both types of love: sometimes loving by healing, teaching, and defending others; at other times loving by enduring sickness, incarceration, and torture in solidarity with others.[30]

Sobrino maintains that these historicizing principles are universally valid throughout history. How can we be sure of their universality? By grasping the praxis of the historical Jesus.[31] As we saw earlier, Cook and Meier questioned precisely how Sobrino arrives at the historical Jesus. These critics

28. Sobrino, *Christology at the Crossroads*, 124.
29. Ibid., 125.
30. Ibid., 126.
31. Ibid., 138.

correctly observe that Sobrino does not identify the historical Jesus through historical criticism. Personal access to the historical Jesus, Sobrino says, is gained "by presenting his [Jesus'] practice in order to re-create it."[32] He argues that this practical knowledge of the historical Jesus is achieved by an affinity and connaturality that the community develops through its own praxis done in the spirit of Jesus. Sobrino's explanation seems to beg the question. How can one know whether one has captured the spirit of the historical Jesus unless one has learned by some means other than praxis?

Jon Nilson sheds light on this. Sobrino, he says, bases his theological reflection on a number of different, but mutually related, sources.[33] Sobrino says that the followers of Jesus grasp the experience of Jesus today in dialectical fashion by allowing the gospel to shape their praxis and by reading the gospel in light of their active commitment. The dialectical process includes community worship, church teaching, and a probing analysis of the social conditions in society. These combined sources help mediate the historical Jesus.

Sobrino's biographical study of Archbishop Romero merits discussion in some detail because Romero's conversion illustrates how the disciple appropriates the historical Jesus and his historicizing praxis. In the biographical work, *Archbishop Romero*, Sobrino describes a man who for most of his life lacked courage, feared conflict, and acted cautiously. Influenced by Opus Dei, he spoke out against priests and bishops who had accepted the Medellín line.[34] And yet Romero was a good person. He meditated on the gospel and carried out his priestly duties faithfully.

The crisis came soon after his installation as archibishop of San Salvador in 1977, when his good friend, Father Rutilio Grande, was assassinated. Gazing dumbstruck at the the the corpse of his friend, scales fell from Romero's eyes. The archbishop observed, "I thought Rutilio's ministry organizing the peasant farmlands was too political. But now I see Rutilio had been right after all."[35]

The archbishop now understood that Rutilio's advocacy for the campesinos that eventually led to his execution imitated the very life and mission of Jesus. Prior to this tragedy, the archbishop suffered from what Sobrino described as an interior division. He possessed high religious ideals and sought the good of his flock according to the social teachings of the church. Yet he

32. Jon Sobrino, *Jesus in Latin America* (Maryknoll, N.Y.: Orbis Books, 1987), 8.

33. Jon Nilson, "A Response to Jon P. Meier," *Proceedings of the Catholic Theological Society of America* 43 (1988): 16.

34. Jon Sobrino, *Archbishop Romero: Memories and Reflections*, trans. Robert R. Barr (Maryknoll, N.Y.: Orbis Books, 1990), 2–3.

35. Ibid., 10.

feared anything that would immerse the church in the conflictive, ambiguous struggle that marked his land. He grew agitated at his priests involved in community organizing and political movements. Now with the lifeless body of his friend before him, Sobrino observed at the wake, the will of God looked very different to Archbishop Romero.[36] Hundreds of peasants stared at the archbishop, wondering what he would do.

Romero made two moves. First, with the help of his priests and people, he undertook an analysis of the sociopolitical situation. Second, he committed himself to the peasants, an action that immediately drew severe conflict, hostility, arrests, and finally his assassination. Sobrino narrates how the poor peasants themselves communicated God's love to Romero and how the archbishop gratefully and generously responded to them. Almost instantly after he visited them, the people accepted, supported, and loved him. The poor literally swarmed about him, Sobrino says. They took him into their heart, and he drew them into his.

Thereafter, Romero read the gospel with a new perspective shaped by his conversion, by his daily contact with ugly repression, and by his social analysis. He began one homily: "I have the job of picking up the trampled, the corpses, and all that the persecution of the church dumps along the road on its way through."[37]

Romero believed that loving the poor called for analyzing the conditions that made them poor and then exposing these structures. His study led him to say in another sermon: "In El Salvador, we really have to say that the gap between the many who have nothing and the few who have everything is actually widening. This is the great evil in El Salvador: Wealth! Private property is an untouchable absolute. And woe to you if you touch this high tension wire. You'll get a bad burn" (August 12, 1979). Although this biography by Sobrino does not explicitly mention the three historicizing principles, the reader can readily recognize them in Romero's solidarity with the peasants, in his preaching like a prophet for a cessation of exploitation and war, and in his openness to change.

One might object that these historicizing principles are not normative guidelines but a strategy for praxis that in shorthand might be stated as follows: "Be partisan, fight against injustice, and be open to change." But what is justice? Whose side does one take when two groups among the poor take opposing positions on an issue? Vincent MacNamara earlier asked whether the experience of Jesus yielded any specific moral directives.

36. Ibid., 26.
37. Ibid., 25.

Sobrino answers that Jesus is not normative for Christians as law but as spirit. "The foundation of Christian morality is not some sort of indoctrination in what Jesus said we must do; rather, it is the experienced meaningfulness of the fact that he lived the life of faith in all its pristine fullness."[38] The disciples' experience of Jesus' life of faith inspires their re-creating the process of living the faith, and within this faith-context moral demands arise.

Certain features begin to emerge from Sobrino's model of discipleship. His discipleship exhibits characteristics of a contextualist ethics reminiscent of Juan Luis Segundo's ethics. Contextualism, according to Christian ethicist Paul Lehmann, begins within a community of faith (*koinonia*) that tries to respond to what God is doing in the world. The disciples respond by discerning what God is doing and then acting to make life more human.[39] Similarly, Sobrino's ethics operates within a community of disciples, which tries to discern how the spirit of Jesus is acting in the world. Sobrino's community asks, "What must be done in order to establish the kingdom of God in history?"

Sobrino's ethics also emphasizes praxis. One learns about justice in the doing, guided by the transforming spirit of Jesus. Yet Sobrino's emphasis assumes that the disciples understand justice and how justice can work to address the complexities of injustices in a concrete situation. Sobrino deals with the practical working of justice in the process he calls "Christian discernment."

Christian Discernment

Sobrino's Christian discernment develops from the historicizing principles of Jesus. In addition to these historicizing principles, Sobrino insists on verification as a part of Christian discernment. The latter weighs interior movements following upon a decision.[40] As the prototype, Jesus shows by his ministry *how* his disciples are to discern, not *what* they are to discern. In general, Christian discernment means hearing the Spirit of God, who utters a no to sinful and dehumanizing actions, and a yes to reconciling actions and acting accordingly.

Sobrino expands the principles into five criteria that he says guided the discernment of Jesus: (1) partial incarnation in history; (2) efficacious love; (3)

38. Sobrino, *Christology at the Crossroads*, 137.
39. James F. Childress, "Situation Ethics," *Westminster Dictionary of Christian Ethics*, ed. James F. Childress and John Macquarrie (Philadelphia: Westminster Press, 1986), 586–88.
40. William C. Spohn, "Discernment," *The Westminster Dictionary of Christian Ethics*, 158.

justice or sociopolitical love; (4) openness to conflictive love; and (5) verification.[41] These criteria may assist today's disciples to discern a course of action, but their own praxis will lead them to other criteria more suitable for their specific context.

The first criterion, partial incarnation, requires that the community first decide in which context it will do its discernment. Sobrino thinks the world of the poor and oppressed serves as the best context. He does not imply this means living with the poor; Sobrino, in fact, lives on a university campus. It means listening to the poor with a critical ear and committing oneself to their full liberation. Why approach discernment through the perspective of the poor? Not because they are more virtuous, more wise, or even more open than the rich, as some theologians have suggested.[42] His primary reasons for deciding on the world of the poor as the theological context (*locus theologicus*) are threefold: it is a graced situation that will move us to see better, to defend life, and to come to life ourselves. "When all is said and done," Sobrino summarizes, "it is the God crucified in the poor who moves us to conversion."[43]

The second criterion, effective love, serves another for the sake of the other. Sobrino illustrates this efficacious love through the parable of the good Samaritan who chooses to become neighbor to the injured traveler, a longstanding enemy. By putting himself in the path of the injured person, the Samaritan becomes his neighbor. His love, born of God's gratuitous love, establishes a new kind of relationship.

The third criterion, justice or sociopolitical love, addresses the whole of society, especially its sociopolitical dimension, but approaches the totality through preference for the particular group whose needs are greatest. Sobrino rejects justice as retribution—"giving to each what is due by virtue of who they are."[44] He defines justice as re-creating a person's or a group's present situation. "The justice of Jesus points toward some new form of social coexistence where class differences have been abolished, at least in principle."[45] Sobrino sees class differences as the fundamental inequality in El Salvador, but he also speaks about the injustices of religious oppression and racism, and injustices done to individual persons.

Justice, in its challenging institutional power, inevitably encounters conflict. The fourth criterion, openness to conflictive love, guides the disciple

41. Sobrino, *Jesus in Latin America*, 135–37.
42. James Tunstead Burtchaell, *The Giving and Taking of Life* (Notre Dame: University of Notre Dame Press, 1989), 191–97.
43. Sobrino, *Spirituality of Liberation*, 113.
44. Sobrino, *Christology at the Crossroads*, 119.
45. Ibid., 120.

through darkness and situations involving repression. Love in this context encourages the disciple to risk in spite of uncertainties and hostilities, including kidnappings, tortures, and guerrilla war. Conflictive love teaches the disciple how to love the enemy. Love means facing up to enemies with winning them over as the long-range goal. In Sobrino's words, it means not closing off their future. Finally, conflictive love means willingness to surrender one's active power to change things. Stricken with illness or rendered immobile by imprisonment, the disciple serves by silent witness.

The second, third, and fourth criteria are three aspects of love that develop organically one from another. Love moves from effective action to a praxis of sociopolitical love, or justice, and then to love as an openness to conflict. Love in these three forms is a gift received from God and a gift to be freely shared with others. It consists of life-giving deeds (praxis) and not simply of good intentions.

The fifth and final criterion, verification, looks at consequences. It weighs how a decision already acted upon affects the actors, the oppressed, and the adversary. The kingdom of God suggests positive signs supporting the decision: an increase of faith, hope, and love over incredulity, despair, and oppression; consolation flowing from the decision that sacrificed on behalf of others; and whether action was done in the spirit of the beatitudes. Sobrino identifies a negative indicator: whether the powerful forces respond by threats and reprisals or by a willingness to discuss the issue.[46]

Issue: Should a University Be Partisan?

In his early writings, Sobrino rarely applied his ethics of discipleship to social problems. In his recent writings, however, he addressed an important issue: whether or not a Christian university should commit itself to the service of the poor and oppressed. He first reflected upon this question at a conference at the University of Deusto, Bilbao, Spain, where he argued that the Christian university must place its scholarly research, teaching, and social projects at the service of and in solidarity with the poor.[47] About two-and-a-half years later, following the assassination of six of his Jesuit colleagues and two coworkers at the University of Central America in San Salvador, he again addressed the issue in a book entitled *Companions of Jesus: The Jesuit Martyrs of El Salvador.*

46. Sobrino, *Jesus in Latin America*, 137.
47. Jon Sobrino, "Inspiración Cristiana de la Universidad," *Estudios Centroamericanos*, 468 (October 1987) 695–705. This article was translated and privately distributed by Simon Smith.

He was answering questions asked about his slain university colleagues. Who were they? Why were they killed? Who killed them?[48]

In this book, Sobrino affirmed what he had said in the first writing about the Christian university's commitment to the poor. These university academics were murdered, he said, because they did what Sobrino had earlier argued all Christian universities should do—namely, promote the liberation of the poor. In defending the mass of poor people, the Jesuits challenged the idols of wealth; in retaliation, the idols crushed them. In both writings Sobrino justified the position taken by the university on the basis of criteria enunciated earlier. In his second writing, Sobrino developed a theological as well as a rare philosophical-ethical defense of his colleagues' corporate commitment to the poor.

In his address at the University of Deusto, Sobrino posed the question whether a university can live in accordance with its Christian inspiration, in particular whether a university's research, curriculum, projects, and policies should embody the values of God's kingdom. Concretely, this means placing the university's whole social weight at the service of the poor. Sobrino argues that to be faithful to its inspiration the university should so commit itself. He first analyzes why Christian universities have not made this commitment. Then he argues his position on the basis of two principles. Finally, he deals with objections.

Sobrino begins with his analysis of why so many universities have not remained faithful to their Christian inspiration: seeking truth, defending life, and working for justice and freedom. In practice, they have more frequently supported values and policies of the antikingdom, preferring falsehood over truth, death over life, oppression over justice, and repression over freedom.[49] The fact that Christian universities have not distinguished themselves by their opposition to unjust social structures can be explained, first, by the university's selective incarnation in social reality and, second, by an unreflective appeal to its autonomy in doing research, writing, and teaching.[50]

First, the university is necessarily incarnated in social reality. But because it requires abundant resources for subsistence and growth, it has often allied itself with conservative, even reactionary, forces within the church and in society. Consequently, the university has become overprudent, unwilling to risk decisions that might threaten powerful forces. As the university drew closer to the centers of power and wealth, it moved away from the reality of the poor and the most marginalized.

48. Jon Sobrino et al., *Companions of Jesus: The Jesuit Martyrs of El Salvador* (Maryknoll, N.Y.: Orbis Books, 1990).
49. Sobrino, "Inspiración Cristiana de la Universidad," 696.
50. Ibid.

Second, the university has appealed to its autonomy in an uncritical way. Autonomy in itself is both good and necessary for a university. Yet without critical reflection on its autonomy, the university can be deceived into thinking it seeks knowledge through the instrumentality of reason alone. It fails to perceive that self-interest often precedes and conditions the quest for knowledge. A university can search for certain aspects of the truth while suppressing other aspects, all for the sake of one interest group over another. In the name of knowledge, the university can serve the social reality around it or abandon it to its own misery. The university's department of theology, for example, may ignore the hopes of the poor by detaching its own investigations from the everyday faith-life of the people.

Moreover, this unexamined sense of autonomy has led the university to treat knowledge simply as noetic, thereby divorcing scholarly insight from ethical and practical responsibility. Reason, however, should never claim immunity from acting responsibly, as Sobrino's colleague, Ignacio Ellacuría, maintained. "To study a situation," Ellacuría said, "is indissolubly linked with accepting the burden of that situation and becoming responsible for the situation."[51] Sobrino's historical-philosophical social analysis concludes that the Christian university *should* commit itself solidly to the poor and marginalized.[52] Social analysis for Sobrino, and for liberation theologians generally, includes an evaluative component. In its exploration of what is, analysis implies what should be.

Sobrino argues that conclusion on the basis of three principles: (1) fidelity to the kingdom of God demands it; (2) the option for the poor requires it; (3) the good consequences of the university's commitment verify the correctness of the policy. These principles are variant expressions of his criteria for Christian discernment. Sobrino relates the option for the poor to the common good as well as to its theological foundations.

Fidelity to the Kingdom

The kingdom of God, Sobrino says, serves as both the horizon and the finality of a Christian university. As horizon, the kingdom throws into sharp relief the crisis and evil of the old world, especially the crisis of meaning and threats to human life. More than one-third (170 million people) of Latin America's total population in the year 2000 will be unable to satisfy its subsistence

51. Ibid., 697.
52. Sobrino provides no historical data to support his analysis, for example, names of universities, periods of close alliances with the state, conservative church, specific policies of the universities, etc.

needs. Unjust and oppressive economic structures effect biological poverty, bringing slow death by starvation. Repression and wars spawned by poverty produce sudden and violent death.[53] This world of death seeks to thwart God's purpose for humankind. In the midst of this sinful situation, the spirit of Jesus proclaims the kingdom of life through his followers.

As the finality of human existence, the kingdom demands that the university seek its center outside itself. This love command urges institutions as well as individuals to reach out to society and lead it toward the ultimate goal of the kingdom. The university serves society by directing its own diverse functions—research, teaching, and social projects—toward the transformation of society and thus toward the ultimate goal of the kingdom. It must also challenge the sin of the antikingdom by unmasking its operations, even at the risk of attacks and persecution. Thus, the university can inspire hope and a sense of meaning in the midst of dire poverty and senseless violence.

The university's commitment to transform society in accordance with God's kingdom enriches the life of the university as well. Its orientation toward the kingdom unifies its understanding of the diverse operations of the institution. The university, for example, can establish its investigations of social reality in accordance with the kingdom, bring the results of its investigations into the classroom, and communicate its findings to the public at large. This kind of service, undertaken in cooperation with other groups and done for the sake of people in society, builds coresponsibility and reconciliation. Moreover, these cooperative efforts give the university a sense of dignity, meaning, and joy.[54]

Option for the Poor

The second principle, option for the poor, specifies the general command to serve society by calling it to assist the most needy in society. Invoking this principle as a guiding norm may baffle some, Sobrino suggests, precisely because the university's partiality toward the poor appears to threaten its universality.

What does the option mean within a university context and in what sense does it oblige the Christian university? Making a choice for solidarity with the poor does not mean inserting itself into the neighborhood of the poor; nor does it mean changing its membership to include more poor students (though such a decision would contribute significantly to this solidarity); and, finally,

53. Sobrino, "Inspiración Cristiana de la Universidad," 698–99.
54. Ibid., 699.

it does not mean abandoning scholarly research and writing. The option does mean that the university take seriously the real problems of the poor.

Sobrino argues that solidarity with the poor obligates a Christian university because Christian faith calls it to make the commitment, because it promotes the common good, and because it benefits the university. Faith obligates in the sense of moving persons to give freely to others what they have been freely given by God. The Christian university should be generous in helping the poor simply because they are poor.

By committing itself to the poor, the university pursues the good of all concerned. Although Sobrino does not use the term "common good," he employs its argument. Option for the poor, he says, does not focus on one part (the poor) while ignoring other groups. Like Saint Thomas's understanding of the common good, Sobrino assumes that the whole (global society) is greater than any one of its parts. Therefore, each of the parts should pursue the good of the whole by cooperative ventures. Then why focus on the poor? Because their need is greatest—the majority of the world faces unemployment and malnutrition. Wide-scale structural problems demand a perspective that views the world from the situation of Third World majorities. Solidarity with poor nations must precede universal solidarity, and this process includes reparation and forgiveness for centuries of oppression. Serving the Third World enables the servant to recover the dignity of being a human person.[55]

Option for the poor benefits the university. Seeing the world from the perspective of the poor instills a universal awareness in the university not obtained elsewhere. In working on behalf of the poor, university members can see the nonbeing, oppression, death, pain, and protest that strike a sharp contrast to life on the university campus. Moreover, engagement with the poor renders the university credible as a Christian university. This in turn enhances its influence in society.

Sobrino responds to the objection that partisanship contradicts the important value of pluralism within the university. If one defines pluralism as neutrality, then a preferential option for the poor would have no place in the university. But pluralism cannot mean neutrality, because a university's mission entails serving society, especially addressing its most severe problems, situations of misery, and injustices. On the contrary, the university's partisanship in favor of society's most vulnerable members can foster pluralism by bringing together diverse disciplines and a variety of religious perspectives to work cooperatively on improving the lives of the poor.[56]

55. Ibid., 705.
56. Sobrino et al., *Companions of Jesus*, 18.

Verification

The principle of verification corroborates or challenges the decision on the basis of its consequences. Certain positive and negative indicators serve as a type of discernment of spirits applied to the social level. Negatively, if praxis on behalf of the poor and oppressed encounters threats, even violent reprisals by the forces of power, and if faith, hope, and love replace incredulity, despair, and oppression, then the university has made a good decision in its option for the poor.

The Jesuits of Central American University, including Sobrino, Ellacuría, and Ignacio Martín Baró, had indeed committed their institution to the service of the poor for well over a decade. And they paid the price. Over fifteen years, the Jesuits at the university received threats, anonymous letters, fantastic accusations appearing in editorials and advertisements, sometimes paid for by the army, demanding the expulsion or annihilation of these Jesuits. Paramilitary forces bombed the university in 1976, and since that time they planted bombs on fifteen other occasions in the print room, the computer center, the library, and the administration building. In 1980 midnight raiders strafed the house with machine-gun fire.

But critics, both in the United States and in El Salvador, have tried to negate Sobrino's principle of verification, supplying alternate reasons why these Jesuits were killed. They accused the Jesuits running this university of being Marxists, antipatriotic, and the ideological front for the FMLN, which the government blamed for the violence and the ten-year-old war. Sobrino provides abundant evidence that the charges are false. Those who killed the Jesuits used these false reasons because they could not justify their actions on moral grounds. In fact, the university sought peace through dialogue and by negotiation, doing "everything it could to enable dialogue to take place by speaking to both sides. President Cristiani knows this perfectly well."[57] Sobrino also points out the signs of hope that grew from the assassinations.

Assessment

In assessing Sobrino's ethics of discipleship, one should bear in mind his primary objective: to show the import for Christian morality of a Christology based on the history of Jesus' own faith. Sobrino's linking Christology with morality provides us with a vision of justice that embodies a coherent set of perspectives capable of inspiring participation in efforts to bring about radical change in society. It neglects a theory of justice that would present specific

---

57. Sobrino et al., *Companions of Jesus*, 20.

principles, relative rights, and mutual duties that address the ethical complexities in political-economic issues.[58] This appraisal concentrates primarily on his more modest aim to construct a vision of justice, specifically, on his efforts to ground moral obligation in his theological convictions and to present his perspectives on God's kingdom.

In his more recent writings, however, he has also tried to develop normative criteria and, in one instance at least, has even applied them. Therefore, it would seem appropriate to comment on, but not to review with the same rigor, his normative ethics.

Strengths

Sobrino presents a remarkably consistent vision of the foundation of Christian morality developed from the kingdom of God. He demonstrates how the imperative (e.g., commit oneself to the poor) arises from a graced encounter with the spirit of Jesus mediated through the Bible, community worship, historical events, and through the poor themselves. His grounding obligation in gratuity respects God's initiative and power, as well as human freedom. By fostering a spirituality that reproduces the message and actions of Jesus as a whole and not simply his prescriptive pronouncements, Sobrino avoids the pitfall of Christian fundamentalism, often found in Latin American church movements, that stresses strict and literal adherence to divine commands in the Bible. The acknowledged differences between the biblical cultural context and the Latin American situation today evince Sobrino's sensitivity toward his use of the Bible as a source to illumine issues, not to prescribe solutions. By relying on general principles found throughout the four Gospels for guiding Christian praxis, Sobrino avoids the pitfall of ethical fundamentalism.

Second, Sobrino handles skillfully the knotty problem of conflict versus class struggle. On the one hand, he does not soften the gospel's radical demand for social justice that inevitably involves conflict with political powers. On the other hand, he neither accepts the Marxist vision of the classless society nor the Marxist strategy that sees class struggle as the necessary path to achieve a socialist society. By upholding God's kingdom as the ethical as well as the utopian standard of societal transformation, Sobrino envisions with the Boffs and Gutiérrez a qualitatively new and interdependent society built on just relationships. This new society operates through dialogue and cooperation,

58. David Hollenbach, "Modern Catholic Teachings Concerning Justice," in *The Faith That Does Justice*, ed. John C. Haughey (New York: Paulist Press, 1977), 214. I follow the distinction Hollenbach makes between a vision of justice and a theory of justice.

even though the full realization of such a society is achieved by partial solidarity involving conflict.

Third, Sobrino steers clear of an individualistic ethics by building discipleship on the basis of the total life of Jesus (his message and his praxis) and not merely on his moral injunctions. The whole life of Jesus, by showing the inseparable unity of God and neighbor, opposes an ethics that emphasizes the vertical relationship between Jesus and the individual. Moreover, Sobrino locates the process of Christian discernment within the Christian base community, which interprets Scripture in light of the people's life and illumines their life in light of Scripture.

Fourth, although Sobrino has not developed a theory of justice, he has proposed a type of eschatological justice that integrates important elements needed for a social ethics. He shows that justice as partial solidarity is not the absolute end point, and so Salvadorans must never lose sight of universal solidarity. Thus Sobrino guards against absolutizing a particular liberative practice.[59] He also sensitizes his people against the temptation to become dogmatic in their analysis, interpretation, and observation of facts. Finally, his emphasis on the eschatological nature of justice cautions the disciple regarding the use of power to change structures. "Power tends innately to serve the interests of self-assertion."[60]

Limitations

Certain limitations of Sobrino's Christian ethics stem from the inherent weakness of discipleship as an ethics;[61] others arise from his use of sources. The ethics of discipleship relies principally on the Bible to shape the identity of the community of disciples and to give it general directives for its mission. Sobrino correctly recognizes that Scripture does not provide disciples with a moral code. He holds fast to his conviction that God's love experienced in conversion generates moral obligations within the moral subject. Hence, he never slips into a heteronomous morality that appeals to biblical injunctions. But, as Sobrino acknowledges, imperatives based on God's gratuitous love are general in nature and so cannot deal adequately with the complexities of agrarian

59. Sobrino, *Spirituality of Liberation*, 28.
60. Ibid.
61. Patricia A. Schoelles, "Discipleship and Social Ethics: Defining Boundaries for the Church of the Diaspora," *The Annual of the Society of Christian Ethics*, ed. D. M. Yeager, 1989: 200–201. The author says that discipleship "does not provide a solution to particular moral dilemmas or public policy issues for the churches." It does, however, offer a context within which to resolve issues.

reform, external debt, and political relationships. Therefore, specific criteria for dealing with issues in Latin America arise from Christian discernment carried out within the community. He says that the praxis of the poor provides moral insight into what ought to be done. But Sobrino remains vague about the nature of this content.

Although option for the poor serves as an adequate general standard for evaluating structures and for proposing alternatives, it does not suffice by itself in more specific dilemmas. It does not tell us how justice for the poor relates to justice for the whole. Sobrino seems to acknowledge this when he invokes an argument based on the common good in order to support the university's option for the poor. Moreover, it does not illumine how the poor themselves resolve issues affecting them, such as whether peasants should support the guerrilla forces or the army in El Salvador. Sobrino maintains that the struggle for justice, even when undertaken in a just manner, elicits some degree of violence and in some extreme instances "legitimate armed insurrection."[62] What legitimates the use of arms in the latter instance? Sobrino does not elaborate on this.

A second limitation deals with Sobrino's use of sources. As Cook and Meier pointed out, Sobrino interprets the historical Jesus as the totality of Jesus' history, and in doing so claims too much. Such a historical picture of Jesus is impossible to retrieve. Meier credits Sobrino for at least examining three criteria of historicity, but faults him for not using them in any detail.[63]

Sobrino's choice of words—"the totality of Jesus' history"—may not be the best language for expressing what he searches for in the gospel. Sobrino seeks access to a personal Jesus, which he feels can be obtained through the practice of Jesus and not simply by his message and knowledge about Jesus. He makes a legitimate claim that a people may know the personal Jesus through mediations other than historical criticism, such as community worship, praxis, and reflection on the praxis. As Jon Nilson replied to Meier's critique of Sobrino, other forms of mediation (e.g., a living tradition) yield reliable knowledge of Jesus. *Dei Verbum* teaches the same.[64] The danger lies in imposing a certain interpretation on Scripture in order to substantiate a theological position, a practice Meier calls "proof-texting." Cook and Meier make an important corrective of Sobrino's hermeneutics.

Meier further objects to Sobrino's tendency to lump together three groups—the poor, the oppressed, and sinners—as the special objects of Jesus'

62. Sobrino, *Jesus in Latin America*, 163–64.
63. Meier, "The Bible as a Source for Theology," 7.
64. Nilson, "Response to John P. Meier," 17.

favor, a partisanship that incurred the hostility of the religious leaders and that
finally led to his death. Two comments should be made about this criticism.
First, Sobrino does distinguish these various groups, though certainly not with
the sophistication of E. P. Sanders in his scholarly work *Jesus and Judaism*, on
which Meier bases his objection.[65] Although Sobrino uses the term "poor" to
include the public sinners, the paralytics, and prostitutes, he more frequently
refers to them as the poor and the oppressed, or the poor and the outcasts.[66]
Second, as Arthur McGovern correctly observed, Sobrino does not argue that
Jesus' solidarity with the poor led to his crucifixion, as Meier asserts.[67] Sobrino,
in fact, acknowledges other reasons for Jesus' death, including accusations of
blasphemy and political agitation. He does maintain, however, that proclaiming
the good news to the poor, sinners, and outcasts, and challenging the forces
of oppression, brought Jesus into conflict with the religious authorities.

Two Tensions

Sobrino's discipleship raises two questions for social ethics: the tension
between the church as prophet and the church as reconciler; the tension between
an ethics that is partisan and an ethics that is impartial.

The first tension, between prophet and mediator, manifests itself in Sobrino's discussion of the Christian university's double commitment of solidarity
and reconciliation. His idea of a university functions something like a church:
it gathers people to reflect on their faith, it teaches its students, it researches
issues affecting the poor and oppressed, and it becomes involved with social
and religious organizations in El Salvador. It operates primarily as a prophetic
church by denouncing the powerful forces exploiting the weak. Even though
this model embodies certain elements of the sect (its emphasis on social justice,
its viewing itself as struggling against an antikingdom, its kinship with the
beatitudes, and its emphasis on praxis), Sobrino's model of church does not,
like the sect, withdraw from society in order to act as a countersign to an evil
world. Rather, it holds this prophetic tendency in tension with a reconciling
spirit that opens itself to dialogue with the adversary and offers to mediate
between the guerrillas and government officials.

Sobrino's prophetic and reconciling church also differs from the traditional Christendom model of church that has sought compromises and alliances
with the state in order to proclaim the gospel without state interference and

65. E. P. Sanders, *Jesus and Judaism* (Philadelphia: Fortress Press, 1985).

66. Sobrino, *Jesus in Latin America*, 140–47.

67. Arthur F. McGovern, *Liberation Theology and Its Critics* (Maryknoll, N.Y.:
Orbis Books, 1989), 81.

even to gain state support for its moral stances (e.g., antiabortion and anti-divorce laws).

Sobrino's prophetic-reconciling church stands midway between the sect and the Christendom type. Choosing neither to withdraw nor to compromise its prophetic mission, the church experiences a pull in both directions. Given the strain inherent in this church, one wonders how it maintains a healthy balance. Can this model long survive as both prophet and mediator, unmasking the unjust operations of the powerful elite and then calling the adversary to dialogue with the very people it exploits?

The second tension exists between Sobrino's ethics of discipleship, which identifies itself as partisan, and the fact that ethics, by its very nature, must impartially or objectively consider each group's interests and make judgments on the basis of fair analysis. Indeed, Sobrino himself argues that discipleship must seek the truth of the situation. This tension raises the issue whether a partisan can be truly objective. In making a case for the university's siding with the poor, Sobrino thinks that the university has been objective, or impartial, by its openness to both sides of the issues. He points out that his own university's willingness to dialogue is a manifestation of its seeking the truth.

Some observers might object that Sobrino did not discuss opposing viewpoints of those groups within and outside the university. He answers that few universities have dealt more openly with their critics on a local and global scale. Central American University has, in fact, brought to the conference table both the FMLN and government forces in an effort to get closer to the truth. Whether partisan ethics can maintain objectivity in situations of conflict, however, is a difficult question for any ethics to answer.

This chapter has examined Sobrino's discipleship as an important model of liberation ethics. Focusing on its foundations, moral content, and application, the examiner recognizes a coherence in this ethics grounded in the kingdom of God, which serves as the horizon, finality, and ultimate standard for followers of Jesus. On the normative level of ethics, this ethics operates as moral discernment within a Christian community. When Sobrino deals with concrete issues in a pluralistic context, such as the role of the university in societal change, he supplements his theological arguments with philosophical reasons. This should not be interpreted as a deficiency, because it strengthens his overall argument. Moreover, as his colleagues Ignacio Ellacuría and Gustavo Gutiérrez have maintained, a connaturality exists between the human and the divine.

Sobrino has built a solid foundation on which Latin American ethicists can develop the normative dimension. Sobrino and his fellow moralists might monitor and reflect upon how Christian communities resolve concrete dilemmas today in El Salvador. This would illumine how the sources of praxis, analysis, and Scripture provide moral insight (and possibly moral norms), which in turn might prove helpful to other communities facing similar dilemmas.

7
Ethics of Power

The second model of liberation ethics addresses power. The best representative of this Christian political ethics is José Míguez Bonino, Methodist minister, professor of systematic theology at the Instituto Superior Evangélico de Estudios Teológicos in Buenos Aires, and former president of the World Council of Churches. His ethics addresses the use of political-economic power, the relation of church and state, and the acquisition of power by the oppressed. Although he makes use of the same foundational sources and perspective of solidarity with the poor as Jon Sobrino, he differs from Sobrino by explicitly attending to political power. Moreover, he presents a distinct perspective among the liberation theologians by integrating his Protestant tradition with a deep knowledge of and respect for the Roman Catholic tradition.

A Passionate and Terrible Experience

Like Sobrino, Míguez Bonino begins with praxis of the people, which he narrates by means of stories. These narratives establish the composition of place wherein a people's commitments, existential questions, and collective wisdom emerge as a font for his theology. His stories also reveal the spirit of the man: his faith, commitment to the poor, and radical approach to doing Christian ethics.[1]

1. José Míguez Bonino, *Doing Theology in a Revolutionary Situation* (Philadelphia: Fortress Press, 1975), xxi–xxv. In the Introduction to this book, he narrates the story of a remarkable gathering of Catholics and Protestants in Santiago, Chile, who participated in the creation of an international group called "Christians for Socialism." In describing this convention aimed at building a democratic socialist society, rethinking its faith, and reexamining its attitude of love for the oppressed, Míguez Bonino reveals his own militancy for liberative change motivated by his radical commitment to the oppressed and the poor. Like these radical Christians, he too analyzes political structures that oppress.

He begins his systematic study of Christian political ethics by telling a story about an anonymous letter that landed on his desk. It described a fifteen-year struggle of Christian activists for political liberation. "These men and women, these groups have to 'process,' they have to 'put in black and white' the experience of these last decades, a passionate and terrible experience—paid many times in blood—of an intensity and complexity that has had no parallel in the Christian history of our continent."[2]

Although Míguez Bonino gives no details about this experience, it must have at least involved severe repression by the Argentine military forces, especially during the "dirty war" from 1976 to 1982. On March 24, 1976, the military junta, in a bloodless coup, overthrew Isabel Perón, who had assumed the presidency after the death of her husband Juan. Like a dragnet, the military forces then systematically swept up and destroyed all radical movements, leftist sympathizers, and dissenters of various stripes. They eliminated the guerrilla movements of the Montoneros and the People's Revolutionary Army (ERP). Dressed in mufti and driving unmarked Ford Falcons, soldiers abducted, tortured, and killed many thousands of people suspected of supporting subversive activity during this six-year period. The regime's repressive measures rivaled in every respect—and in some ways exceeded—the terror in Chile following Pinochet's coup in 1973.

Whatever this "passionate and terrible experience" involved, it brought home to these activists how ill prepared they were to engage in this conflictual, violent work.[3] They also discovered "how crudely ambiguous and dirty political life is." Even more disconcerting, they could not grasp the deeper significance of their political activity. The theological language of their confessional world was a foreign tongue in the world of politics.

But for all their disillusionment, they held fast to this conviction: they must "name and confess" God "from within the womb of politics, from within the very heart of commitment." Naming the true God meant first denouncing the false ones; confessing God called for staking "one's life with and for the poor." Míguez Bonino gained an insight from their political praxis. Their engagement, he said, bears witness to a reality that no Christian can escape: living the faith involves political struggle. Yet the struggle is colored with ambiguity. "[Political struggle] both confers meaning on and denies meaning to human plans and actions, encompasses and invades all areas of human existence, and offers and dispenses both life and death to thousands of millions."[4] Liberation pursued in solidarity with the oppressed changes faith itself.

2. Míguez Bonino, *Toward a Christian Political Ethics*, 7.

3. For details on the "dirty war," see John Simpson and Jana Bennett, *The Disappeared and the Mothers of the Plaza* (New York: St. Martin's Press, 1985), 15.

4. Míguez Bonino, *Toward a Christian Political Ethics*, 8.

Faith dies in the struggle and then is reborn. The rebirth in turn transforms the way the disciples confess Christ, pray, receive the sacrament, and wait for eternal life. For all the moral ambiguity and meaninglessness in their battle for liberation, these Christians felt empowered and led by the Spirit of God.

The political ethics of José Míguez Bonino, therefore, encompasses both the transformation of the human subject and the changing of institutions. The source for both transformations is the Spirit of God, who is the ultimate power that addresses earthly powers and powerlessness. God's Spirit is active in the world through Christ, and Christ's active presence in the world constitutes the kingdom of God. Pervading all political existence, the kingdom serves as the ultimate standard of truth and justice.[5] The crucified and risen Christ protects the powerless, judges the unjust, and encourages all to commit themselves to the poor.[6]

Míguez Bonino's theological project involves creating an ethics that relates God's power to political power. More specifically, he is intent on showing how the kingdom of God addresses the dominating power of the elite and the subordinate power of the masses. In presenting the political ethics of Míguez Bonino, I shall first show how he grounds ethics in the kingdom. Then I shall discuss his method of doing ethics within the framework of the hermeneutical circle. Finally, I shall discuss his strategies for social change, with special concern for the problem of violence.

God's Kingdom as the Standard of Justice

Beginning with the eschatological foundations, Míguez Bonino undertakes the task of showing how God's actions relate to human efforts. He asks himself and the reader: "How are we to understand the active and dynamic presence of God's kingdom in our history so that we can adapt our witness and activity to it?"[7] He searches for an answer by examining two historical answers: monism and dualism.

The monistic perspective, represented by Ireneaus and Origen, emphasized the immanence of God by closely relating eschatological time with historical time, and God's action with certain events in history. The Marx and Engels critiques of religion rejected eschatological reality. Their radical monism envisioned human liberation occurring entirely within history.

5. Míguez Bonino, *Doing Theology in a Revolutionary Situation*, 150.

6. Míguez Bonino, *Toward a Christian Political Ethics*, 96.

7. José Míguez Bonino, "Historical Praxis and Christian Identity," in *Frontiers of Theology in Latin America*, ed. Rosino Gibellini, trans. John Drury (Maryknoll, N.Y.: Orbis Books, 1979), 266.

Liberation theologians have rejected radical monism and, in fact, would not regard their theology as monistic at all. Yet their close weaving of God's justice with liberating praxis, and their strong opposition to dualistic approaches, have led some theologians to brand their theology "monistic." Even Míguez Bonino expressed reservation about Gutiérrez's infelicitous expression: "there is only one history—a 'Christo-finalized' history."[8] Míguez Bonino insists upon always making explicit the two reference points of divine revelation and human transformation. In doing so, he feels he avoids the pitfall of absolutizing all praxis as liberative and Spirit-directed.[9]

Furthermore, he thinks the one-history notion of Gutiérrez presupposes a natural law framework in which grace builds on nature and in this nature God's will can be discerned. His perception of a natural law presupposition in the theology of Gutiérrez may be correct, though the monist label seems misplaced.[10] Míguez Bonino seems to be operating in the same theological key as Gutiérrez by using the praxis of Christians and social analysis to find out what God wants and how human beings should respond. He feels, as does Gutiérrez, that God's action in the world cannot be adequately understood without using these tools. This basic similarity causes me to wonder whether his insistence on making explicit his twofold referent constitutes a real or a linguistic disagreement with Gutiérrez.

If the latter's eschatology seems tinged with monistic elements, European theologies appear to Míguez Bonino as exhibiting traces of dualism. The Europeans do this, he says, by relegating secular history to a secondary role and by not examining concrete political realities. For them historical liberation appears to be an inauthentic type of freedom. Moreover, their eschatologies fail to connect the action of God with the action of human participants.[11] The prophetic word, Míguez Bonino says, must ring "with the authenticity of God's proclamation in Jesus Christ while also addressing the reality of human historical existence."[12]

8. Gutiérrez, *Theology of Liberation*, 86.

9. Gutiérrez distinguishes three dimensions of the one salvific history (political, human, religious).

10. Although Gutiérrez does not identify himself with the natural law tradition, he speaks about the middle personal dimension of his tripartite division of liberation that in some respects functions as a kind of natural law: it mediates faith and politics. As for Míguez Bonino's criticism that Gutiérrez's "one history" notion carries monistic connotations, the latter carefully argues against such a reductionism. See Gutiérrez, *Theology of Liberation*, xxxix.

11. Míguez Bonino, *Doing Theology in a Revolutionary Situation*, 139–40.

12. Míguez Bonino, *Toward a Christian Political Ethics*, 33.

He regards Moltmann's political theology as the best of the European theologies. He feels indebted to his European colleague for showing how God's kingdom relates to the political world. Christian hope, symbolized in the resurrection of Jesus Christ, engenders hope in the faithful and casts judgment on unbelievers. Hope inspires people to transform their political reality.[13] God identifies himself with the poor, the estranged, and the forsaken through the suffering of Jesus Christ. Experiencing abandonment in his crucifixion and death, Jesus demonstrated his solidarity with those who feel abandoned in their own suffering. Moltmann's Christology explains how oppressed and suffering Christians today live in solidarity with Jesus, the crucified God. By accepting their own cross in the manner of Jesus, imitators of Christ thereby enter into the hope of the resurrection. Moltmann's drawing a closer connection between the cross and the resurrection enables believers to see better how Christ's promise of resurrected life leads a suffering people to a mission involving resistance to and denunciation of social evils.[14]

Although Míguez Bonino endorses the general structure of Moltmann's political ethics, he criticizes it because it describes contemporary social evils only in an abstract, superficial way. His theology fails to uncover the roots of poverty, racism, and the destruction of the ecosystem. Lacking a coherent socioanalytical instrument, Moltmann's theology does not show how demonic circles of death oppress people through historical institutions or how one exploitive corporation conspires with another. Nor does his theology analyze how Christian churches became enmeshed in and compromised by their relationship with the state and private corporations. Consequently, his political ethics has an idealistic ring.[15] Míguez Bonino would endorse Gutiérrez's observation that Moltmann's theology of hope cannot find a language sufficiently rooted in concrete experience and in the possibilities of liberation.[16]

In response to this critique, Moltmann admonished Míguez Bonino for seeing the speck in the eye of the European political theologians while failing to see the beam in his own. The beam was Míguez Bonino's dualistic eschatology—the same shaky foundation supposedly sighted by him in the European theologies. Writing in 1976, Moltmann fired this volley into the Argentine theologian's court: "Your Barthianism always lets you distinguish neatly between what God does and what human beings do. But at the same time, you reproach Barth, the Europeans and thus, in the same breath, also yourself for

---

13. Jürgen Moltmann, *Theology of Hope: On the Ground and Implications of a Christian Eschatology* (New York: Harper & Row, 1967), 15–36.

14. Míguez Bonino, *Doing Theology in a Revolutionary Situation*, 145.

15. Ibid., 149.

16. Gutiérrez, *Theology of Liberation*, 124.

not overcoming this dualism through a new, historical-dialectical way of think-ing."[17] Moltmann judged that Míguez Bonino's eschatological ethics had not advanced beyond what Barth, Bonhoeffer, Metz, and Moltmann himself had already developed. Míguez Bonino had shown that eschatological promise revealed the meaning of human existence and that it had guided believers in their work of transforming the temporal order. But European theologians Barth and Moltmann had already said that. What was distinctive about the Latin American approach?

Given his differences with both Gutiérrez and Moltmann, one may won-der where Míguez Bonino locates himself on the eschatological continuum relative to the monistic and dualistic polarities. I would place him between the dualistic-leaning Moltmann and the monistic-leaning Gutiérrez. Like Molt-mann, he insists on making explicit God's revelation as the power pushing and pulling oppressed people toward liberation. But Míguez Bonino stands closer to Gutiérrez in his underscoring emancipatory praxis by human beings in response God's action. Both theologians use social sciences and praxis to gain a deeper understanding of the concrete world in which God's word is revealed. They strive to see the face of God in the faces of the wretched and oppressed.

Míguez Bonino is more cautious than Gutiérrez in steering clear from identifying projects with the kingdom of God. Hence, he avoids language such as "building the kingdom" that would seem to equate liberating activity with the kingdom itself. Yet Gutiérrez does not identify God's reign with historical embodiments of human liberation, but distinguishes between the "growth" and the "coming" of the kingdom of God. "Growth of the kingdom" for Gutiérrez means salvific activity that points to the fullness of the kingdom; whereas the "coming of the kingdom" means fullness or complete salvation. Although historical, liberating actions contribute to the growth of the king-dom, they must not be equated with the coming of the kingdom.[18]

Whether Gutiérrez's distinction would satisfy Míguez Bonino is doubtful. The latter uses the metaphor of imitation, but not growth, in order to link human action and God's kingdom. Liberating historical projects imitate the kingdom; they do not contribute to its growth or advancement. Liberating events possess "eschatological permanence insofar as they represent the quality of human existence which corresponds to the kingdom."[19] This carefully qual-ified statement appears to say that human activity is kingdomlike activity

17. Jürgen Moltmann, "An Open Letter to José Míguez Bonino," *Christianity and Crisis* (March 29, 1976): 58.

18. Gutiérrez, *Theology of Liberation*, 15–16.

19. Míguez Bonino, *Doing Theology in a Revolutionary Situation*, 150.

provided it follows the values of the kingdom. The expression "corresponds to the kingdom" implies that human liberation is like liberation in God's kingdom and intrinsically linked to it; but it does not express the kingdom's fullness. "An eschatological faith," he says, "makes it possible for the Christian to invest his life historically in the building of a temporary and imperfect order with the certainty that neither he nor his effort is meaningless or lost."[20] That the human work is meaningful in terms of the kingdom demands an act of faith. Hence, the analogy between God's reign and human liberation rests on faith and not on recognizing concrete fulfillment in historical reality. Even the response done in obedience to God's purpose falls short.

Míguez Bonino uses the Pauline metaphor of the body to explain the continuity between the kingdom of God and the political praxis of Christians. Just as the risen body is continuous and discontinuous with the earthly body, so also is the transformation of our present historical life continuous and discontinuous with the plenitude of the kingdom. The resurrection does not rescue the soul from a corruptible body. If it did, this would mean total discontinuity. Rather the resurrection cleanses the whole person from self-deception and self-seeking, and makes one's bodily life perfect in singleness of purpose and in full community with God.[21] The risen body is no longer corruptible, weak, and sinful, but fully communicative, loving, and worshiping. In this life, the kingdom transforms and perfects the corporality of history (e.g., removes the selfishness from persons) through a forgiveness of sins. Christ's forgiveness cleanses, burns, and excludes elements that do not belong in the new age. The body metaphor illumines the continuity and discontinuity between the kingdom and political activity. Yet this explanation does not clarify how God's self-revelation and guidance become known in particular historical events. Míguez Bonino needs to show, as Moltmann challenged him to do, how the kingdom of God manifests itself within Latin American realities.

Another way of approaching the eschatology of Míguez Bonino is through his treatment of praxis, examining how he sees the transformative activity of Christians contributing to the work of the kingdom. He wants to build a theology in which Latin Americans understand themselves as conscious, responsible subjects forging a path toward liberation. Yet human agents must not arrogate God's initiative and efficacious power as though they themselves were bringing about liberation and redemption. The issue becomes how to encourage human initiative and creativity without diminishing God's role as liberator.

20. Ibid., 152.
21. Ibid., 141.

He sculpts his own theological anthropology by contrasting its features with traditional Catholic and Protestant forms, characterizing the first as "anthropological optimism" and the second as "anthropological pessimism."[22] The Catholic optimists maintain that, in spite of a nature damaged by original sin, human beings can know the good through reason and with God's grace follow right reason. Thus, through the instrumentality of reason, individuals and groups can cooperate with God's salvific work of the kingdom.

Protestants, in contrast, view human nature as totally sinful. Consequently, the human capacity to know and to do the good is severely limited. The assumption of a handicapped nature shackles one's political ethics; it does not envision a program of creating just social structures or qualitatively better human relationships. Because a depraved imagination and will contribute nothing to liberation and redemption, one must depend entirely on God's grace. This anthropology leads to an ethics of the lesser evil, a political realism that offsets dominance by evil empires through a balance of power.[23] Protestant theologians habitually have invoked the eschatological reservation, which reminds zealous social changers that the kingdom is also a "not yet" reality. Consequently, Protestant political ethics has become primarily a negative endeavor that tries to preserve order against the forces of evil.

In light of the optimistic and pessimistic models, Míguez Bonino unveils his own paradigm that protects God's sovereignty and initiative while setting in bold relief human participation and creativity. Against his own Protestant tradition that emphasized doing the lesser evil, he proposes an ethics of doing the greater good by building solidarity based on love and justice. Doing the greater good does not imply moral purity, for all human projects and ethical choices are freighted with moral ambiguity and incertitude.[24] It does mean that people should dream of better ways of living in cooperation with God's inspiration and assistance. Míguez Bonino strives to implant the marrow of hope and creativity in the bones of Latin Americans by encouraging people "to name their world" and participate in God's creative activity. The Spirit of God instructs persons to exercise power for others and not use power to impose one's will.[25] The active power of the Spirit works with the creativity of human beings.

22. José Míguez Bonino, "The Shape of a New Society: Power and Solidarity" (lecture at San Francisco Theological Seminary, San Anselmo, California, April 23, 1987).

23. Míguez Bonino, *Toward a Christian Political Ethics*, 28–31.

24. José Míguez Bonino, *Christians and Marxists: The Mutual Challenge to Revolution* (Grand Rapids, Mich.: Eerdmans, 1976), 123.

25. Ibid., 8.

Yet Míguez Bonino does not speak of human participation in obediential response to God's intitiative as the "work" of the kingdom (Gutiérrez) or as "building" the kingdom (Leonardo Boff).[26] Rather he describes the praxis of Christians as "anticipating" God's reign. The metaphor of building the kingdom is nonbiblical, naively optimistic, and fails to protect the primacy of the divine initiative.

He also rejects the expression "discovering and interpreting the signs of the kingdom." Interpreting the signs implies that history in relation to the kingdom is a riddle to be solved rather than a mission to be fulfilled. The Christian does not figure out what must be done, but listens to what God's Spirit prompts, aided by Scripture, which points a person toward the kingdom of love, justice, and peace. Historical projects should be chosen and evaluated on the basis of these values.[27]

His rejection of the metaphor of discovering–interpreting the kingdom sets his theology apart from the approach of both Sobrino and Gutiérrez, who try to discern the signs of the times in historical events. Rebecca Chopp has noted a difference between Míguez Bonino and Gutiérrez regarding their respective interpretations of the option for the poor. For Gutiérrez, the option for the poor is based first upon God's own choosing to be with the poor; solidarity with the poor is itself a religious experience. Míguez Bonino bases the option for the poor on the obedience of faith to a God of love, which necessarily implies justice. Said differently: for Gutiérrez, the poor manifest God's presence; for Míguez Bonino, Christians are in solidarity with the poor out of obedience to the proclamation of God's word.[28] She aptly identifies the Catholic theologian's approach as a "manifestation model" and the Protestant theologian's as a "proclamation model."

As a general characterization, Chopp is correct. Míguez Bonino does follow a proclamation model whenever he discusses his theological ethics. But he switches to a manifestation model whenever he does social analysis, which he says discloses the evil structures and identifies more humane alternatives. In his dialogue with Latin American Marxists, for instance, he maintains with the Marxists that "truth is found . . . in the scientific analysis of the activity

26. Gerhard Lohfink, "Die Not der Exegese mit der Reich-Gottes-Verkündigung Jesu," *Theologische Quartal Schrifte* 168, no. 1 (1988): 4. Lohfink argues, based on solid biblical evidence, that one can say that the coming kingdom is both "totally, completely, and entirely" the work of God and "totally, completely, and entirely" the work of human beings.

27. Míguez Bonino, *Doing Theology in a Revolutionary Situation*, 152.

28. Rebecca Chopp, *The Praxis of Suffering* (Maryknoll, N.Y.: Orbis Books, 1986), 167 n. 43.

of human beings within the conditions of their social situation."[29] In other
words, truth is manifested in history through scientific, rational inquiry.

On the theological level, however, Míguez Bonino conveys a distrust of
the manifestation model because of its kinship with natural law, a tradition he
eschews. Natural law looks for God's footprints on earthly soil. The search
for God's path, some contemporary natural law adherents say, consists in
pursuing universal value through rational inquiry. Although Míguez Bonino
explicitly rejects this approach, he searches for God's design by examining the
praxis of Christians and by doing social analysis. These keys open doors to
worlds the theologians would not otherwise see and understand: the struggling
world of the poor and the dominating world of the rich. In the world of the
disenfrancised, he says, the Christian "deeply experiences the reality of love,
fellowship, sacrificial commitment, solidarity, and hope within this community
in which the name of Jesus Christ is not invoked."[30] His analysis identifies
programs judged to be more humane and, together with theological sources,
judges them to be in accord with God's will. Although he says history is not
a riddle to be solved, he scrutinizes complex political entities in order to
understand what must be done. Hence, evidence from his own writings contradicts his earlier statement that his theology does not involve discovering
and interpreting the signs of the kingdom. An examination of his theological-
ethical method may illumine this inconsistency.

Hermeneutical Circle

The theological-ethical method of Míguez Bonino, like the hermeneutical
circle of Segundo and Gutiérrez, asserts that God's revelation must be interpreted by means of multiple sources. This section will examine these sources
of praxis, social analysis, and tradition-Scripture, showing what each source
contributes to moral decision making. The hermeneutical circle follows the
sequence of steps in his normative ethics. It begins with political praxis and
then moves to theological investigation either by way of a praxis undertaken
by Christians or via social analysis aided by social theorists. He distinguishes
political praxis from the praxis of Christians, who, like their counterparts, are
engaged in critical-reflective activity, but who also bring religious faith to bear
upon their active engagement.

29. Míguez Bonino, *Christians and Marxists*, 93.
30. Míguez Bonino, *Doing Theology in a Revolutionary Situation*, 158.

Míguez Bonino's Hermeneutical Circle

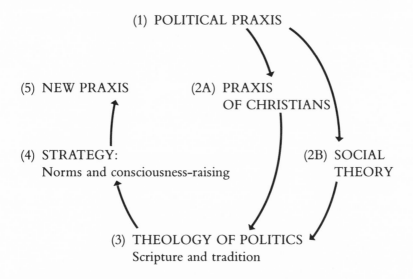

(1) POLITICAL PRAXIS

(5) NEW PRAXIS   (2A) PRAXIS
                              OF CHRISTIANS

(4) STRATEGY: (2B) SOCIAL
    Norms and consciousness-raising   THEORY

(3) THEOLOGY OF POLITICS
    Scripture and tradition

Two fruitful approaches:
   (A) political praxis ⟶ praxis of Christians ⟶
       theology ⟶ strategy
   (B) political praxis ⟶ social theory ⟶
       theology ⟶ strategy

Two misguided approaches:
   theology ⟶ political praxis
   praxis of Christians ⟶ social theory

Praxis of Christians

Míguez Bonino cautions theologians against bypassing this important step of Christian praxis because doing so isolates the theologian from the faith-life of the people and thus weakens the authority of his or her theological assertions.[31] The church base community serves as the locus of praxis for many

31. Míguez Bonino, *Toward a Christian Political Ethics*, 48–49. Some Christian activists, Míguez Bonino points out, are tempted to bypass theological-ethical reflection and so move directly from Christian praxis to analysis and then to action. This procedure gives rise to confusion and disorientation because they lack a solid understanding of their faith. The most fruitful theological-ethical method moves along both pathways, involving the theologian in communication with Christians engaged in political praxis and with social theorists who help him or her understand the mechanisms of political structures.

Christians. In this community of faith, participants are encouraged to read the gospel, reflect on its message, and relate it to their lives and to the world. Speaking, sharing, praying, and then strategizing over what the community should do often bring remarkable results.

Míguez Bonino told the following story illustrating how a woman claimed her rightful dignity as a child of God:

> A poor, illiterate woman, who had been battered by her husband, was invited by her neighbor to a meeting of the small congregation, where each member took turns reading the Bible. The illiterate woman listened in silence, but then decided to learn to read. Then she took her place at one of these meetings reading a lesson from the Bible. One day, she faced her husband: "I can now read. Now listen to me. I know the gospel. I have read what Jesus says. You won't hit me anymore. Things will be different now."[32]

The woman's praxis, inspired by the gospel, transformed her life and the relationship with her husband. Her action also encouraged other women to esteem their own dignity and wisdom.

A second and complementary route from political praxis to theology involves using social theory to explain institutions and their policies. It plumbs greater depths than the praxis of Christians by examining power relations and ideologies. Social-scientific research examines problematic areas, such as the dominant behavior of foreign-based corporations and political regimes. Theological investigation reflects critically on issues set forth by the analysis, such as the power of transnational corporations, examining what should be done in light of certain alternatives. Moving around the circle, the theologian moves to a step that Míguez Bonino calls "strategy," where he discusses how normative principles and a strategy of consciousness-raising guide a people's praxis. Finally, a new praxis, the fruit of theological process, completes the circle.

The entire process is "dialectical," by which he means that theory and praxis challenge each other. "Action overflows and challenges the theory that has informed it; and thought, projecting the shape and future of reality, pushes action to new ventures."[33] Praxis, including social analysis, presents the complexities of the political world, which theological theory addresses.

Social Analysis

Social analysis, Míguez Bonino says, is a "constitutive moment" within theological-ethical method because it provides necessary knowledge about the

32. Míguez Bonino, "The Shape of a New Society" (lecture).
33. Míguez Bonino, *Toward a Christian Political Ethics*, 39.

political world that theological ethics cannot otherwise obtain.[34] In defining the proper tasks of social science and theology, he follows Christian ethicist Paul Lehmann, who says historical analysis *identifies* priorities, and theology *determines* priorities.[35] In other words, social science explains the concrete options, and theology makes a judgment about them. In practice, Míguez Bonino's social analysis tries to give a coherent explanation of how a structure works. It also unfolds the contradictions, ideologies, and social consequences of its operation.

Like the Boffs, he describes his type of analysis as dialectical. He acknowledges that the selection of any analysis is itself an ethical move. As we have already seen in chapter 4, the dialectical model includes both Marxist analysis and dependency analysis. He finds dialectical analysis a better instrument than the functionalist type, because it more adequately explains Latin American reality and because it offers a possibility of systemic change. The choice of an analytic instrument is an ethical decision because one makes the decision on the basis of certain values one wishes to defend.

A key value in Míguez Bonino's ethics is solidarity with the poor. The dialectical model, in contrast to the functional approach, takes the perspective of the poor classes and groups. It perceives major, long-standing problems as indicators of systemic problems and not simply as malfunctioning elements that can be repaired by reform measures.[36] Furthermore, dialectical analysis focuses upon institutional power, especially upon the dominance of one group over another. Although he is sensitive to the limitations of dialectical types of sociology, such as its association with a Marxist worldview, he judges it to be an apt instrument to understand the reality within Third World nations.

To see how he actually does analysis is instructive. Using a historical-dialectical analysis, he traces the struggle of the Latin American people from the colonial period to the neocolonial period of the nineteenth and twentieth centuries, and finally to the modernization period following World War II. His extensive analysis shows how political-economic domestic and foreign powers came to conquer and control the people of Latin America. Moreover, it explains how Catholic and Protestant churches cooperated with these powers until the 1960s, when both churches suddenly became aware that their people were not becoming junior partners with opportunity for advancing in the world economy. On the contrary, underdeveloped nations remained dependent apprentices.

34. Ibid., 44–45.
35. Ibid., 54.
36. Ibid., 44–47.

Religion played an important role in the structures of dependency. In the neocolonial period (especially between 1870 and 1890), Protestantism gave religious approval to the liberal-modernistic project. Unlike Latin American Catholicism, which identified more with the medieval, prescientific, feudal, and aristocratic world, Protestantism emphasized freedom, culture, democracy, and progress.[37] Hence, the latter fitted nicely as the supporting actor of the free-enterprise capitalist economy. Roman Catholic resistance to these liberal values gradually weakened, beginning at the end of World War I when the masses entered public life. Catholic conservatives and liberals came together in defense of the capitalist economy. Gradually Catholics became supportive of the capitalist order and its values of modernization.

The Second Vatican Council was a watershed that also encouraged Latin American Catholics to alter their conservative outlook. The council taught participatory democracy in the governance of the church and recognized the values of autonomous culture, science, and the state. It upheld religious freedom and human dignity as distinctively Christian values. Thus, the council reinforced the developing rapprochement with Protestants, who joined hands with Catholics to support a democratic, enlightened, and liberal Latin American society.

But as structures of modernization developed, the masses—Catholic and Protestant alike—grew suspicious of the emerging economy. Aided by social-scientific studies, the people became aware that the modernization project, called "development," did not enhance their livelihood. Quite the opposite, their lives became more impoverished and their national economy more tightly controlled by outside centers of power. Latin Americans discovered the basic fact of dependence and the fraudulence of the so-called democracy.[38]

The awareness of dependence arose through the efforts of social scientists (mostly Latin Americans), who showed that the development programs did

37. Míguez Bonino, *Doing Theology in a Revolutionary Situation*, 12. Protestantism in Latin America carries an Anglo-Saxon and North American ethos, whereas Catholicism in Latin America is markedly European and Mediterranean.

38. Gary J. Dorrien, *Reconstructing the Common Good* (Maryknoll, N.Y.: Orbis Books, 1990), 139. Dorrien thinks that Míguez Bonino is on solid ground in using dependency theory to critique the domination of Latin America by North Atlantic powers, yet criticizes him for adopting the theory of André Gunder Frank, who overstated the relationship between domination and dependence between North and South America. Although Dorrien is correct in showing the parallel between Míguez Bonino and Frank on this issue, it should be pointed out that Míguez Bonino does not cite Frank, but the more sophisticated theories of F. H. Cardoso, Celso Furtado, Theotônio dos Santos, R. Stavenhagen, and Orlando Fals-Borda. See Míguez Bonino, *Doing Theology in a Revolutionary Situation*, 36 nn. 6–10; *Toward a Christian Political Ethics*, 123 n. 10.

not deliver the goods promised. On the contrary, they simply expanded the Anglo-Saxon neocolonial project. Great Britain had in the nineteenth century changed the relatively self-sufficient agrarian economy to a one-crop exporting economy. "Argentina was supposed to supply corn and meat; Brazil, coffee; Chile, saltpeter and copper; the Central American countries, bananas; Cuba, sugar; Venezuela, oil; and so on."[39] In its modernization project, the United States continued the basic pattern of domination by means of transnational corporations, which invested relatively little capital in the host-country economy, while drawing out disproportionate amounts of resources and profit. Under the influence of U.S. development, Latin American countries continued to serve as suppliers of foodstuffs, raw materials, and cheap labor, as well as to function as an outpost of an integrated and controlled world economy.

Democracy held up as a characteristic element of modernization, was exposed as a hoax, even though it was inscribed into Latin American constitutions. The rights that national-democratic constitutions promised to protect—free press, free trade, opportunity to participate in politics—benefited only the elite. The indigenous masses remained undernourished, illiterate, exploited; and, when they fought back, they were repressed.

In practice, Míguez Bonino's historical-dialectical analysis concentrates more on ideologies that support power than on the structures of power. The ideology of development, he argued, is fallacious. It maintained that the North Atlantic nations became prosperous because of moral achievement (frugal and industrious living) and because its citizens followed principles of democracy, free enterprise, and education. Underdeveloped countries could attain economic prowess, such as the United States, England, and Germany had achieved, provided they fostered the same civic virtues and adopted the same principles. Such reasoning, however, overlooked important historical facts. The rise of the developed nations occurred at a particular historical moment when conditions were favorable and when resources and a vast cheap labor market offered possibilities for development. Míguez Bonino debunked the evolutionary theory of moving from colonial underdevelopment to modern development. Development and underdevelopment, he said, are inversely related—the growth of developed nations occurs at the expense of undeveloped countries. Domination and dependence, not development, accurately describe the relationship.

Heightened awareness of their economic-political dependence led certain groups and nations to resist. Certain populist governments, such as Goulart's

39. Míguez Bonino, *Doing Theology in a Revolutionary Situation*, 14.

Brazil, Torres's Bolivia, and Allende's Chile, moved radically to the left. Revolutionary movements came forth in Uruguay, Colombia, and Nicaragua. This set the stage for the national security state, which was adopted by many Latin American countries: Argentina, Brazil, Chile, and Uruguay.[40]

We have already seen the analysis of the national security state by José Comblin. Míguez Bonino builds on Comblin's thesis that heads of state, often military dictators, justified their repressive actions against dissidents in the name of freedom, democracy, and Christianity. Thus, their official statements often contradicted their actual strategy. While the state proclaimed freedom and democracy as supreme values of its regime, it tried to exercise total control by suppressing all forms of dissent. In addition, military regimes regarded themselves not only as the last bastion of Western and Christian values, but also as guardians of the multinational corporations and implementers of liberal economic philosophy. These military regimes created and consolidated authoritarian and antijuridical governments that were controlled and directed by the armed forces.

As a cloak over its design to dominate and to expand its sovereignty, the national security regime dressed its goals and activities in religious garb using words like "sacred," "sacrifice," and "purging." It denounced its enemies as "diabolic," "sacrilegious," and "anti-Christian." The authoritarian regime co-opted religious language in order to institutionalize itself as a permanent organization of society. It also aimed to persuade the church that it shared the same goals. Since the state was fighting atheistic communism, supporting family values, and establishing an ordered and stable society, it believed it could count on the church to support its program.[41] Although some churches were hooked by the bait, many of them identified the machinations of the state in which it was claiming for itself the church's proper role of interpreter and teacher of religion and morality. Subsequently, churches became critical of the state, denouncing its violation of human rights. Míguez Bonino's extensive analysis brought into sharp resolution this dilemma: whether his nation and other southern cone nations should continue to support the capitalist transnational project or choose a democratic socialist project of liberation. Writing in the early 1980s, he observed that most of these national security states faced a desperate situation of economic paralysis, permanent repression, and mounting opposition by citizens. The capitalist project would continue the controlled development within the world capitalist system and a limited democracy managed by technocratic elites. Ethical considerations aside, he

40. Míguez Bonino, *Toward a Christian Political Ethics*, 68.
41. Ibid., 72–73.

thinks this project will not work, primarily because the transnational system has found it increasingly difficult to incorporate Third World economies into the world system.

The socialist project entails societal appropriation of the means of production, political power, and freedom. It fosters the creation of a new social consciousness. Míguez Bonino summarizes the liberation project as "socialist in the organization of its economy, democratic in terms of the political participation of the people, and open in the sense of insuring the conditions for personal realization, cultural freedom and opportunity, and the mechanisms for self-correction."[42] Within the economy a people must determine how to structure central planning while maintaining sufficiently small group and personal initiatives.

These indicators of a new and free society represent only priorities and very general ones. Míguez Bonino's lack of specificity in proposing a democratic socialist society is one of his liabilities, as Gary Dorrien earlier observed.[43] Because he has criticized present regimes for their misuse of power, one would expect him to discuss at greater length the structures of power in his socialist proposal. Míguez Bonino fails to identify which of the many theories of dependency he is following. His analysis of foreign corporations relies on a general type of dependency theory, echoing the approach of André Gunder Frank, who related Third World impoverishment to First World enrichment as opposite sides of the same coin. He rightly identifies the exploitation of Third World countries by transnational corporations, but fails to explain the relationship of foreign corporations to entrepreneurs and politicians within the host country.

Theology of Politics

His analysis raises the question for church groups, "What should we do?" Although churches in the 1960s generally opposed the practices of national security states, they were hesitant to change the system. Their hesitancy, Míguez Bonino suggested, stemmed partly from their theological perspective rooted in an Augustinian political ethics. Augustine viewed history as the place in time where God's eternal city and the human city intersect. The foundation stones of the eternal city, justice and love, order the human city. Justice gives legitimacy to the earthly ruler and establishes proper relationships within the city. Love provides the inner motivation and points the direction for human

42. Ibid., 77.
43. Dorrien, *Reconstructing the Common Good*, 137.

action. Thus, justice as the objective basis and love as the motivating force enable Christians to discern God's active presence in history and, in light of this discernment, to determine further what to do.

Yet Augustine's practical dealing with political moral issues reveals a fundamental premise that, in Míguez Bonino's mind, inhibits social transformation: peace is based on order. The peaceful society, like an organism, ought to function harmoniously. Injustices, which harm order, must be addressed but in a manner that does not endanger order and peace. This perspective, Míguez Bonino suggests, grew out of an anthropological pessimism and a natural law perspective that interpreted society as an organism. Changing its basic parts would constitute a crime against nature.

In summarizing Augustine's political ethics, he says, "theologically, justice and love are supreme, but historically both are subordinated to order."[44] Ingrained with this Augustinian tradition, the Latin American church has resisted supporting radical change. This contributed to the church's conservative position on maintaining the established order even in the face of long-standing oppression.

Míguez Bonino thinks the prophetic theological tradition that emphasizes radical transformation of society will better serve the Latin American people. In this tradition, justice, understood as fidelity to the exclusive claims of God within a covenantal relationship, shows a special concern for the poor and oppressed. Thus, justice for the poor serves as his theological premise, the "fixed point" and standard of God's redeeming presence, and the hallmark of human justice.[45] Therefore, in determining priorities as the first step in the moral decision-making process, the church should ask, "Which order of society is compatible with the exercise of justice?" and not "What degree of justice is compatible with maintaining the basic order of society?" (the Augustinian priority). The alternative chosen should foster the liberation of the poor and protect their basic human rights.

Strategies of Social Change

Strategy completes the ethical reflection process by bringing together the relevant sources to make a synthetic moral judgment about what should be done concretely.[46] The ultimate concern for Míguez Bonino is whether his country (and other Latin American countries) should remain with the status

44. Míguez Bonino, *Toward a Christian Political Ethics*, 83.
45. Ibid., 84–85.
46. Ibid., 101.

quo or choose a democratic socialist type of government. His social analysis identified the options and the relative strengths and weaknesses of each program. Social analysis also informs the theologian whether conditions are ripe for changing the infrastructure. His critical theological reflection enunciated a prioritizing principle (justice over order) that ranked the options. Strategy must weigh the options in light of the relevant conditions and gospel values. An important condition is the awareness and readiness of the people for change. Their level of conscientization and commitment, and the probable consequences of the revolution, are important considerations in deciding what should be done.

Assuming that the social-political-economic conditions are ripe for change and that the people favor a radical transformation, Míguez Bonino proposes an ethical criterion. The basic ethical criterion, or principle of justice, is "the maximizing of universal human possibilities and the minimizing of human costs."[47] By "universal human possibilities" he means the realization of distinctively human goods, such as freedom; better human conditions, such as employment and housing; and space for human community, guaranteed by respecting human rights. Under "human costs" he would include the loss of human goods, material conditions, and human rights. It might well involve bloodshed, torture, and imprisonment as people struggle for change. In sum, a people and the church must weigh the probable consequences of each option. This principle applies to revolutionary struggle and to everyday political actions.

At first glance, the political ethics of Míguez Bonino seems to have evolved from an eschatological ethics in which God is the judge to a utilitarian ethics in which human agents calculate what must be done on the basis of probable effects. Because of his emphasis on consequences, critics Dennis McCann and Charles Strain labeled his ethics a "utilitarian calculus."[48] However, his ethics should be regarded as a "mixed consequentialism." A "mixed" consequentialism attends to norms as well as to the projected results. Míguez Bonino's principle assumes the a priori conviction of preferential option for the poor. Therefore, maximization of human goods and minimization of human costs are measured especially with regard for the poor and oppressed in Latin America. Classical utilitarianism, in contrast, does not favor any sociological group, but chooses on the basis of whatever action produces the greatest amount of good for the greatest number of people, which may or may not include the poor.

47. Ibid., 107.
48. Dennis P. McCann and Charles R. Strain, *Polity and Praxis* (Minneapolis: Winston Press, 1985), 151.

Moreover, he upholds the dignity of persons, which, again in opposition to utilitarianism, rules out certain actions as antecedently wrong, such as torture and exploitation of others. Respecting human dignity also means regarding the enemy with a basic respect. Hatred of the enemy is "functional" because one hates the hostile agent only because of and only as long as the enemy continues to oppress others. The people should remain open to the possibility of affirming the humanity of the enemy before, during, and after the struggle.[49] Hence, his theological convictions—option for the poor and respect for persons, which are grounded in the covenant and the kingdom of God—remain the basis of his ethical standard.

In discussing radical transformation, he explicitly mentions just war criteria as relevant to the discussion of revolutionary change.[50] Indeed, his maximization principle is strikingly similar to the principle of proportionality within just war theory, which tries to estimate antecedently whether the costs incurred by the war would be proportional to the good expected as an outcome. Similarly, in the context of revolutionary struggle, the maximization principle tells revolutionaries to weigh the human cost of their realization (e.g., the sacrifice of many lives, physical and psychological suffering) against the cost of their postponement (ongoing oppression, miserable living conditions, violation of human rights). Benefits and losses, however, must be calculated not simply on the basis of short-term results, but on the basis of long-term consequences. Although Míguez Bonino criticizes natural law and its reasoning, he borrows principles developed from such reasoning, such as the principle of proportionality, to make a case against absolute pacifism.

Issue: Violent Revolution

Strategizing for revolutionary change must consider the ethical aspects of violence. Míguez Bonino does indeed address the issue, but insists with other liberation theologians that discussion of violence should be located within a broad historical context. Like the mythical monster Hydra, violence has many heads: structural violence that punishes or exploits by institutional policy; repressive violence that coerces by incarceration and torture; and revolutionary violence, which subverts the infrastructure. Genetically linked, one type of violence spawns another, as Dom Helder Câmara has demonstrated in Brazil. Likewise, the historical analysis of Míguez Bonino revealed the contours of violence from the conquest to the contemporary national security state. In

49. Míguez Bonino, *Toward a Christian Political Ethics*, 113.
50. Ibid., 106–10.

Argentina, Chile, and Uruguay, long-standing oppression led to resistance movements today, including organized efforts by peasants to gain farmland or by industrial workers for better wages. Such initiatives were met with the policeman's club, disappearances, rape, and death. Repressive action by land-owner and soldier nurtured the seeds of revolution planted in the long season of oppression.

Given the panoramic picture of violence in Latin America, Míguez Bonino addresses the ethics of revolutionary violence. The Bible, church tradition, and Marxist thought all help illumine his thinking on this issue. The biblical-ecclesiastical sources point to two understandings of peace in relation to vi-olence: the priestly and the prophetic.[51] The first equates peace with an ordered, nonconflictual, and harmoniously integrated society; the second views peace as a dynamic process in which justice is established amid the tensions of history. The priestly perspective, which has shaped the theological tradition since Au-gustine, judges in a positive light the physical use of force that preserves law and order in society and judges negatively any force that disrupts that order. The second perspective, best represented by the prophets and Jesus, evaluates physical coercion on the basis of justice. The prophetic understanding is, of course, the perspective of Míguez Bonino, who sees peace as inextricably linked in the ongoing march toward justice. Paradoxically, the pursuit of peace, prophetically viewed, invariably involves conflict and often physical violence.

The prophetic tradition found in the Old and New Testaments gives a direction by proclaiming the kingdom of God. It does not, however, present universal principles related to violence. Within the Old Testament the law of God forbids violence in certain situations, but authorizes, even commands, other forms of violence in others. God sometimes commands wars even against Israel, but forbids other wars even on behalf of Israel. Míguez Bonino identifies a pattern within God's just war perspectives: "Do whatever tends to 'open space' for foreigners, widows, orphans, and families—conditions allowing people to be human."[52]

The expressions to "open space" and "to be human" need clarification. The former seems to mean establishing conditions that foster justice. Although he does not define what it means to be human, he implies that the human consists of freedom expressed in love for others and of living in solidarity with others in community. Perhaps "solidaristic love" best captures Míguez Bonino's understanding of the human. This means committing oneself freely to the liberation of the poor, exploited, and vulnerable members of society.

51. Míguez Bonino, *Doing Theology in a Revolutionary Situation*, 116.
52. Ibid., 118.

The criterion of the normatively human—pursuing and protecting self-determination and solidaristic love—may justify using physical violence. The Old Testament, Míguez Bonino says, seems to support using violence in order to protect the humanity of God's people. Violence (and by extension revolutionary war) is justified in certain conditions to free people from bondage.

Rebecca Chopp faults his interpretation of the Old Testament for failing to employ "specific historical, sociological, or literary arguments for either the foundations or the principles of his hermeneutics of the Word." He proposes no arguments to substantiate the claim that violence in the Old Testament is permitted or condemned depending on whether it hinders or promotes freedom.[53] It is true that Míguez Bonino does not substantiate his claim with biblical evidence, though he seems confident that the evidence for his position is considerable.

When he moves to the New Testament, Míguez Bonino perceives a difference in Jesus' stance toward violence. Whereas God in the Old Testament enjoins the Israelites to embark on a holy war against the enemy, Jesus renounced the role of a messianic leader. "Renouncing power meant for him renouncing the exercise of divine power to settle men's affairs."[54] The incarnation terminated the justification of the holy war. Jesus taught his people to conduct their own affairs and to create responsibly their own history by engaging in analysis, strategy, and tactics to determine what they should do. In summary, the prophetic biblical perspective instructs one to examine the concrete situation from a historical perspective rather than to base one's strategy on fixed principles governing the use of violence.

Turning to Marx's writings, Míguez Bonino finds there a historical contextualism rather than a dogmatic assertion about the necessity of violence in revolution. Violent revolution for Marx was a hypothesis drawn from the history of revolutionary praxis and not a dogmatic principle, as some have interpreted Marx. As historically conditioned strategy, violence as an ingredient of revolution must be considered anew in different historical situations. This means that Latin Americans must weigh the long-term results of both nonviolent and violent means.

Although Míguez Bonino approaches the issue of violence from a contextualist perspective, he is not without religiously inspired guidelines indicated by his assertion that Christians generally should adopt nonviolent action because it shows greater respect for persons than violent measures, which exacerbate hatred, resentment, and rivalries. In addition, the nonviolent approach

53. Chopp, *The Praxis of Suffering*, 97.
54. Míguez Bonino, *Doing Theology in a Revolutionary Situation*, 123–24.

achieves more effectively the goal of revolution because it provides greater space for internalizing the project of liberation and for fostering solidarity among the people. Victorious revolutionary violence runs the risk of substituting one type of oppression for another. However, he would reject an absolute pacifism as well as an absolute violence, because both exact a terrible human cost.

Concretely, Míguez Bonino outlines three steps in the process for revolutionary change. First of all, the poor and the oppressed themselves exert pressure for change. This involves a growth in awareness (conscientization) of themselves as active participants in society. Second, the churches include in their evangelization an exposition of oppressive ideologies. This would help unblock the resistance of middle- and upper-class Christians and might even enlist their support for social change. Third, some measure of violence is inevitable. Therefore, the people must assess the expected benefits of change versus the costs, following the proportionalist principle. At each stage of social transformation, the people must seek the best possibilities for enhancing the human potential of the majority. Finally, it should be noted that he recognizes the validity of just war principles as helpful for illuminating whether a certain revolutionary project ought to be undertaken.

Although the gospel of Jesus Christ does not provide concrete norms for revolutionary change, it does contribute moral content, in Míguez Bonino's view, to the process of moral discernment. Following the road of the cross involves the followers of Jesus evaluating prudently and courageously the cost of violence, fighting against the destructive spirit of hate and revenge, and aiming toward reconciliation between oppressor and oppressed when both lay down their rifles.[55] The followers of Jesus exercise power in the service of others. This means defending the weak, judging the unjust, and strengthening those working on mission. Service may involve surrendering one's life for the sake of the liberation of others, as Jesus gave his own life for the ransom of the many.

Assessment

This chapter has examined the eschatological foundations of José Míguez Bonino's Christian political ethics, his method and normative principles, and finally how he views revolutionary violence. The skeletal structure of his ethics consists of the kingdom of God and the political world. An adequate ethics, he maintains, must show how God's kingdom relates to all sociopolitical

55. Ibid., 128.

activity without either reducing the kingdom to human liberation achieved
entirely within history, or elevating liberation to such transcendent heights
that it leaves day-to-day politics untouched.

The kingdom operates through conscienticized, faithful, and responsible
persons, who, like the biblical prophets, are called to perform a dual task.
They deconstruct the dominating relationships and then reconstruct them anew
according to God's justice. Using a broad brush, Míguez Bonino paints for
us the general lines that move from kingdom to politics and from politics to
kingdom. He shows how revelation, social sciences, and the lived faith of the
people connect the two realities. The specific task of painting the subtleties of
political ethics are left to other theological artisans.

His ethics demonstrates a remarkable consistency in upholding the kingdom of God as the ultimate standard by which present institutions and future
projects are to be judged. Scripture, especially the New Testament, provides
general pointers that give general directives and guidance for judgment and
future planning. Unlike Jon Sobrino, he offers little detailed biblical exegesis
and argument to support his perspectives on important themes, such as Jesus'
understanding of power as service and his rejection of violence. Nonetheless,
his interpretation of Scripture is balanced and judicious. His theological analysis
of Jesus' understanding and use of power as service of the people challenges
the use of power in politics. Power as service should be exercised on behalf
of the poor and oppressed.

Míguez Bonino fails to explain how power as service fits with his statement that God empowers human agents "to execute God's righteous judgments
of deliverance and of punishment."[56] He allows for revolutionary violence if
it brings justice for the poor without a disproportionate cost. Yet he recognizes
that nonviolence is the more appropriate way. His values of power as service
and radical change through nonviolence function more like ideals that temper
revolution than as absolutes that determine whether to begin a revolution.
Although he views his own theology as different from the political realism of
Reinhold Niebuhr, he recognizes with Niebuhr the moral ambiguity of political
action even as a people tries to follow the kingdom.

In his debates with Moltmann and Gutiérrez, he seems to be pulled to
and fro by a Barthian proclamation theology in which God more directly
illumines what must be done and by Gutiérrez's manifestation theology where
human agents discern through social analysis and God's Spirit what must be
done. This evinces conceptual strain demonstrated by his emphasis on God's

56. Míguez Bonino, *Toward a Christian Political Ethics*, 97–98.

will and human obedience in his theological reflection, and by his underscoring scientific rationality and human initiative in the search for truth and liberation.

Although he sees himself as a biblical ethicist, Míguez Bonino draws his moral principles from nonbiblical as well as biblical sources. The principle of option for the poor enjoys a solid biblical foundation. On the other hand, he invokes rational principles (e.g., proportionalism of just war reasoning) and social analysis when addressing the specifics of a revolution. While he insists with Barth that all moral criteria be grounded in revelation, he pursues truth in dialogue with Marxists even though they reject his eschatology. This implies that he recognizes a basis for dialogue with nonbelieving Marxists. Although I find his use of multiple sources for constructing his ethics to be a strength, it does not fit coherently with his proclamation model of theological ethics.

Míguez Bonino wrestles with and departs from the pessimistic Protestant anthropology that focuses on limits and the lesser-evil ethics. He favors a post–Vatican II Roman Catholic emphasis on human creativity, subjectivity, and the greater good ethics. His language, however, holds fast to a Barthian structure and rejects with Barth any semblance of natural law. In brief, this ecumenical theologian has tried to integrate two Christian traditions, and to a certain degree he has done this successfully even with the tensions noted earlier.

Yet even with his oscillation between two traditions, Míguez Bonino maintains a fairly well balanced eschatology and ethics. Building his eschatological ethics on biblical notions of love and justice, he conceives of justice as solidarity with the poor in fidelity to God's covenant. Hence, ethics is undertaken by a church, or community of believers, who worship and work together as God's covenant community. This biblical vision of justice then becomes translated into two principles of justice that offer general guidance to moral decision making: justice takes priority over law and order; maximize universal human possibilities over the costs.

Míguez Bonino more clearly than other liberation theologians defines the proper tasks of social analysis and revelation. With the other theologians, such as the Boffs and Comblin, he sees the twin functions of social sciences as determining *the what* and *the why* of institutions: understanding what is going on and explaining within a coherent framework the deep causes behind the phenomena. He goes beyond his colleagues by showing more clearly than they how the fruits of analysis and praxis feed into the evaluative process on the theological–ethical level.

Critics McCann and Strain express an appreciation for his two general moral norms. The first principle (maximizing universal human possibilities) is concerned with ends, and establishes a priority of justice over order. The second principle tests the appropriateness of the means taken to bring about social change. Míguez Bonino's development of these general moral principles proves that he recognizes the importance of criteria for making moral judgments, even though McCann and Strain correctly point out the absence of a full normative system. These critics, however, fail to show sufficient appreciation of his ethics, which calls for making prudential judgments about complex political policies only after having become involved on the grass-roots level with the issues, after having done the necessary social analysis, and after having listened to the word of God.

Míguez Bonino recognizes with many Christian ethicists that universal principles effectively screen out the essential guidance of the Spirit and diminish the responsibility of those actually involved in the situation. He also understands that biblical values and norms do not yield criteria that can guide today's complex political dilemmas. The praxis of Christians, social analysis, and the social teaching of Christian churches all serve as important sources for discerning what must be done. Míguez Bonino keeps these sources in balance as he constructs his political ethics.

Another strength is Míguez Bonino's habitually availing himself of the insights of the poor and oppressed as he does his theology. Although he draws upon their stories and insights, he does not examine their theological-ethical reflection process. Doing so might reveal helpful criteria that people actually develop in deliberating over and resolving concrete issues. One does not find in his writings any discussion about how people themselves have resolved some of the complex social issues in local and national politics.

He shows better than most liberation theologians how social analysis is done and how it relates to the entire process. But as critics Chopp and Dorrien note, his analysis lacks concreteness. Although he has gone beyond Moltmann in closing the gap between God's word and the political world, one may ask Míguez Bonino, as he asked Moltmann, about the concrete politics in his political theology. Analysis of specific institutions and practices is lacking. The lack of specificity may be due to a recognition of his own limits in analyzing social-political structures; or it may be due to the real danger to his own life, and to the lives of his friends and collaborators in Argentina, should he undertake more concrete types of analysis.

The tension mentioned earlier between his theology of proclamation and the theology of manifestation needs to be addressed. Although he underscores human agency in the struggle toward liberation, he is suspicious of discernment that identifies the ought in the empirical reality. Yet he seems dissatisfied with Moltmann's language, which sees liberating praxis as approximating the promise of God's full reign. For Moltmann, hope liberates persons for committed action on behalf of others. But the liberating activity does not seem to participate substantively in God's kingdom. Míguez Bonino recognizes this tension and seeks to establish a closer link. Human liberation is analogous to God's liberation, but it is genuine liberation. But if it is authentic liberation participating in God's action, then it would seem that liberating praxis expresses the presence of the kingdom, though not in its fullness. José Míguez Bonino brings us close to showing the intersection of human action and God's action.

Part
Four

NORMS

8
Status of Moral Norms

This book has pursued two major questions about the adequacy of liberationist ethics. It first explored how comprehensively representative liberation theologians actually use the foundational sources of praxis, social analysis, and Sacred Scripture, and second how coherently they interrelate these same sources to develop an ethics. The criterion of coherence judges how well the liberation theologians integrate the principal sources in their Christian ethics. Do they integrate revelation and the practice of faith so that both sources contribute to a unified vision of liberation and justice? Which source is the more authoritative? Does their use of social analysis in general and a Marxist analysis in particular fit with Christian values?

The issue of the highest authority among the sources becomes more complex in a dialectical theology. Liberation theologians see these sources revealing truth in a dialectical relationship with each other. Theology constructs its theoretical foundations from historical praxis. But then new experiences and knowledge gained from social analysis and from reflection on Scripture challenge the old theology. The new praxis critically assesses whether theory adequately explains the reality. Theological themes and norms (theory) emerge from a critical reflection on the faith-life of the people of God in light of Scripture and church tradition. As the starting point and goal, praxis conditions theory by raising the consciousness of the community, by influencing what kind of social-scientific tools should be used for deeper study, and by posing questions to theology and Scripture.

A key aspect of coherence is whether theological principles and moral norms serve as the highest authority, or whether in practice liberation theologians allow the praxis of the people and social-scientific analysis to carry greater weight. Critics of liberation theology have posed the question whether praxis functions as the decisive source when theologians assess the truth or justice of a given situation, or whether theology has the final say.

Using the two criteria of coherence and comprehensiveness, this final chapter addresses one of the central concerns in the ethics of liberation theology: the status of moral norms. The specific concerns relate to the role of norms for shaping analysis and the presence of norms for evaluating institutions and social practices. The first concern inquires whether Christian ethics guides and shapes the method of analysis. The second concern asks whether liberation theology has moral norms precise enough to guide its moral judgments, or whether it functions like a situational ethics. In evaluating the role of moral norms regarding analysis and issues, I shall offer a suggestion about what I think needs to be done to strengthen this ethics.

Does Christian Ethics Guide Analysis?

Liberation theologians hold that social analysis contributes constitutively to their theological method. Without analysis, Christian ethics cannot adequately understand the sociopolitical realm and cannot, therefore, provide a comprehensive understanding of the Christian faith.[1] Christian ethics by itself lacks the capacity to understand the sociopolitical and economic forces related to wealth, poverty, and oppression. Without social analysis, Christian ethics could not intelligently address issues in public life.

Liberation theology's concern with institutional power, ideology, and social change has led to adopting radical sociologies, primarily dependency and Marxist analysis. Selecting these modes of analysis led critics to ask whether these modes, especially a Marxist scientific analysis, are consonant with Christian theology and ethics.[2] One important critic, the Congregation for the Doctrine of the Faith, or CDF, challenged liberation theology's use of Marxist analysis and Marxist categories such as class struggle and partisan praxis. CDF thinks this analysis is so epistemologically bound to a materialistic and totalitarian vision of reality that theologians cannot employ it without compromising Christian faith, hope, and charity.[3] The analysis interprets history as a struggle between rich and poor classes, and this struggle foments hatred. The analysis also assumes that only those engaged in the struggle for liberation possess the true consciousness, and so they alone are able to work out the analysis correctly.[4]

The CDF thinks that certain theologies of liberation, by adopting a Marxist analysis, have thereby subverted the truth and radically called into

1. Míguez Bonino, *Toward a Christian Political Ethics*, 45.
2. A few critics, such as Michael Novak, have criticized the theologians' use of dependency theory. See McGovern, *Liberation Theology and Its Critics*, 132.
3. CDF, *Instruction*, pt. IX, 3, 5–7.
4. Ibid., pts. VII and VIII.

question the nature of ethics.[5] These theologies seem to assume that authentic truth emerges from praxis—that is, struggle on behalf of the oppressed makes the truth. Consequently, theological-ethical criteria fall by the wayside, yielding the right-of-way to the class struggle that becomes the chief ethical criterion.

Since that critique in 1984, many liberation theologians, including the Boffs, Juan Luis Segundo, Gustavo Gutiérrez, and Ignacio Ellacuría, responded to the critique. All have denied that they and their colleagues hold that struggle in solidarity with the oppressed by itself presents us with the truth. From the origins of this theology, the theologians defined their theology as a critical reflection on praxis in light of the word of God. Furthermore, the theologians rejected the CDF's indictment that they have advocated or encouraged class struggle as a strategy to bring about social change. Gutiérrez pointed out that in his first major work, *Theology of Liberation*, he was speaking of "the class struggle as a fact," not as a strategy, and certainly not as a praxis endorsing hatred of oppressors.[6]

The exchange between the theologians and the CDF about Marxist analysis can be analyzed on two levels: the historical-ethical and the epistemological. The historical-ethical level of discourse dealt with the question whether or not the theologians have in fact subverted Christian ethics by giving too much purchase to a dialectical social analysis and to a conscientizing praxis. The epistemological level deals with the question whether conceptually it is possible to separate the scientific analysis from the materialist philosophical vision and strategy of class struggle. The CDF called for "a careful epistemological critique" prior to the employment of any scientific instrument.[7] Its chief concern was whether liberation theologians integrated their theology and social analysis in such a way that theory—namely, Christian dogma and moral principles—function as the decisive authority over praxis. How do liberation theologians respond to these critiques?

First Response: Ethics Directs Analysis

Ethics relates to social analysis at three junctures: first, when selecting a specific type of social-scientific instrument; second, when deciding whether to accept or to reject the causal explanation of the phenomena provided by the instrument; third, when considering whether to follow the strategy presented by the analysis. Do liberation theologians call upon theological-ethical

5. Ibid., VIII, 4, 9.
6. Gutiérrez, *Truth Shall Make You Free*, 38.
7. CDF, *Instruction*, pt. VII, 4.

guidelines at these decisive moments, or do they follow the Marxist principle that whatever promotes the class struggle to break down the class barriers between rich and poor is justified?

Any careful reading of the liberation theologians should convince the questioner that class struggle is not the linchpin of liberation ethics. Earlier chapters provided solid evidence that the theologians do, in fact, appeal to theological-ethical as well as to sociological criteria when choosing a mode of analysis and interpreting its findings. The analyses of the Boffs, Comblin, and Ellacuría in chapter 4, as well as that of Míguez Bonino in chapter 6, have provided us with at least four criteria. The first three guide the selection of the scientific instrument, and the fourth helps evaluate whether to follow a particular strategy indicated by the social analysis.

The first criterion calls for comprehensiveness: choose the intrument that provides the most comprehensive data and causal explanation of social problems. Comprehensiveness should include historical and structural understanding of how structures operate and an explanation of the deep causes of problems that have arisen. Liberation theologians seek the kind of instrument that can explain both historically and structurally the roots of poverty and oppression. Míguez Bonino explains why he and many of his colleagues have chosen the dialectical approach: "It corresponds more adequately to the perspective, the understanding, and the concerns that emerge in an option for solidarity."[8] Comprehensiveness includes the perspective of the poor, which is often overlooked in other types of analysis.

A functionalist type of sociology, in the judgment of liberation theologians, is not as comprehensive, because it fails to explain contradictions between rich and poor, and because it reinforces the status quo. The theologians rightly note that functionalism provides no guidance or strategy for addressing these structural contradictions. Although I agree with their critique of functionalism, other radical non-Marxist sociologies might be used by theologians in their analysis of institutions.

The second criterion requires coherent explanations.[9] To be coherent, a mode of analysis must demonstrate whether concepts and principles are grounded in practice. In other words, a coherent interpretation must indicate whether ideologies distort or hide the truth of the situation.

The third criterion for selecting an instrument is justice for the poor. Choose the type of analysis that will enhance social awareness of deep structural problems and that will also indicate alternatives for dealing with the problems.

8. Míguez Bonino, *Toward a Christian Political Ethics*, 47.
9. Ibid., 46.

This means that the scientific instrument should include in its interpretation the perspective of those being adversely affected by the system.

The fourth criterion relates to strategic alternatives. We examined this criterion earlier in the theology of José Míguez Bonino. It has two principles. First, the exercise of justice should have priority over maintaining the order. Second, a community should choose the strategy that will maximize universal human possibilities and minimize human costs. Included in the costs are various types of psychological and physical repression, loss of life, social dislocation, and ecological damage to the country.

In summary, liberation theologians as a group have provided us with a coherent set of criteria for choosing a type of social analysis and for guiding the alternatives it presents. One may disagree with the choice of criteria, but it would be incorrect to criticize them for lacking guidelines for using analysis. These criteria refute the criticism by the CDF that liberation theologians have given primacy to a Marxist type of social analysis that rejects transcendent values and subverts Christian ethics. How does theology relate to social analysis? Míguez Bonino summarizes the relationship in this manner: social analysis identifies the priorities in society; theology has the responsibility for judging which priorities are just.[10] In a word, theological ethics is the decisive source.

Yet not all liberation theologians are consistent in giving the highest priority to theological sources. Pixley's interpretation of four stages of exodus in light of a Marxist analysis seems to contradict his statement that the Bible serves as the highest authority. He reduces in importance the authority of certain passages of the Pentateuch that do not support the liberation struggle of the Hebrews for the egalitarian, socialist society. His social theory, in other words, overrides the work of certain biblical authors, such as the Priestly account of the exodus.

Pixley aside, the theologians considered in this book give the highest authority to biblically based values for choosing and interpreting analyses. In some instances, such as in the analysis by Comblin, there is a tendency to blur the difference between scientific explanation and ethical evaluation. The deficiency here lies not with subverting ethics, but with mixing ethics with analysis.

Finally, it should be noted that in practice few liberation theologians have used a Marxist analysis, though most have borrowed Marxist concepts. One theologian who has effectively used a Marxist analysis to study land distribution without compromising Christian values is Ellacuría. Neither he nor his colleague Jon Sobrino ever recommended a strategy of class struggle between the

10. Ibid., 54.

landowning oligarchy and the peasants. On the contrary, even in the thick of the revolutionary struggle between the FMLN and Salvadoran government forces in 1980, both theologians argued against the guerrilla war in El Salvador. They maintained that the revolutionary struggle would only end tragically for the entire country. The same stance was adopted by Gutiérrez toward the revolutionary violence of the Shining Path in Peru.

Second Response: Different Epistemologies

The epistemological issue underlies the disagreement over Christian ethics and method of analysis. The CDF argued that a "separation of the parts of this epistemologically unique complex" is impossible.[11] It maintains that scientific analysis cannot be disengaged from its philosophical presuppositions, including unacceptable atheistic and deterministic presuppositions. Liberation theologians disagree. Building on Paul VI's letter *Octogesima Adveniens*, which distinguished the various types of Marxism, liberation theologians hold that the Marxist scientific method of examining social and political reality is not inseparably linked to the Marxist metaphysical materialism or to its political totalitarianism.[12] In accord with Paul VI, these theologians recognize the dangers as well as the values in adopting this instrument. The liberation theologians recognize with all social scientists, as well as with the Vatican Congregation, that no social-scientific instrument is value-free.

Liberation theologians maintain that they have conducted an ongoing epistemological critique of both Marxist and non-Marxist types of analysis. Gutiérrez, in his earliest writings, urged that the contributions of Marxist analysis be "critically situated within the framework of the social sciences," lest these contributions be given undue importance by both defenders and adversaries of the Marxist approach.[13] Likewise, Míguez Bonino urges theologians to adopt a critical attitude toward all scientific analyses. However, he cautions, this should not deter the theologian from using these instruments.[14]

"The evil," Segundo writes, "is not in doing an analysis of the class system or in doing it from a partisan praxis. It is in not having another education or other moral principles beyond the results of such an analysis."[15] It is quite

11. CDF, *Instruction*, pt. VII, 6.
12. Pope Paul VI, *Octogesima Adveniens*, nos. 33–34. Gutiérrez, *Truth Shall Make You Free*, 62–63.
13. Gutiérrez, *Truth Shall Make You Free*, 62.
14. Míguez Bonino, *Toward a Christian Political Ethics*, 47.
15. Juan Luis Segundo, *Theology and the Church: A Response to Cardinal Ratzinger and a Warning to the Whole Church*, trans. John W. Diercksmeier (Minneapolis: A Seabury Book, Winston Press, 1985), 132.

possible, Segundo acknowledges, to make unsound judgments, but errors in judgment that fail to grasp the complexities of a situation should not be attributed to a defect in the instrument. Furthermore, he said, Christians possess a spiritual tradition enabling them to evaluate the analysis and the praxis.

The epistemological differences between the liberation theologians and the CDF manifest a different understanding of how theory relates to praxis. I agree with Joseph Kroger's thesis that "the truth of the charge [by the CDF] that liberation theology is reductive and subversive rests on certain assumptions about the relationship between theory and praxis, science and action, theology and faith."[16] I shall explore only the relation between theory and praxis that separates liberation theologians and the Vatican. As I read the two instructions by the CDF (1984 and 1986), it consistently gives primacy to theory (dogmatic and moral theology) while giving a subordinate status to praxis (pastoral practice and *consensus fidei*). By way of contrast, the CDF in its 1984 Instruction implied that liberation theology gave primacy to praxis by its holding that class struggle, not charity, served as the moral mainspring in history.[17] But the evidence presented above suggests that liberation theologians do not follow a primacy of praxis paradigm. How do they relate theory and praxis, and how does their approach differ from the Vatican's?

Theologian Matthew Lamb's development of five types of theory-praxis relations helps clarify how both the Vatican Congregation and liberation theology relate theology to practice. Lamb's description of the "primacy-of-theory" model aptly describes the CDF approach. In this model, theory consists of knowledge of necessary and eternal truths, as in Aristotle; whereas praxis is action (*actio*) or the empirical situation (*factio*) that has an extrinsic relationship to theory.[18] Theory guides praxis, but praxis contributes little to the formation of theory. In the words of the 1984 Instruction, "the ultimate and decisive criterion for truth can only be a criterion which is itself theological."[19] We must, therefore, judge the validity of what other disciplines teach us according to teachings of Christian faith.

Christian teaching about God, human persons, and their ultimate destiny determine the validity of social analysis and a community's reflection on praxis. The way we understand theory, whether dogma or natural law teaching, is influenced by praxis; but praxis does not challenge the truthfulness of the

16. Joseph Kroger, "Prophetic-Critical and Practical-Strategic Tasks of Theology: Habermas and Liberation Theology," *Theological Studies* 46 (March 1985): 4.

17. Ibid., 7.

18. Matthew L. Lamb, *Solidarity with Victims: Toward a Theology of Social Transformation* (New York: Crossroad, 1982), 67.

19. CDF, *Instruction*, pt. VII, 10.

principles or values of Christian teaching, though it makes persons more aware of "certain aspects of truth."[20]

In this respect, the Vatican Congregation would interpret its social teaching and natural law principles in a manner similar to Jacques Maritain, who distinguished two basic elements in natural law: the ontological element, which is the unwritten law in the hearts of all that indicates the ends toward which persons should move; and the gnoseological element, which is the natural law as actually known. Maritain taught that human reason discovers the essential inclinations of the human heart by discerning its inner melody of the abiding tendencies. The natural law does not change, but through a discernment process over many generations, people progressively come to know the essential inclinations of human nature and to refine them.[21] Similarly, for the Vatican Congregation, the basic dogma and moral principles do not change, but people come to a deeper understanding of them through pastoral practice.

Lamb locates liberation theology not within a primacy of praxis type, as the CDF interprets the new Latin American theology, but within a type called "critical praxis correlation." In contrast to the primacy of praxis type in which theory emerges as an extrinsic relation to praxis, critical correlation links theory and praxis in an intrinsic relation. Praxis serves not only as the goal but also as the foundation of theory. Theory is critical in the sense that it develops its own foundations in transformative praxis.[22]

Modifying Lamb's theory-praxis typology, I would distinguish the two epistemologies in this manner: the Vatican Congregation understands theory as program, whereas liberation theologians see theory as grammar. As program, theory implements itself by interpreting reality, organizing society by its law, and guiding behavior. Thus, the church presents a social doctrine for a Christian practice of liberation that flows from Sacred Scripture, dogma, and natural law.[23] As grammar, theory provides the rules of language that articulate what is happening in the lives of the people. While theory as grammar interprets through its rules of inflection and syntax, it is constantly being adapted. Similarly, as Scripture and tradition give direction to a people's life, worship, and conversion, new awareness and understanding about God's presence, about human relationships, and about the devolution of persons corrupted by power create new ways of understanding the truths of faith and morality.

20. CDF, *Instruction*, pt. XI, 13–14. See also CDF, *Instruction*, in *Origins*, vol. 15, no. 44 (April 17, 1986): 713, 715–28.

21. Jacques Maritain, *Man and the State* (Chicago: University of Chicago Press, 1951), 85–90.

22. Lamb, *Solidarity with Victims*, 82.

23. CDF, *Instruction*, reprinted in *Origins*, chap. 5.

Liberation theologians reject all theory-as-program approaches to Christian ethics, whether they derive formal principles solely from theory or whether they develop themes and strategies for action entirely from practice without the benefit of theory. The theologians hold that historical praxis (the way the world is structured) must be the point of departure for theology, and that liberating praxis (the way the world should be restructured) must be its goal. Yet both types of praxis must be challenged and guided by theory, understood as grammar. As Segundo says, social analysis and praxis illumine whether certain Christian norms are applicable or not in a specific context. "Once any truth-seeking analysis of reality is undertaken, Christian moral rules do not seem clear enough to determine definitely what the spirit of the norm indicates."[24] Either values become distorted or the situation changes to such an extent that certains norms cease to be relevant.

In summary, liberation theologians find inadequate any theological ethics that draws moral obligations exclusively from theory: whether from convictions intrinsic to faith that fail to account for the people's practice of faith, such as the divine command ethics of Karl Barth; or from Christian philosophical systems that deduce moral principles primarily from human nature informed by faith, such as the new Christendom ethics of Jacques Maritain; or from the theology represented by the CDF. They reject as idealist theological approaches that give primacy to theory, including moral principles that guide reflective action, but that remain unchanged by it.

In agreement with the Vatican Congregation, liberation theologians discount empirically based ethical approaches that make judgments solely on the basis of praxis. A Marxist ethics, for example, approves or disapproves of activity on the basis of its effectiveness in liberating a people from political-economic oppression. It spurns as ideological any transcendent standard that would question the means used to achieve liberation, such as a strategy of class struggle or the use of terrorist tactics. In a word, liberation theologians reject ethical systems based on *sola theoria* or *sola praxis*.

In contrast to an overspiritualist or overmaterialist ethics, mainline liberation theologians work toward an ethics that gives a primacy, though not an exclusive one, to praxis, which is engaged in a mutually challenging dialogue with social theory and divine revelation. In this reciprocal exchange, praxis tells the social scientists whether their theories are on target and tells the theologians how well they are interpreting the people's faith. Praxis by itself is an insufficient source for doing ethics. It cannot be its own judge. That praxis should be evaluated in the light of praxis is a tautology. Certain projects,

24. Segundo, *Theology and the Church*, 129.

in some instances, may be self-serving rather than other-regarding; or they may be liberating for one exploited village, but detrimental to other oppressed communities. Therefore, as Gutiérrez and Míguez Bonino point out, the ultimate criteria for judging rightness or wrongness come not from praxis but from revealed truth accepted in faith.[25]

Evaluation

Most liberation theologians are critical and discriminating in their use of social sciences. They do not subordinate Christian ethics to social-scientific investigation; on the contrary, they have developed criteria for choosing and guiding social analysis. On the epistemological level, they generally demonstrate a solid understanding of the values at stake in working with a Marxist analysis.

One value to which liberation theologians have given insufficient reflection is the arrangement and distribution of power in the new society. Although they wisely maintain that theologians cannot construct a priori moral principles based on theory alone for justifying and guiding revolutionary change, theologians can antecedently grapple with foreseen issues of power. This would include reflection on the organization of the new society: its infrastructure, the role of the state, church, and private organizations. Liberation theologians have not reflected sufficiently on power in the utopian society, probing in the light of past and present forms of socialist economies such questions as: Who controls? How should the new society be structured to allow greater economic-political participation and self-dominant activity among all people?

Reflecting on power in a socialist society, Reinhold Niebuhr observed that property held in common within a classless society must necessarily be administered by certain officials who would exercise enormous power and consequently be tempted to assume dictatorial rule, forgetting the ideals "which originally endowed their power with moral legitimacy."[26] Niebuhr applied Marx's principle—whoever controls the means of production controls society—to the inevitable situation in a socialist state in which someone must manage the means of production. He feared the probable situation of a centralized power establishment becoming a totalitarian state. Even with the abolition of private property, administrators of the means of production can

25. Gutiérrez, *Truth Shall Make You Free*, 100; Míguez Bonino, *Toward a Christian Political Ethics*, 109–110.
26. Reinhold Niebuhr, "Two Forms of Tyranny," *Christianity and Crisis* (February 2, 1948): 3–5.

enforce such a state by using every means at their disposal to enforce the laws of the ideal society. Sin, Niebuhr emphasized, is deeply ingrained in all persons. The oppressed, even though working toward an equalitarian ideal, do not by that fact become sinless carriers of the revolution. Nor would the managers of the ideal society be so disciplined and so rigorously just that they would not require checks and balances by other powers.

Given his pessimistic view of sinful human nature, Niebuhr's overriding concern was that economic and political power be shared, checked, and balanced by other powers.[27] Liberation theologians generally disagree with Niebuhr's theological anthropology and his Christian realism that overemphasize human sinfulness and that consequently put limits on social change. Nonetheless, what he says about the distribution and balance of power and its relation to citizen participation in a revolutionary society needs to be dealt with.

A second issue deals with liberation theologians' rejection of functionalist analysis. Liberation theologians such as Clodovis and Leonardo Boff and Míguez Bonino have upheld a radical dialectical type of social analysis as the only adequate approach for understanding the injustices in Latin America. They imply that systemic change requires either a dialectical Marxist analysis or a radical form of dependency analysis and not a functionalist analysis that supports the status quo. Gutiérrez, in his later writings, shows an openness to other modes of analysis.

Although I agree with liberation theologians in their rejection of functionalist analysis, I think their social analysis would be strengthened by adopting other nonfunctionalist and non-Marxist modes. Sociologist Herbert Gans, for example, has shown through a non-Marxist conflict analysis that poverty persists not only because it reaps a number of positive goods, but also because many of the functional alternatives to poverty would be quite dysfunctional for the wealthy. Poverty satisfies thirteen positive functions for various nonpoor groups, one of which involves the creation of a low-wage labor pool that is willing ("or rather, unable to be unwilling") to do the dirty work at low wages.[28] Poverty also supports the laissez-faire ideology of a capitalist economy, which alleges that a certain population of the poor is unwilling to work and that another is inferior. Therefore, both groups must accept charity or welfare in order to survive. This alleged deviancy painted by capitalist ideology reduces

27. Thomas L. Schubeck, "Liberation and Imagination: A New Theological Language in Response to the Marxist Critique of Religion" (diss., Ann Arbor, Mich.: Ann Arbor Microfilms, 1975), 88–89.
28. Herbert J. Gans, "The Uses of Poverty: The Poor Pay All," in *Social Problems Today: Coping with the Challenges of a Changing Society*, ed. James M. Henslin (Englewood Cliffs, N.J.: Prentice-Hall, 1990), 31–35.

the moral pressure on the present political economy to make radical changes. This capitalist ideology makes the socialist alternatives look unappealing to the nonpoor, who are persuaded that the beneficiaries of the new system (the poor) are inherently lazy, spendthrifts, dishonest, and promiscuous.[29]

If these positive functions served by the poor were to be replaced by eliminating poverty, then the nonpoor, especially the affluent, would bear the extra cost. This nonfunctionalist analysis implies that no structural transformation within a capitalist economy would change the ways of the poor. Thus, Gans's more radical analysis makes manifest the type of structural contradiction that a functionalist approach would describe as latent.[30] Liberation theologians, by employing a Gansian or other mode of analysis, would, in my judgment, corroborate their critiques and demonstrate greater objectivity in their search for truth.[31] Thus they would also undercut criticism that charges that liberation theology's use of Marxist analysis is no less ideological.

Does Liberation Ethics Have Concrete Norms?

Critics have judged liberation ethics to be situationist and utilitarian. Brian Hebblethwaite interpreted liberation theology "as an instance of situation ethics in the social and political sphere." He said that its basic principle of love as justice, precisely because of its abstract quality, can be easily manipulated to endorse a Marxist analysis or to give moral support to violent revolution or guerrilla warfare.[32]

Ethicists McCann and Strain found the theological ethics of Míguez Bonino, among all the liberation ethics, to be the most promising. Nonetheless, they said his ethics was "utilitarian," implying that he made moral decisions on the basis of a utilitarian calculus. Hebblethwaite, McCann, and Strain fault liberation theologians for not developing concrete moral principles.

Liberation theologians have not responded as forcefully as they might to

29. Ibid., 34.
30. Robert K. Merton, *Social Theory and Social Structure*, 1968 enlarged edition (New York: Free Press, 1968). "*Manifest functions* are those objective consequences contributing to the adjustment or adaptation of the system which are intended and recognized by participants in the system; *Latent functions*, correlatively, being those which are neither intended nor recognized" (105).
31. For a functionalist analysis that shows the limits of economic systems in bringing about social changes in sexual exploitation through prostitution, see Kingsley Davis, "The Sociology of Prostitution," *ASR*, 2 (1937): 744–55.
32. Brian Hebblethwaite, *Christian Ethics in the Modern Age* (Philadelphia: Westminster Press, 1982), 93–94.

the critique that they are situationists.[33] But their discussion of norms indicates that the critics may have missed something. Liberation theologians are neither situation ethicists nor utilitarians who measure goodness or badness of acts solely on the basis of consequences. It would be more accurate to call liberation theologians "mixed consequentialists" (though they do not identify themselves as such), because they do account for concrete norms as well as consequences in their ethical judgments.

They interpret and judge social consequences on the basis of two types of principles, which I shall call "categorical" and "concrete." The categorical imperatives are general and universally valid perspectives, whereas the concrete imperatives are specific guidelines and context-specific. Both types of imperatives are measured by their purpose, which is the reign of God. The urgency of all imperatives in liberation theology is directly proportional to the way in which they bear upon or embody the kingdom of God. The kingdom is the ultimate goal (telos) that empowers, guides, and finally judges human behavior. The following figure illustrates the relationship of the kingdom to moral norms.

33. Segundo has addressed the issue of situation ethics. See Segundo, *The Liberation of Theology*, 170–81.

Normative Structure in Liberation Theology

Ultimate Goal:		KINGDOM OF GOD	
Mediations:	Revelation (SS and trad.)	Praxis of faith	Social analysis
Categorical Imperatives:	Witness to the truth!	Opt for the poor!	Foster freedom!
Concrete Imperatives:	Common good: all persons must enjoy conditions for human flourishing	Criteria for just revolutionary war	Basic human rights
Example:	Common good prohibits monopolization of land	Proportionality	Right to life and self-determination

In this figure, we see that liberation theology is a teleological ethics. It evaluates human action and institutional policies on the basis of the kingdom of God, which is the ultimate goal and supreme good of all people. All other obligations are good insofar as they participate in the absolute and unconditional demand of the kingdom.[34] The mediations help the people to discern how the kingdom calls them to live in faith. Liberation theologians define the call in terms of two types of imperatives.

The categorical imperatives embody values of the kingdom, calling people to proclaim truth, freedom, and compassion for the poor. Because these imperatives participate in the kingdom, they share its urgency and its unqualified and universally binding nature. Hence, the imperatives may be called categorical. As universal obligations, they apply to all situations.

Liberation theologians think of categorical imperatives as virtues as well as guiding principles.[35] All persons should be truthful, free, and committed to the poor. Although I focus here on truth, freedom, and preferential option as

34. Segundo, *Liberation of Theology*, 177.
35. Categorical imperatives are similar to what ethicists sometimes call formal norms. For a distinction between formal and material norms, see Richard M. Gula, *What Are They Saying about Moral Norms?* (New York: Paulist Press, 1982), 55.

norms, it should be remembered that liberation theologians emphasize these virtues in their spirituality of liberation.

Witnessing the Truth

Liberation theologians begin with experience. Truth is a primordial human experience so fundamental that nothing else can ever substitute for it. A person cannot demonstrate the actuality and goodness of truth, but can only point to it and expect others to acknowledge its presence.[36] The poor come to understand and appreciate truth in its absence—in those negative experiences where truth is distorted, withheld, or blotted out. They learn truth in the negative contrast experience of seeing what truth is not, which includes the graced experience of being called by God to be truthful witnesses.[37] Hence, liberation theologians interpret the meaning of truth and its normative nature in light of the people's historical experience (praxis) and revelation.

Gustavo Gutiérrez, following the biblical concept in his book *The Truth Shall Make You Free*, defines truth in terms of a personal relation and not as a correspondence between reality and a person's concept of the reality. Truth does not reside in the essence of things, but within interpersonal relationships where what happens is equally important as what is. In the interpersonal, covenantal relationship between God and God's people, truth is measured by fidelity, reliability, and trustworthiness.[38] Jesus Christ is the full and unexpected fulfillment of God's promise and so becomes the truth incarnate, who acts faithfully in history to fulfill God's covenantal promise to give life. God's people are truthful and act truthfully by recognizing through Christ that God is the father/mother of all people and by accepting other human beings as brothers and sisters.[39] Like Gutiérrez, Míguez Bonino describes truth as fidelity or obedience to Christ—as the act of responding to the demands of the covenantal relationship.[40]

36. Michael J. Buckley, "Authority," unpublished article.

37. Edward Schillebeeckx developed the notion of negative contrast experience as the basis for moral norms. Certain liberation theologians have developed this notion. See Leonardo Boff, "¿Qué es hacer teología desde América Latina?" in *Liberación y cautiverio: Encuentro Latinamericano de teología* (Mexico City: Comité Organizador, 1975), 129–54; Ricardo Antoncich, *Christians in the Face of Injustice*, trans. Matthew J. O'Connell (Maryknoll, N.Y.: Orbis Books, 1987), 58–59. See also Patricia McAuliffe, *Fundamental Ethics: A Liberationist Approach* (Washington, D.C.: Georgetown University Press, 1993).

38. Gutiérrez, *Truth Shall Make You Free*, 94–95.

39. Ibid., 97.

40. José Míguez Bonino, *Christians and Marxists: The Mutual Challenge to Revolution* (Grand Rapids, Mich.: Eerdmans, 1976), 40.

Truth as fidelity to the covenantal relationship is closely linked with justice. In this biblical-liberationist perspective, truth is grasped through a creative event or God's efficacious word.[41] In response, human beings speak the truth by proclaiming what they have heard and by standing behind what they have said. Witnessing the truth, therefore, involves speaking honestly and acting in fidelity to one's word. In this sense, one does the truth, which for liberation theologians involves justice. Doing the truth and doing justice in the Christian context means following Christ and accepting others as one's brothers and sisters.

Doing the truth also means uncovering falsehoods and deceptions. Negative experiences of oppression lead to a people's suspicion of the lie, especially the institutional lie. It assumes various forms: a public declaration contradicted by institutional practice, a lie of silence by a government that pretends to know nothing about disappearances of citizens.

Liberation theologians try to expose the lie by identifying ideologies suspected of concealing or distorting the true situation. Segundo carries out his confirmation process by means of the hermeneutical circle, Comblin by ideology critique, and Ellacuría by the historicization of concepts. Each of these methods scrutinizes truth claims made by theologies and institutions and then examines their fruits: whether the results bear out what is proclaimed or projected.

Respecting Freedom

The second categorical imperative commands that all human beings foster freedom for others as well as for themselves. Like truth, freedom is a primordial human experience that is understood by struggling against its opposite—coercion. Long-standing oppression and tyranny push a people to resist and eventually to claim their God-given right to determine their own destiny. Yet biblical narratives and contemporary history demonstrate that individuals and groups require the freedom of others to assist them. The God of an oppressed people leads them in their exodus; Jesus gives others a profound understanding of freedom by surrendering his life on behalf of the others. Pastoral leaders in Latin American base communities help people who are afraid to risk their lives to be free.

Freedom, understood as a struggle for self-determination in solidarity, calls persons to be self-directive and creative subjects. Thus, liberation theologians distinguish their understanding of freedom from the liberal notion of

---

41. Míguez Bonino, *Doing Theology in a Revolutionary Situation*, 89.

protecting individual rights. Freedom entails self-determination and self-ac-
tualization achieved in relationship, and especially in solidarity, with the poor.
Because human freedom is indivisible, it must extend to the whole of society.[42]

Persons, in dialogue with others, become aware of their subjectivity, that
they are responsible agents who have been called by God to assume responsibility for shaping their lives, including the shaping of social conditions.
Liberation theologians see freedom as a historic achievement for the oppressed
in Latin America because it marks a unique moment in history when an
oppressed people takes responsibility for living as self-dominant, creative beings.

Brazilian theologian Yvone Gebara has written about the awakening of
Latin American women, who, while struggling with their poor neighbors,
became cognizant that they as women suffered oppression at the hands of their
male colleagues even as they collaborated with them in the social struggle for
liberation. Women became aware that they needed to opt also for themselves
within their larger option for the poor. This meant fighting those false self-
images that they had acquired from a macho society and to discovering and
loving themselves.[43]

Opting for the Poor

The third and most distinctive categorical imperative in liberation ethics
is the preferential option for the poor. The option implies an encounter with
the poor and at the same time an experience of God's grace. Option for the
poor is fundamentally God's concern. As Jorge Pixley and Clodovis Boff
express it, "God is the first to opt for the poor, and it is only as a consequence
of this that the church too has to opt for the poor."[44] Preference for the poor
means a recognition that God's gracious empowerment precedes a person's
commitment to the poor even in instances of those who work in a disinterested
and magnanimous way but who have no awareness of encountering Christ.
In a word, recognizing God's prior concern for the poor as the antecedent to
a human person's concern for the poor manifests again liberation theology's
basic premise that categorical imperatives are grounded in the kingdom of
God.

42. Gutiérrez, *Truth Shall Make You Free*, 143.
43. Yvone Gebara, "Option for the Poor as an Option for the Poor Woman," in
Women, Work and Poverty, ed. Elisabeth Schüssler Fiorenza and Anne Carr (Edinburgh:
T & T Clark, 1987), 111–12.
44. Boff and Pixley, *Bible, the Church and the Poor*, 109.

Concrete Norms

Truth, freedom, and option for the poor, precisely because of their universality, are limited guides to specific and complex problems. They shape the general direction the moral agent should follow by insisting that truth, human dignity, and especially the poor should never be violated under any circumstances. Yet these categorical imperatives do not illumine the intricacies of dilemmas involving fair trade, ecological issues, and guerrilla warfare. Concrete norms, which contain more moral content, are needed. Precise moral concepts counsel the agent regarding protectionist barriers against foreign agricultural goods of poor nations; or deforestation by the military-industrial state; or the exploitation of domestic servants.[45]

But concrete norms, say the critics, are scarce in liberation theology. Are the critics correct? As we have seen, liberation theologians have identified concrete guidelines related to violence, land distribution, and human rights. As we examine the concrete norms, we see that these theologians do not create something entirely new, but give a new perspective to old principles that take into account the uniqueness of situations. Preferential option for the poor modifies the theologians' way of articulating imperatives of the common good and human rights. The experience of oppression leads theologians to see revolutionary war in a wider context of violence. The theologians insist that concrete norms must not be separated from historical context. In the following illustrations, Ellacuría and Segundo develop concrete norms within situations of El Salvador and Uruguay.

Land and the Common Good

In chapter 4 we examined Ellacuría's analysis of agrarian land reform in El Salvador. The National Association of Private Enterprise had argued that private property was just because it produced more goods and fostered greater initiative than an agrarian reform program. Ellacuría countered this position, showing that the present system of vast landholdings has not produced humane conditions for millions of Salvadorans. Moreover, increased production did not bring about fair distribution. Finally, he said the present system has not brought personal initiative on the part of the majority who possess no property.

---

45. For details on each of these three issues, see the editorial in *The Plain Dealer*, "Don't Scorn the Plea of the Poor," *The Plain Dealer* (Cleveland, August 6, 1991); José Ramos Regidor, "Wanted: A New North-South Ethic that Demands Ecological Justice," trans. IDOC, "Ambiente e Sviluppo nei Rapporti Nord-Sud," in *Volontari e Terzo Mondo* (Rome, December 1988); Mabel Sardón-Filippini, "Domestic Service in Latin America," in *Women, Work and Poverty*, 51–55.

Ellacuría then developed his moral position that the present land distribution in El Salvador was unjust because it violated the common good. The church fathers emphasized the right of all human beings to enjoy goods of this world over the right to possess anything privately. Thomas Aquinas taught that private property was devised by human reason to preserve the proper finality of goods in the most ordered manner. Reason, therefore, should be used to determine which forms of property are the more just and the more rational in each instance.[46] Recent Catholic social teaching insisted on the universal and common destiny of the earthly goods. In sum, the church's position over two millennia has consistently taught on the basis of the gospel that the goods of the earth are common to all, that all human beings should be allowed to share fairly all the available goods, and that this primary right must be respected.

The present system of landholding in El Salvador, Ellacuría argued, violated the common good. Following Thomas Aquinas, he showed that the common good refers to the whole of society and not to the parts. If a particular structure seeks its own gain to the detriment of the whole, it runs counter to the common good and therefore is wrong. In El Salvador, the monopolization of farmland and the permanent violation of human rights by landowners in order to maintain their vast tracts of land vitiate the common good of El Salvador.

The common good consists of structural conditions that bring about human flourishing for all. Ellacuría identified the criteria for verifying whether a society is supporting these conditions and thus promoting the common good. The criteria are, first, that all citizens must enjoy the conditions for personal development; second, that society, aided by the state, should prevent persons and groups from appropriating for themselves what is common to all. Expressed in its negative formulation, the norm states that any permanent denial of access to basic human goods, such as farmland, is wrong. Moreover, repeated violation of human rights of those who legally try to obtain or maintain farmland constitutes a denial of the common good and therefore is unjust.

Ellacuría's argument demonstrates careful ethical reasoning that appeals to concrete norms based on the common good. Thus, he complements his theological critique of farmland monopolies by using philosophy informed by historical analysis. His philosophical-historical approach identifies the ideology of the landowners and the fallacy of their arguments. Like Segundo, Ellacuría measures the truth of historical concepts and abstract principles by their impact on the lives of the poor. He demonstrated that the defense of private property

46. Ignacio Ellacuría, "La historización, 443.

on the basis of its contribution to the good of all was false. The present
distribution of property protected the interests of the elite while discriminating
against the majority.

Segundo and Norms Governing Revolutionary War

In analyzing oppression and guerrilla war in his own country of Uruguay,
Juan Luis Segundo identifies material norms that offer guidance to right use
of force within a revolutionary situation. He begins his analysis with a discussion of structural violence, which he sees as instigating a civil war in his
own and other Latin American nations. Beginning in the 1950s government
leaders and entrepreneurs debated various programs to stimulate a stagnant
economy. Various plans were proposed including industrialization, various
models of development, agrarian reform, and a Latin American common
market.[47] Gradually university students, workers, professionals, and church
people became suspicious of what was going on in programs of development.
Foreign powers, using the rules of the common market for their own benefit,
exploited the poor countries.

The chief concern of this new awareness, Segundo said, was not the
injustice, but the lie. One ideology in particular tried to conceal the lie: the
political search for a *third-way approach*. It claimed to be a real democratic
alternative to capitalist and socialist economies.[48] In Argentina this alternative
political structure developed as Peronism; in Chile, Christian Democracy; and
in Peru, a military evolution. Segundo called these plans "lies" because the so-
called third-way movements were simply modified capitalist approaches operating according to the same international rules. The movements did not
deliver the economic goods and structural change they had promised, but
actually exploited laborers and managers, who were gradually ground down
by the rules of the market economy.[49]

Economic failure was followed by a period of desperate violent action.
In order to repress subversion, regimes exacted terrible retribution, "more
thoroughgoing in its disturbing effects on the social ecology and more inhuman
in its use of reasons." People felt caught in a vicious circle. The result of these
wars, especially by the repressive violence carried out by military governments
in Uruguay, Chile, and Argentina, was the destruction of social ecology. By
"social ecology" Segundo means the whole system of relations between human

47. Juan Luis Segundo, *Faith and Ideologies*, trans. John Drury (Maryknoll, N.Y.:
Orbis Books, 1984), 277.
   48. Ibid., 279.
   49. Ibid., 278–79.

beings and their environment. The spiral of violence involving oppression cloaked in lies, subversion by guerrillas, and especially the repression did incommensurate damage to the families, friends, and professional contacts. Segundo judged the guerrilla wars and repression to be more destructive than war between nations because of widespread suspicion and mistrust. No one knew who was friend or foe.[50]

Reflection on these historical experiences led Segundo to formulate criteria for interpreting the justice of guerrilla war. Following Paul VI and the bishops' conference at Medellín, Segundo identified three conditions for justifying the use of armed violence in a revolutionary situation. First, counterviolence, in response to long-standing institutional violence, must be motivated by justice and solidarity (right intention). Second, revolutionary insurrection can be justified in the case of manifest and prolonged tyranny in violation of fundamental human rights and because of damage to the common good of the nation (just cause).[51] Third, proportionality that places the social ecology over all other goods must be observed. The consequences must not destroy the social ecology even in its praiseworthy goal of seeking justice under the first two conditions. When a prolonged guerrilla war involving severe repression by government forces produces consequences destructive of the social ecology, engagement in this conflict is wrong.[52] Using this last criterion, Segundo condemned the guerrilla warfare in his own land of Uruguay in the 1970s.

Evaluation

Liberation theologians have given greater importance to moral norms than is generally believed. Ellacuría's evaluation of private property in El Salvador as a violation of the common good and Segundo's judgment that guerrilla wars in Latin America have severely damaged the social ecology illustrate arguments that employ concrete moral norms. Other theologians, including Leonardo Boff and Gustavo Gutiérrez, appeal to norms of human rights and respecting human dignity as the basis of their moral judgments. Liberation theologians are not situationists who reject all a priori concrete norms. They are, however, contextualists who insist on rigorous historical-structural analysis before bringing norms to illumine the concrete dilemma.

50. Ibid., 286.
51. Second General Conference of Latin American Bishops, *The Church in the Present-day Transformation*, vol. 2: *Conclusions* (Washington, D.C.: Latin American Bureau, 1968), "Peace," no. 19.
52. Segundo, *Theology and the Church*, 130.

Ellacuría provides us with the strongest analysis and evaluation because he employs in his argument many foundational sources, including the social teaching of the church as well as philosophy. He makes a special contribution by analyzing ethical concepts historically to see whether they are being used ideologically to justify the actions of the powerful. He argues that theologians must undertake the task of reinterpreting the meaning of moral norms and ethical concepts before using them in contemporary moral issues.

Both Segundo and Ellacuría have made valuable contributions to social ethics by showing how institutions can mask intentions and motives through ideologies. By presenting a declared policy that differs from its actual policy, the state or private institution engages in deception. But making informed judgments about the institutional lie is a long and difficult process, as these liberation theologians realize.

Segundo's analysis of violence establishes a linkage between truth and justice or between the lie and injustice. The systematic lie (that Latin American nations were on a path to development that was neither capitalist nor socialist) surrounded and perpetuated the injustice done to the poor majority. The lie compounded the evil of injustice. The people felt caught in a vicious circle, frustrated at every turn. When the truth was discovered that the type of development proposed was structurally impossible even from the start, the people grew indignant and organized subversive activity against structural injustice compounded by the lie.

Segundo's analysis is well done. Implied in his analysis is the distinction between an ideology of a false consciousness, in which agents erroneously thought development would help the nation, and an ideology in which the agents knew that their program was a dependent capitalism that could only benefit the local elite. Segundo's calling the development programs systematic lies in the moral sense assumes that the agents intended from the start to deceive the public for the sake of personal or corporate benefit. He implies that the architects of the "third-way" approaches in Argentina, Chile, and Peru deliberately intended to deceive the people. Unclear in Segundo's analysis is whether the planners presented the third-way approaches with good intentions, or whether they conceived the programs as ways of achieving power and wealth for the wealthy entrepreneurs and landowners. Segundo says that people became aware somewhere along the twenty-five-year process that they were being sold a bill of goods and consequently found themselves farther away from the goal of development than when the programs were first launched.[53] Awareness of the lie led to subversion, followed by the violence of repression.

53. Segundo, *Faith and Ideologies*, 281.

Although he stops short of imputing blame to particular actors, he suggests that both the devisers of the plan and the military regimes who supported it deliberately deceived the people.

What is needed, says Segundo, is a "critical-minded awareness": reason must "unmask illusions and fight to destroy them as it seeks justice and truth and proclaims that reality can be changed."[54] But identifying the illusion must include naming the agents or groups who created the illusion and showing the deliberate deception. At the same time, ascertaining the intention and motives of heads of institutions who work behind closed doors is difficult.

Ellacuría has suggested an indirect way of demonstrating deliberate deception. The truth of affirmations, he says, is measured by their results. If a government says it stands for freedom of the press as a fundamental right, but in practice allows only the powerful to exercise this right, then the government is lying. Objective judgments are difficult to make in this regard. But, says Ellacuría, one stands a greater chance of being right when one judges actions on the basis of whether they seek the good of the whole. Seeking the good of the whole, or the common good, must be measured, he says, both by the intentionality of the government and by its action: by establishing conditions and laws and by upholding the law.[55]

Final Comments

Following the method of liberation theology, I have examined how the theologians actually used the foundational sources rather than how they theorized about how the sources should be used. These dozen theologians, whose works I have examined, are consistent in affirming the importance of integrating praxis and theory. In practice, most of the theologians, especially Gutiérrez, Míguez Bonino, Sobrino, and Gebara, incorporate the people's experience of oppression and faith in their theology and ethics. More could be done in the theological writings that incorporate how church base communities and voluntary organizations actually resolve ethical issues. The normative dimension of liberation ethics has not adequately reflected the people's value system or decision-making process. Liberation ethics has not realized its goal of reflecting critically on the people's praxis of decision making.

Liberation theology has undergone considerable change over the course of its thirty-year history in Latin America. It has grown increasingly ecumenical, involving a diversity of Protestant and Catholic theologians. Women

54. Ibid., 283.
55. Ellacuría, "La historización," 434.

theologians over the past dozen years have brought important perspectives, including a greater concentration on local issues as well as issues dealing with sexism and patriarchal structures. Liberation theologians have changed their minds on some issues. Some have altered their Marxist terminology; others have moved away from dependency-theory analysis. All attend more to domestic issues, though they approach these issues with an awareness of how international mechanisms influence them.

For all the change in liberation theology, the theologians have remained steadfast in their commitment to the full liberation of the poor. Although fewer liberation theologians see socialism as the better alternative, most liberation theologians continue to view capitalism as an exploitive system. This raises a question of what kind of analysis they will develop for the future and what kind of new society liberation theologians envision.

The shift in many international alliances beginning in the late 1980s and continuing into the 1990s has made the question of a different kind of political-economic structure more difficult to address. Cuba began to lose its financial support from the Soviet Union. With the collapse of the Soviet Union, Cuba has become increasingly isolated within the Western hemisphere.[56] Fidel Castro attended the Latin American Economic Conference in the summer of 1991. Nicaragua's socialist government was voted out of office in 1990. After the collapse of the Soviet Union following its failed coup in August 1991, the global socialist alliance disintegrated rapidly. Satellite countries of the former Soviet Union, especially Czechoslovakia, Hungary, and Poland, have dismantled their socialist political economies and have moved toward the market system.

What impact this will have on Latin America is difficult to predict. Some political observers think this may sway economic powers, such as the United States, Germany, and Japan, to switch the bulk of their Latin American trade to these eastern European countries, which could lead to greater impoverishment of Latin America. The shift from socialist economies toward capitalism may further widen the economic gap between developed and undeveloped nations. As the countervailing power of the Eastern bloc nations evanesces and the capitalist economies grow stronger, prospects for Latin American economies moving into a radically different system seem dim.

Although these shifts suggest change in the type of social analysis needed by liberation theology, they do not mean liberation theology will disappear. As I view it, liberation will be needed even more urgently, for this theology

56. Kevin P. O'Higgins, "Liberation Theology and the 'New World Order,'" *America* (November 24, 1990): 389.

and ethics does not rise or fall with Marxism and the viability of socialist economies. Rather, it rose and continues to thrive because of its commitment to the poor and oppressed. As poverty increases among Latin Americans and throughout the world, so will the work of the liberation theologians.

Index

Liberchon theol seen as = L. A. Liberchon theol